GROUND STUDIES FOR PILOTS
Volume 1

By the same authors:

Ground Studies for Pilots, third edition
Volume 2, Plotting and Flight Planning
Volume 3, Navigation General

Aviation Law for Pilots, third edition

By H. A. Parmar:

Navigation General and Instruments
(published by H. & J. Parmar)

GROUND STUDIES FOR PILOTS

Third Edition
Volume 1

RADIO AIDS

S. E. T. Taylor

formerly British Airways and Chief Ground
Instructor, Malaysia Air Training, Kuala
Lumpur; Chief Ground Instructor, London
School of Flying

H. A. Parmar

Senior Tutor, Bristow Helicopters Ltd
formerly Chief Ground Instructor, Malaysia
Air Training, Kuala Lumpur; Specialist
Instructor, London School of Flying

GRANADA
London Toronto Sydney New York

Granada Publishing Limited – Technical Books Division
Frogmore, St Albans, Herts AL2 2NF
and
3 Upper James Street, London W1R 4BP
515 Madison Avenue, New York, NY 10022, USA
117 York Street, Sydney, NSW 2000, Australia
60 International Boulevard, Rexdale, Ontario R9W 6J2, Canada
61 Beach Road, Auckland, New Zealand

ISBN 0 246 11169 0

First published in Great Britain by Crosby Lockwood & Son Ltd 1970
Reprinted 1972
Second edition 1974, reprinted 1976, 1978
Third edition, in three volumes, 1979
Reprinted 1981, 1983 by Granada Publishing

British Library Cataloguing in Publication Data
Taylor, Sydney Ernest Thomas
  Ground studies for pilots. – 3rd ed.
  Vol. I: Radio aids
  1. Airplanes – Piloting
  I. Title   II. Parmar, Hasmukhlal Amritlal
  629.132'5216   TL710

Text set in 10/12 pt IBM Press Roman, printed and bound
in Great Britain at The Pitman Press, Bath

Granada ®
Granada Publishing ®

Contents

Preface

The text of *Ground Studies for Pilots* has been completely revised and brought up-to-date: it is now produced in three volumes:

        Vol. 1   Radio Aids
        Vol. 2   Plotting and Flight Planning
        Vol. 3   Navigation General

All matter for the Commercial and Airline Transport Licences is covered, but the problem of inter-relationship remains; frequent reference from one section to another and occasional simultaneous reading will be needed.

We have added further exercises which are typical of the present vogue, but again we must stress that speed with accuracy is an essential ingredient of the ground examinations, so continual timed practice from recent exam papers is quite vital. These are obtainable from CAA, 37 Gratton Road, Cheltenham.

January 1979

                                      S. E. T. Taylor
                                      H. A. Parmar

1: Introduction

The word 'radio' means the radiation of electromagnetic waves conveying information, and detection of such waves. Within this meaning, such applications as telegraphy, telephony, television and a host of navigation aids are all classified as radio. Our present study will be primarily concerned with the air navigation aids commonly used world-wide.

The existence of electromagnetic waves was suspected long before Heinrich Hertz conducted his famous experiment in 1887 and demonstrated their presence. As early as 1865 James Clerk Maxwell of King's College, London University produced a paper in which he predicted the existence of these waves. Later, in 1886, a year before Hertz' experiment, Professor Hughes, a scientist in London came very close to the discovery.

However, Hertz not only verified Maxwell's prediction but also established the speed of the radio waves and other properties. He showed that they can propagate in vacuum, and that they are stopped by a metallic screen (the foundation of our present day radar). He calculated wavelengths for various frequencies and determined the relationship between the two.

Propagation of radio waves

If a source of alternating voltage is connected to a wire (i.e. an aerial) an oscillating current will be set up in the wire, the electrons of which move about a mean position. The electric field present in the wire is accompanied by a magnetic field and at a suitable frequency (in relation to the length of the aerial) both fields radiate efficiently outward from the wire in the form of electromagnetic or radio waves. In the earth environment these disturbances travel approximately at the speed of light, that is,

186 000 statute miles per second or
162 000 nautical miles per second or
300 000 000 metres per second.

As the waves are alternating fields, the terminology involved with alternating currents will be looked into first, extending this to radio terminology.

An a.c. voltage in a wire reverses its direction a number of times every second. Consequently, if a graph of the current in the wire is plotted against time, it will be found that it is a sine curve (see fig. 1.1).

Cycle.   A cycle is one complete series of values, or one complete process.

Hertz.   A hertz is the number of cycles per second. (This term is a recent adoption in honour of the eminent scientist.)

Amplitude.   Amplitude of a wave is the maximum displacement, or the maximum

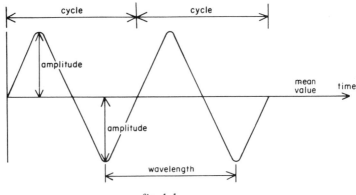

fig. 1.1

val ʼ it attains from its mean position during a cycle. It is both positive and negative. (Th part of the curve in fig. 1.1 above the mean or time axis is called positive and that ırt which is below the line is negative.)

Frequ ıcy.   Frequency of an alternating current or a radio wave is the number of cycles ccurring in one second, expressed in hertz (Hz). For example, 500 Hz means 500 cy s per second. Since the number of cycles per second of normal radio waves is very h h it is usual to refer to them in terms of kilohertz, megahertz and gigahertz as follow.

$$
\begin{aligned}
1 \text{ cycle per second} &= 1 \text{ Hz} \\
1\,000 \text{ Hz} &= 1 \text{ kHz (kilohertz)} \\
1\,000 \text{ kHz} &= 1 \text{ MHz (megahertz)} \\
1\,000 \text{ MHz} &= 1 \text{ GHz (gigahertz)}
\end{aligned}
$$

Wavelength.   This is the physical distance travelled by the radio wave during one complete cycle f transmission. It is defined as the distance between successive crests or the distance b ween two consecutive points at which the moving particles of the medium have the same displacement from the mean value and are moving in the same direction.

Wavelength-frequency relationship
A radio wave travels at a speed of 186 000 statute miles per second, or 162 000 nautical miles per second or 300 000 000 metres per second. The relationship between the frequency and its wavelength is established when it is considered that if a transmission of one hertz is made, the wave will cover a geographical distance of 300 000 000 metres. If two hertz were transmitted (that is, two cycles in one second), two complete cycles will occupy a space of 300 000 000 metres between them. This means that one cycle will occupy 150 000 000 metres, which is also its wavelength. Thus, as frequency is increased, the wavelength is decreased in the same proportion and vice versa; putting this in a formula:

$$
\text{wavelength} = \frac{\text{speed of radio waves}}{\text{frequency}}
$$

and

$$
\text{frequency} = \frac{\text{speed of radio waves}}{\text{wavelength}}.
$$

By use of the above formula it is possible to convert frequency into wavelength and wavelength into frequency. To avoid any errors, at least at the beginning, basic units should be used in the formula. The use of hertz for frequency gives metres for wavelength; the use of metres for wavelength gives hertz for frequency which may then be expressed as kHz or MHz as appropriate for the answer.

Examples

1. If the wavelength is 1.5 kilometres, what is the frequency?

$$\text{Frequency in hertz} = \frac{\text{speed in metres per second}}{\text{wavelength in metres}}$$

$$= \frac{300\,000\,000}{1\,500}$$

$$= 200\,000 \text{ Hz}$$

$$= 200 \text{ kHz}$$

2. If the transmission frequency is 75 MHz, what is the wavelength?

$$\text{Wavelength in metres} = \frac{\text{speed in metres per second}}{\text{frequency in hertz}}$$

$$= \frac{300\,000\,000}{75\,000\,000}$$

$$= 4 \text{ metres}$$

3. If the wavelength is 3 cm, what is the frequency?

$$\text{Frequency} = \frac{300\,000\,000 \times 100}{3}$$

$$= 10\,000\,000\,000 \text{ Hz}$$

$$= 10\,000 \text{ MHz or } 10 \text{ GHz}$$

(Note that the factor 100 in the solution above converts 3 cm to metres.)

4. If the frequency is 13 500 MHz, what is the wavelength?

$$\text{Wavelength} = \frac{300\,000\,000}{13\,500\,000\,000}$$

$$= \frac{3}{135}$$

$$= 0.0222 \text{ metres}$$

$$= 2.22 \text{ cm}$$

5. How many wavelengths, to the nearest whole number, of frequency 150 MHz are equivalent to 52 feet?

$$\text{Wavelength} = \frac{300\,000\,000}{150\,000\,000}$$

$$= 2 \text{ metres}$$

$$= 2 \times 3.28 \text{ ft}$$

$$= 6.56 \text{ ft}$$

The number of times 6.56 ft will go into 52 ft $= \dfrac{52}{6.56}$

$$= 8 \text{ (approx.)}$$

Now try these.

1. Wavelength is 3 metres, what is the frequency?

Answer: 100 MHz

2.   Express 100 KHz in metres.
Answer: 3 000 metres
3.   Wavelength is 3 520 metres, what is the frequency?
Answer: 85.23 KHz
4.   Frequency 325 kHz, what is the wavelength?
Answer: 923.07 metres
5.   Frequency 117 000 kHz, what is the wavelength?
Answer: 2.56 metres
6.   Wavelength 3.41 centimetres, what is the frequency?
Answer: 8 797.6 MHz
7.   How many wavelengths to the nearest whole number is equivalent to 60 feet if
the transmission frequency is 100 MHz? (1 metre = 3.28 feet)
Answer: 6 wavelengths
8.   If wavelength is 2.739 metres, what is the frequency?
Answer: 109.53 MHz
9.   Give the frequency appropriate to a wavelength of 2 222 metres.
Answer: 135.01 kHz
10. If the frequency is 1 439 kHz what is its wavelength?
Answer: 208.47 metres

Phase and phase difference
Consider a vector, rotating about central axis O and producing an AC waveform. As
the vector OR, starting from its position of rest, R, completes one revolution, it will
produce one complete cycle of AC. This cycle may be plotted on a horizontal axis,
representing 360° (fig. 1.2).

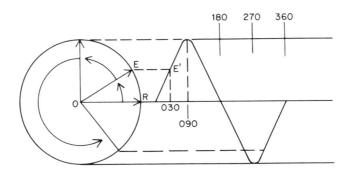

fig. 1.2

If the vector is stopped at some stage of its revolution, say at point E (30° anti-
clockwise from OR position), it will have traced the cycle from zero position on the
horizontal axis up to point E′. E′ is then the instantaneous phase of that cycle. In
other words, any stage in the cycle of an alternating current is referred to as its
phase.
    If two transmissions were taking place on the same frequency, two waveforms
would superimpose each other, providing the transmission commenced at the same instant
Then, the two waveforms are said to be 'in phase'. A fractional delay in sending off

the second transmission would cause them to be out of phase. To define the term —
if two alternating currents of the same frequency (therefore, their amplitudes need
not be the same) do not reach the same value at the same instant of time, they are
out of phase. The phase difference is the angular difference between the corresponding
points on the waveform and is measurable. This forms a principle of some of the
navigational aids. Two waveforms having any number of degrees of phase difference
between them can be drawn by considering revolutions of two vectors placed similarly
apart and by tracing their instantaneous values. The point is illustrated in fig. 1.3(a)
and (b).

fig. 1.3(a)

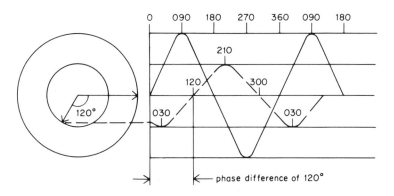

fig. 1.3(b)

Fig. 1.3(c) is a further illustration showing two signals 240° out of phase. (With
regard to the shapes of the a.c. waves in these diagrams it should be noted that in strict
theory, the waves take the shapes of a sine curve.)

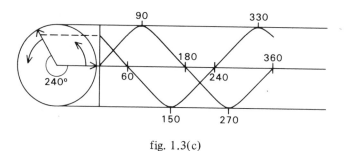

fig. 1.3(c)

Polarisation

As mentioned earlier in the chapter, when a suitable alternating current is applied to an aerial, electromagnetic waves are radiated from the aerial. These waves alternate with the same frequency as that of the a.c. applied to the aerial. The two components, electric and magnetic, thus radiated travel together at the speed of light. Both travel at right angles to each other (see fig. 1.4) and also at right angles to the direction of propagation.

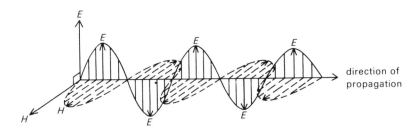

fig. 1.4 A vertically polarised signal

When the transmission is being made from a vertical aerial the electrical component, E, travels in the vertical plane and its associated magnetic component, H, in the horizontal plane and the emission is called vertically polarised. Similarly, for a horizontal aerial the electrical component travels in the horizontal plane, the magnetic component in the vertical plane and the emission is horizontally polarised. Where the electrical and magnetic components spin about the axis of advance, the signal is circularly polarised. This technique is used in reducing rain clutter in radar.

The importance of knowledge of polarisation lies in the orientation of the receiver aerial. A vertical aerial will efficiently receive the electrical component of a vertically polarised signal. If the receiver aerial, on the other hand, was perfectly horizontal it would receive no electrical component. Similarly a horizontal aerial will efficiently receive a horizontally polarised signal.

The vector lengths in fig. 1.4 represent the field intensity of the signal at a given instant. As the signal travels further the energy spreads out in an ever-increasing volume of space. This is one form of attenuation of the signals — attenuation due to spread out. The reduction in field strength is governed by the inverse square law in experimental conditions in vacuum. Thus, if the field strength of a point at a given distance from the transmitter measures, say 80 microvolts, then the reading at another point twice the distance from the transmitter will be a quarter of the value, that is, 20 microvolts.

Polar diagram

A polar diagram can be drawn up for any aerial or aerial system to represent the relative values of either field strength or power radiated at various points in both horizontal and vertical planes. For example, the polar diagram of a simple vertical aerial, radiating equally in all directions, is a circle. The polar diagram of two such aerials placed half a wavelength apart would be a figure of eight. Directional aerials radiate most strongly in the required direction and consequently, in any other direction the energy transmitted will be less than the maximum value, see fig. 1.5.

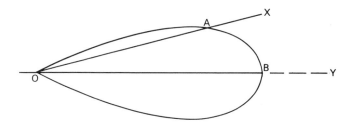

fig. 1.5 Example of a polar diagram

The strength of transmission in the predetermined direction is shown by vector OB. On the same scale, vector OA represents the transmission strength in the direction of X.

The polar diagram of a receiver aerial similarly gives indication of reception from various directions. An aerial with a circular polar diagram would receive signals equally from all directions whereas an aerial with a polar diagram of a figure of eight (ADF loop aerial) would receive maximum signals from one direction and no signals if the aerial were turned 90° from the original position. In fig. 1.5, if the receiving aerial was at O, it would receive maximum signals from a transmitter in the direction of Y and reduced signals from direction X.

Modulation

A page left blank in a newspaper conveys no information. To convey information it must be impressed with print. A plain radio wave may be likened to the blank newsprint. It can neither be heard nor can it convey information. If it is made audible by use of special components (BFO: this will be considered in a later chapter) the only signal heard is a constant audio tone but still nothing is 'read'. Therefore, some form of intelligence must be impressed upon such a wave if it is to convey information. The process of impressing such intelligence is called 'modulation'. It is done in a variety of ways, but since in all cases the radio waves simply act as a vehicle for the information, they are commonly called 'carrier waves' (CW). The waveform of information which is being impressed on this carrier is called a 'modulating wave'. Some of the ways in which the carrier wave may be changed to transmit information are given below.

Keying.   This is radio telegraphy. It consists of starting and stopping the continuous carrier so as to break it up into the form of dots and dashes. The communication is by a code, groups of dots and dashes having been assigned particular meanings. The technique is primarily used for long-distance communication; a radio navigation facility may break its carrier to identify itself by dots and dashes. The receiver requires BFO facility to make the signals audible.

Amplitude modulation.   This method may be used in one of two ways: to transmit coded messages at audio frequencies (AF) or to radiate speech, music, etc.

As the name suggests, in this method, the amplitude of the carrier is varied in conformation with the amplitude of the audio modulating signal, keeping the carrier's frequency constant. To transmit coded information, e.g. ident of a navigation facility, breaks must be caused in the audio. This is done either by keying on/off just the audio tone, or both audio and the carrier.

In fig. 1.6, audio signal B is impressed on radio frequency (RF) A. Suppose the amplitude of both A and B is one unit. It will be noted that the resultant envelope

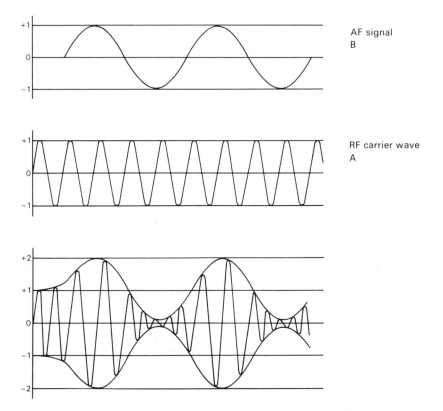

fig. 1.6 100% modulated RF signal

of the carrier wave is the picture of the modulating audio wave and that its amplitude has increased to 2 units, now varying between values 0 and 2.

When a signal is amplitude modulated, its resultant amplitude varies between the sum and difference of the amplitudes of the two waves. In fig. 1.6 the sum of the amplitudes of A and B is 2 and the difference is 0 and the amplitude of the audio being carried varies between values 2 and 0. This is a measure of the modulation depth. Modulation depth is the extent to which the carrier is modulated and is expressed as a percentage. It is the ratio

$$\frac{\text{amplitude of B}}{\text{amplitude of A}} \times 100$$

In fig. 1.6 the modulation depth is 100%. If the carrier's amplitude was 2 units and the audio's 1 unit, the resultant audio would vary between 3 and 1 and the modulation depth would be 50%.

The degree of modulation is an important design consideration. Here we are concerned with two factors: the strength of the outgoing audio and the power required to produce it. The variation in the amplitude of the outgoing modulated signal controls the strength of the audio being carried. Thus, a signal with 100% modulation depth will be stronger compared with a 50% modulated signal. High modulation depth would appeal to broadcasters whose speech and music would be heard loudest when 100% modulated. In practice they keep their modulation depth to slightly below 100%. Over-modulation causes distortion in the reception.

As for the power considerations, extra power must be supplied to amplitude-modulate a carrier. The power requirement increases by half for a 100% modulated signal but it falls rapidly when the modulation depth is decreased. Thus, for a given power output and the other conditions being equal, an unmodulated signal will travel further than an amplitude-modulated signal.

Broadcasters in LF and MF bands employ amplitude modulation, so does the civil aviation in VHF RT.

Frequency modulation
This technique of conveying information was developed in the U.S.A. after the shortcomings of AM transmission due to external unwanted noise became apparent during the First World War. It is achieved by varying the frequency of the carrier in accordance with the change in the amplitude of the audio, keeping the amplitude of the carrier constant (fig. 1.7). The extent of frequency deviation depends on the modulating audio; it is more than the mean carrier frequency when the audio amplitude is positive, and less than the mean when it is negative. The maximum deviation occurs at the positive and negative peaks. In the receiver a frequency discriminator unit detects these deviations and converts them into useful information.

Comparing the technique of frequency modulation with amplitude modulation, FM transmitters are simpler than AM transmitters, the necessary modulating power is relatively lower and the reception is practically static free. This last benefit is due to the fact that the VHF band is practically free from static, and where it is present, it is normally an amplitude oriented disturbance which enters freely into a vertical receiving aerial. Of the disadvantages, FM receivers are more complex and the modulated transmission calls for a much wider frequency band to cover its multi-

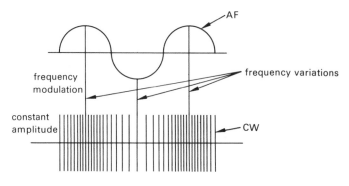

fig. 1.7

sidebands (see below). This is why FM broadcasters operate in the VHF band: the congestion in lower frequency bands would not permit accommodation of the necessary bandwidth. Being in the VHF, as a side benefit they can cover a complete range of human audio frequencies (up to 15 kHz) and thus provide high fidelity reception whereas in the MF band they would have to be content with staying inside the limit of a spread of 10 kHz.

In civil aviation this technique is employed in radio altimeters which measure height above the surface, and VOR transmits a frequency-modulated carrier. A CW Doppler may find its height using this technique.

Pulse modulation
Pulse modulation is used in radar, and there is a variety of forms of pulse modulations in current use. The modulating pulses in the simplest form amplitude-modulate the carrier, giving it the shape of the pulses.

Sidebands
Sidebands are additional frequencies which occur whenever a carrier is modulated by a frequency lower than itself, particularly audio frequencies.

When a carrier wave is amplitude-modulated, the resultant radiation consists of three frequencies made up as follows:

carrier frequency

carrier frequency + audio frequency

carrier frequency − audio frequency.

All these frequencies travel together and the new frequencies are called 'sidebands'. In fig. 1.8, a carrier frequency of 500 kHz is shown being amplitude-modulated by an audio tone of 2 kHz. The resultant side frequencies are: 498 kHz and 502 kHz. The former is called 'lower sideband' and the latter is called 'upper sideband'. The complete range, from 498 kHz to 502 kHz is called 'bandwidth', which is 4 kHz in this illustration.

Unlike AM, a frequency-modulated signal carries with it a multiple of sidebands and consequently its bandwidth is greater.

In the process of modulation, it is the sidebands and not the carrier which carry the intelligence. Therefore, the receiver must be capable of admitting an adequate

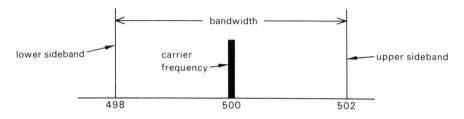

fig. 1.8 Production of sidebands

range of frequencies on either side of the carrier when the carrier frequency is being tuned in. The receiver's bandwidth may be broader than necessary for a particular reception. In this case, by means of a bandpass control this may be narrowed down to reduce external noise or interference from another station.

And because of the sidebands associated with carrier frequency, two stations operating on the same or similar frequencies must have sufficient geographical separation between them to prevent an overlap. This is the primary cause of congestion in the MF and LF bands. The precious frequency space may be utilised more economically by radiating just the single-banded transmission with an additional advantage of economy in the power requirement, or even both sidebands but each carrying different information, and utilising a common carrier. The following are examples of bandwidth requirements:

> speech transmission — 3 kHz
> music — between 10 and 15 kHz
> radar — 3 to 10 MHz.

Designation and classification of emissions

All radio transmissions are designated by ICAO according to their description and required bandwidth. We are concerned with the following:

(a)   Methods of modulating the carrier

   (i)   amplitude modulation — code letter A
   (ii)   frequency modulation — code letter F
   (iii)   pulse modulation — code letter P
   (Pulse structure will be discussed in a later chapter.)

(b)   Types of emission

These are coded in figures from 0 to 9 (inclusive); we are interested in the following:

   (i)   absence of any modulation intended to carry information — that is, a continuous wave without any modulation } code 0

   (ii)   telegraphy without the use of a modulating radio frequency, continuous wave keyed on/off without modulation } code 1

   (iii)   telegraphy by the on/off keying of a modulating audio frequency/frequencies, or by the on/off keying of the modulated emission } code 2

   (iv)   telephony (including sound broadcasting) — code 3
   (v)   cases not covered by 0 to 8 — code 9.

Examples of classes of emission are given in fig. 1.9 on page 12.

Emission	Facility
A0	None
A1	Communication by radio telegraphy (MF and HF), Consol
A2	Radio ranges, ILS and marker beacons
A3	Communication by radio telephony (VHF and HF RT), broadcast
A0A1	Long-range NDBs (Class A0 emission is keyed to give ident-A1)
A0A2	Short and medium range NDBs (ident by audio)
A9	VOR
P	Loran, DME

fig. 1.9

Test questions

1.   Describe an A3 emission and give one radio facility which you associate with it.

2.   Show by means of a diagram two radio signals of the same frequency and wavelength but one 330° out of phase and twice the amplitude of the other.

3.   In what plane does the magnetic field of a radio wave lie if it is

(a)   vertically polarised?

(b)   horizontally polarised?

4.   By means of suitable diagrams show the following radio emissions:

(a)   a frequency-modulated wave;

(b)   an amplitude-modulated wave.

5.   What do you understand by the terms (indicating type of emission) A2, P, A0A2? Suggest one facility to which it might refer.

6. Show by means of a diagram a radio wave which has A1 emission.

7.   What is an A1 emission?

8.   What do you understand by the term 'frequency modulation'? State one facility which might use this type of emission.

9.   What do you understand by

(a)   sideband?

(b)   an A0A1 emission?

10. Explain briefly the terms 'phase' and 'phase difference'.

2: Propagation and Properties – 1

Simple transmitter

The basic components of a simple radio transmitter are shown in fig. 2.1.

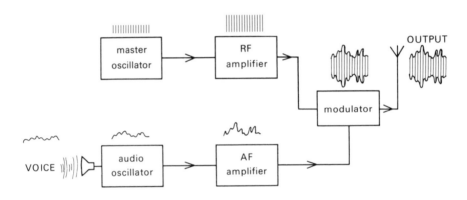

fig. 2.1 Simple transmitter

Oscillator.   The purpose of an oscillator is to provide a radio carrier wave. At very high frequencies a unit called a magnetron may be used to produce the oscillations.
Radio frequency (RF) amplifier.   The signals produced by the oscillator are too weak for transmission and they must be amplified. This amplification is done at the RF amplifier which is coupled to the oscillator, and the outgoing amplified signals are fed to the modulator.
Microphone and audio frequency (AF) amplifier.   Similarly, a microphone produces weak audio signals which are amplified by the AF amplifier unit. The amplified signals are then fed to the modulator.
Modulator.   In this unit the audio signals modulate the carrier waves by varying the amplitude (amplitude modulation) or the frequency (frequency modulation); the resultant modulated signals are fed for further amplification to the power amplifier.
Power amplifier.   Modulated signals arriving at this unit (not shown in fig. 2.1) are finally amplified (by stages if necessary) to the transmission level.
Aerial.   Modulated and amplified signals are fed to the aerial by the power amplifier and the electromagnetic radiation takes place.

General properties of radio waves
    (a)   In a given medium, radio waves travel at a constant speed.
    (b)   When passing from one medium to another of different refractive index, the

velocity of the waves changes. The waves are also deflected towards the medium of higher refractive index, that is, they change their direction.

(c)   Radio waves are reflected by objects commensurate with their wave lengths.

(d)   Uninfluenced, radio waves travel in a straight line.

Radio spectrum

The electromagnetic spectrum starts at the lower end of the radio frequencies, that is 3 kHz, and stretches to over ten million million gigahertz where the radiation takes the form of gamma radiation. In this vast spectrum, radio frequencies occupy only a very small part. Different frequencies are found to have different characteristics and in order to identify frequencies having similar characteristics the full range of the radio spectrum is divided into various groups called frequency bands. The following frequency bands are internationally recognised.

	Frequency band	Abbreviation	Frequencies	Wavelength
Com. & nav. aids	very low frequency	VLF	3–30 kHz	100–10 km
	low frequency	LF	30–300 kHz	10 000–1 000 m
	medium frequency	MF	300–3 000 kHz	1 000–100 m
	high frequency	HF	3–30 MHz	100–10 m
Radar	very high frequency	VHF	30–300 MHz	10–1 m
	ultra high frequency	UHF	300–3 000 MHz	100–10 cm
	super high frequency	SHF	3 000–30 000 MHz	10–1 cm
	extremely high frequency	EHF	30 000–300 000 MHz	1–0.1 cm

It will, however, be appreciated that these divisions are not 'water-tight' divisions and the characteristics of a particular band may overlap above and below its demarcation line.

The earth and its surround

Before we set out to discuss the type of propagation, properties and the ranges available in the above frequency bands, let us take a quick look at the physical elements present on and around the earth.

First of all, the shape of the earth: it is a sphere. This means that the horizon curves away with distance from the transmission point, and if the radio waves travelled only in straight lines (as they would, by their basic property) the reception ranges would be limited to 'optical' distance only. This distance is given by the formula $D = 1.05 \sqrt{H}$, where D is the range in nautical miles and H is the height in feet. Fortunately, we will soon see that radio waves do curve to a greater or lesser extent with the surface of the earth and in the atmosphere, which means that the above formula is seldom used.

The conductivity of the earth's surface itself varies: sea water provides a medium of high conductivity whereas the conductivity of the land surface depends on its composition. It is fairly high where the soil is rich, and very poor in the sands of a desert or the polar ice caps. The terrain itself varies from flat plains to tall mountains, from deserts to dense jungles.

Surrounding the earth our atmosphere is rich in water vapour right up to the height of the tropopause. Water vapour is the major cause of the weather and the weather means precipitation, thunderstorms, lightning and so forth. Electrical activity may be expected in any of these attributes of the weather. The other characteristics of the atmosphere, pressure, density, temperature, all vary continually, both horizontally along the surface and with height.

And finally, well above the earth's surface we have electrically conducting belts of ionised layers caused by the ultra-violet rays of the sun.

Radio waves travel best in the free space. On and around the surface of the earth they are influenced to a varying degree by the factors discussed in the preceding paragraphs. We will now study these influences in detail.

Propagation: surface waves

When electromagnetic waves are radiated from an omni-directional aerial, some of the energy will travel along the surface of the earth. These waves, gliding along the surface are called 'surface waves' or 'ground waves'. As we learnt earlier, it is the nature of radio waves to travel in a straight line. However, in appropriate conditions they tend to follow the earth's surface giving us increased ranges. But, what causes them to curve with the surface?

Primarily there are two factors. One, the phenomenon of diffraction and scattering causes the radio waves to bend and go over and around any obstacles in their path (see fig. 2.2(a)). As the earth's surface is full of large and small obstacles, the waveform is assisted almost continually to curve round the surface. The extent of diffraction depends on the radio wave's frequency (see fig. 2.2(b)). The diffraction is maximum at the lowest end of the spectrum and it decreases as the frequency is increased. At centimetric wavelengths (SHF) an upstanding obstacle stops the wavefront, causing a shadow behind it. It is because of this effect that low frequency broadcasts give good field strength behind a range of hills but there is no reception on your car radio when going under a railway bridge.

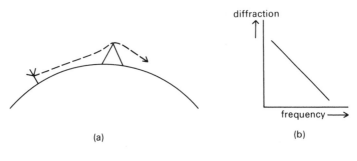

(a)   (b)

fig. 2.2

This bending downward is further assisted (the other factor) by the fact that as a part of the waveform comes in contact with the surface it induces currents in it, thereby losing some of its energy and slowing down. This is called surface attenuation. This slowing down of the bottom gives the waveform a forward and downward tilt encouraging it to follow the earth's curvature (see fig. 2.3(a)).

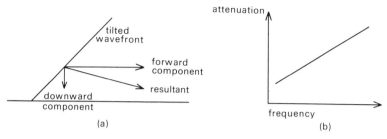

fig. 2.3

Thus, bending due to diffraction and tilting due to attenuation (imperfect conductivity of the surface) cause the waves to curve with the surface. Waves continue until they are finally attenuated, that is, become undetectable.

Attenuation, in its turn, depends on two factors.

(a)   The type of the surface. As mentioned earlier, different surfaces have different conductivities. For a given transmission power a radio wave will travel a longer distance over the sea than over dry soil. The example is Consol navigation aid. Its range over the sea is nearly double of that over the land.

(b)   Frequency in use. The higher the frequency, the greater the attenuation (see fig. 2.3(b)).

In combating attenuation, we have no control over the surface over which the propagation is to be made. The primary consideration therefore, is the choice of frequency. We are now ready to summarise the ground ranges expected from frequencies in various frequency bands.

VLF. Attenuation is least, maximum bending is due to diffraction. Given sufficient power, ranges of several thousand miles may be obtained.

LF. Attenuation is less and the signals will bend with the earth's surface; ranges to a distance of 1 500 nm may be expected.

MF. Attenuation is now increasing, signals still bend with the surface and the ranges are approximately 300 to 500 nm, maximum is 1 000 nm over the sea.

HF. Severe attenuation, bending is least. The maximum range obtainable is around 70 to 100 nm.

VHF and above. The signals do not bend and the radio waves travel in a straight line, giving line-of-sight ranges.

Disadvantages at low frequencies.   Although low frequencies produce very long ranges there are considerable drawbacks which prohibit their inconsiderate employment.

(a)   Low efficiency aerials. Ideally the length of the transmitter and receiver aerials should each be equal to the wavelength. An aerial approximately half the size of the wavelength is also considered to be suitable for satisfactory operation. Any further reduction in the aerial size would result in a loss of efficiency. The largest aerials are found in the lowest frequency band – VLF.

(b)   Static is severe at lower frequencies and additional power must be supplied to combat its effect. The effect of static decreases as the frequency is increased: VHF is considered to be practically free from static.

(c)   Installation and power. The cost of initial installation is high and subsequent power requirement to maintain the desired range giving satisfactory reception is very large.

3: Propagation and Properties – 2

Sky waves

We saw in the previous chapter how surface waves may be transmitted to varying distances in VLF to HF bands. In these bands, signals may also be received having first been reflected from a huge reflecting layer surrounding the earth known as the ionosphere. These reflected signals are referred to as 'sky waves' and they form the principal mechanism for long range communication.

The ionosphere

The ionosphere is an electrically conducting sphere, completely surrounding the earth. The ultra-violet rays from the sun impinging upon the upper atmosphere cause electrons to be emitted from gas molecules. These free electrons are believed to form a reflecting layer (positive ions would be too heavy to influence electromagnetic waves). Because the absorption of the solar radiation is uneven at different levels in the upper atmosphere, several distinct and separate layers, rather than one continuous zone, are formed. They are given code names D, E and F (see fig. 3.1). During the period 1901–30, the E layer was more commonly known as the 'Kennelly-Heaviside'

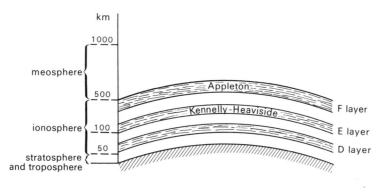

fig. 3.1

layer, named after its discoverers. The presence of the F layer was established simultaneously by E. V. Appleton in England and A. F. Barnett in the U.S.A. and direct measurements were made in 1925, hence the name of F layer. At present, these belts may be identified either by the code letter or the layer names. Average heights of these layers are as follows, and there are diurnal and seasonal variations.

> D layer : 50–100 km, average 75 km
> E layer : 100–150 km, average 125 km
> F layer : 150–350 km, average 225 km

The maximum daylight density of the E region is around 10^5 free electrons/cm^3. During the day time the F layer may exist in two separate regions, when the layers are called F_1 and F_2. The maximum value of the electron density in the F layer is around 10^6/cm^3. When they are separate, F_2 is more persistent than F_1. The electron density in the D, E and F layers varies with time of the day, season of the year and geographical location, as explained below. The overall variation in the E layer is relatively small, but abnormal, sporadic fluctuations may occur all year round, but are more pronounced in summer months. Fluctuations in the F layer are relatively large and irregular, more so during magnetic storms, sun-spot activities and flares. Ionisation in these layers causes refraction, reflection and attenuation of the radio waves, which we will now discuss.

Refraction

Since atmosphere and ionosphere constitute different media, a signal travelling upward will be refracted. If the conditions are suitable it may bend sufficiently to return to the earth. By the accepted usage, the process is called 'ionospheric refraction'. It should be noted that the waves may be refracted by the lower layer and then further refracted by an upper layer. The wave may then return or escape.

Density

The degree of refraction varies directly as the intensity of the ionisation.

The higher the altitude, the lesser the atmosphere. At a height of 60 km the atmospheric pressure is about 0.35 mbar. At such altitudes the solar radiation has a greater effect in breaking down the gas molecules than at lower altitudes where the atmosphere is denser.

Electron density in the E layer is higher than in the D layer; the density in the F layer is higher than in the E layer. Variations in the density occur as follows.

Diurnal activity.   In the day-time the solar radiation increases ionic density in all layers and the reflective height moves down. As the sun crosses the meridian the maximum density will be reached. At night as the sun goes below the horizon the process of recombination begins. The D layer, being nearest to the earth and having relatively denser atmosphere, completely disappears. In the E layer the intensity decreases and the reflecting height rises. The F layer similarly decreases in intensity and finds an intermediate level as one single layer (fig. 3.2). Sunrise and sunset produce unstable conditions as the layers start falling or rising. These are critical periods for the operation of the radio compass.

Seasonal activity.   The amount of intensity depends on where the sun is with regard to the position under consideration. There is maximum activity when the sun is closest. Sporadic ionisation occurs in the E layer in summer.

11-year sun-spot cycle.   Very marked changes in ionisation occur during this sun-spot activity period. This is due to enhanced ultra-violet and X-radiation from the sun. At this time, ionisation in D and E causes an increase in absorption disrupting communication, and signals at VHF frequencies may return.

Attenuation

As mentioned earlier, radio energy is absorbed in the ionosphere. The extent of attenuation depends on various factors.

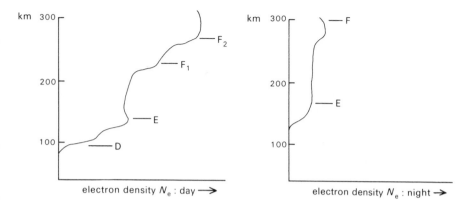

fig. 3.2

(a)   Density of the layer. The greater the density, the greater the attenuation. Maximum attenuation occurs around mid-day.

(b)   Penetration depth. The deeper the signal penetrates into the layer, the more loss of energy due to attenuation will occur.

(c)   Frequency in use. The lower the frequency, the greater the attenuation. This is one of the reasons why a higher frequency is used for communication in the HF band during the day.

Conditions of refraction

Critical angle.   The angle at which the signal strikes the layer decides, among other factors, whether the signal will return or not. If it strikes the layer at a small angle it will not be refracted sufficiently to return. As this angle of incidence is progressively increased, the signals will bend progressively more until an angle is reached for a given frequency and ionospheric distribution when the first reflection will occur. The angle this wave makes with the normal at the transmission point is called the 'critical angle' (see fig. 3.3) and the returned wave is called the 'critical ray' or 'first sky return'. At this angle, and higher than this, there will be an uninterrupted flow of skywaves.

Frequency in use.   A higher frequency requires a higher electron density to refract it. As ionic density increases with height, higher frequencies will penetrate more deeply into the layer than lower frequencies before returning.

The D layer is not heavily ionised and it will reflect only low frequencies – up to around 500 kHz. For any planned usage of sky waves in this frequency band it should be remembered that the attenuation is predominant.

The E layer is relatively more heavily ionised and will reflect frequencies up to around 2 MHz.

F layer.   Frequencies higher than 2 MHz will not be sufficiently refracted in the E layer to return. They will travel to the F layer before returning, thus giving very long ranges. Above 30 MHz, that is VHF and above, the refraction in the layers is insufficient and the signals escape into free space. (The UHF band is used for communication with astronauts in the outer space.) An exception arises in the cases of VHF and UHF during the high solar activity period when the ionisation is extremely dense.

Ranges available

The ranges available from the sky waves depend on the following factors.

(a)   Transmission power.

(b)   Depth of penetration. This depends on the frequency in use and the iono-spheric distribution. The deeper a signal travels before being refracted, the larger the ranges it produces. (Higher frequencies require a higher density to refract them.)

(c)   Critical angle and angle of incidence. The critical angle will determine the range at which the first sky return occurs, and the prevailing conditions might produce a dead space (see below) where no reception is possible. Similarly, maximum range is given by that wave which leaves the transmitter tangential to the earth.

Fig. 3.3 illustrates the propagation through the ionosphere at various frequencies during day and night.

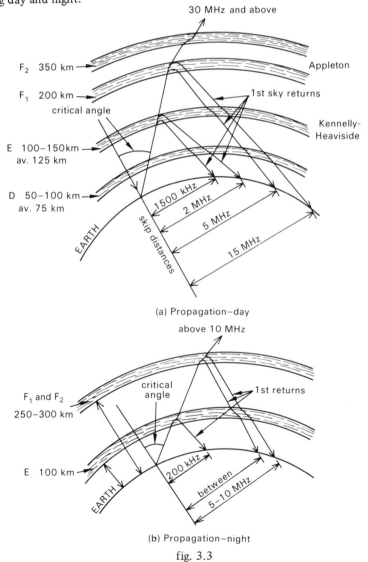

(a) Propagation—day

(b) Propagation—night

fig. 3.3

Skip distance and dead space

The distance between the transmitter and the point on the surface where the first sky return arrives is called the 'skip distance'. For a given frequency the skip distance varies with the time of day and also the seasons.

Where a signal produces both surface wave and sky wave, there may be an area where no reception is possible. This is because the surface wave's limit has been reached and the sky waves have not started returning (see fig. 3.4). This area, that is, the area between the limit of the surface wave and the point of reception of the first sky wave is termed 'dead space'.

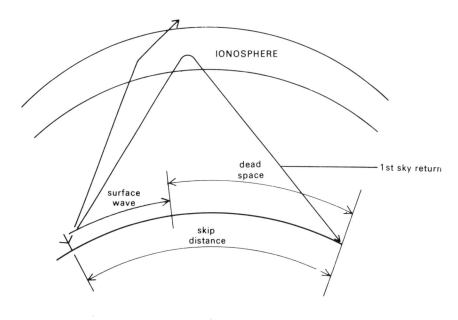

fig. 3.4

Dead space is possible in HF where the surface wave is very short and the refraction occurs at higher layers. As the frequency is lowered to MF and LF the surface wave increases whereas the sky wave is returned from lower layers at low critical angles. In these circumstances generally there is no dead space.

Multi-hop refraction

If the returning signals are sufficiently strong they will be reflected from the earth's surface back to the ionosphere where they will be refracted and returned again. This process may continue several times until the signals are finally attenuated by passage through the ionosphere and contact with the earth's surface at the point of reflection (fig. 3.5). This phenomenon is known as 'multi-hop refraction' and very long ranges are obtained using this type of propagation. When multi-hop propagation is taking place the first return is called the 1st hop and its subsequent reflections are called 2nd hop and so on. If the angle of incidence is right, the signals can travel round the world and an 'echo' of the previous reception may arrive 1/7th second later.

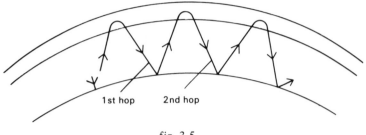

1st hop   2nd hop

fig. 3.5

Fading

Fading is always present, to a greater or lesser extent in sky wave reception because of continuous fluctuations in the ionosphere. The relative phases of the sky waves arriving at a receiver vary in random fashion affecting the amplitude of the output.

It is also possible to receive two sky waves which have travelled different routes or to receive both 1st hop and 2nd hop signals. Since they have not travelled the same distance there will be a phase difference between them. When the two incoming signals are in phase they augment each other giving stronger reception; when they are directly in opposition they cancel themselves out.

Summary of properties, using sky waves

VLF, LF. Some sky waves are present during the day, also at night. Low frequencies reflect at relatively low heights, ionospheric attenuation is very large and the propagation is mainly by surface waves.

MF. This frequency band is in mid-position between surface wave and sky wave. Surface wave distances are getting shorter (compared with VLF and LF); the sky waves increase these distances, particularly at night. Sky wave attenuation is less, atmospheric interference is also less but still troublesome. Sky waves in this band are a blessing to such facilities as Loran and Consol but are a nuisance to ADF operation.

HF. Surface waves travel only a short distance but very great ranges are achieved using sky waves. Comparative power requirements are less, ionospheric attenuation being only slight.

VHF and above. All frequencies above 30 MHz escape into free space. The ionospheric density is not sufficient to refract them back to the earth.

4: Propagation and Properties – 3

Space waves

We learnt in the previous chapter that above HF neither sky waves nor ground waves may be usefully employed. At frequencies in VHF and above, the only radiated wave which can be used is the one which travels in a direct line from the transmitter aerial to the receiver aerial. This type of transmission is called 'line-of-sight' transmission and it means that if a straight line can be drawn joining the transmitter and receiver, the signals can be received (but see below). The signals thus received are called 'direct waves'.

Sometimes an aircraft may pick up the same signal from two directions: one having travelled direct to the aircraft and the other having first been reflected by the surface (fig. 4.1). Such a signal is called a 'ground reflected wave'. The direct waves and the

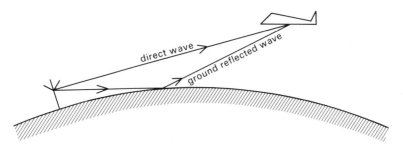

fig. 4.1

ground reflected waves are collectively called 'space waves'. It will be appreciated that when signals are being received from two directions as above, the receiver output will be the vector addition of the two: maximum strength when the two signals are in phase, and fading of signals when the signals are out of phase. The phase relationship between the two signals is governed by the lengths of the two paths and the phase shift at the reflecting point. This phase shift, in its turn, depends on the angle of incidence, polarisation of the incident signal and the conductivity of the reflecting surface.

Ranges

VHF and frequency bands above VHF are straight-line propagation. However, the actual range is slightly better than mere optical range. As we mentioned earlier the distance to the horizon is given in the formula $D = 1.05 \sqrt{H}$. The improvement to this range is from the refraction or curving of the waves in atmosphere, due to 'atmospheric refraction'.

The refractive index of the atmosphere, n, is a function of pressure, temperature and humidity. These elements vary significantly in the vertical plane giving rise to diminishing density with increasing height. This means that the refractive index decreases with height. The result is that the radio wave curves away from it towards the regions of higher density, that is, towards the surface. Thus, signals in VHF and above will be received beyond the optical horizon and the working formula for calculating maximum ranges is:

$$D = 1.25 \sqrt{H_T} + 1.25 \sqrt{H_R}$$

where D is the range in nautical miles, H_T is the height in feet of the transmitter (amsl) and H_R is the height in feet of the receiver (amsl).

Ground waves

The term 'ground wave' is used to describe all types of propagation except sky waves. Thus, a surface wave is also a ground wave, so is a space wave.

$$\left.\begin{array}{l}\text{direct wave}\\ \text{and}\\ \text{ground reflected wave}\end{array}\right\} = \left.\begin{array}{l}\text{space wave}\\ \text{and}\\ \text{surface wave}\end{array}\right\} = \text{ground wave}$$

Duct propagation or superrefraction

In the above discussion on ranges we saw how a ray curves towards the earth's surface due to the varying refractive index of the atmosphere. If the curvature were slightly greater, the ray would curve sufficiently to travel parallel to the earth's surface and would give very long surface ranges. In normal conditions, however, this is not so, but meteorological conditions can exist from time to time at an altitude which could produce an increased curvature.

The rise of temperature with height results in an inversion layer only a few thousand feet above the earth's surface. Immediately above such a layer an abrupt fall in the temperature would be noticed. This condition is sufficient to create a negative refractive index and signals passing through would be refracted and returned to the earth's surface. A similar effect would be produced by evaporation of water and its diffusion into a layer above the surface. These types of phenomenon occur in the VHF band and above and cause freak reception at ranges of several hundred miles. The meteorological conditions suitable for such propagation are:

(a)   warm, dry air blowing over cool sea
(b)   subsidence
(c)   pronounced radiation cooling.

This type of propagation is called 'duct propagation' or 'superrefraction' (see fig. 4.2).

The climatic conditions most conducive to the formation of duct propagation are usually found in tropical and sub-tropical latitudes. This is because the land mass can get extremely hot during the day followed by a rapid cooling at night.

Sporadic-E reception

Patches of intense ionisation occur from time to time in the E layer. The effect occurs all year round but is highly pronounced in summer. The patches are comparable

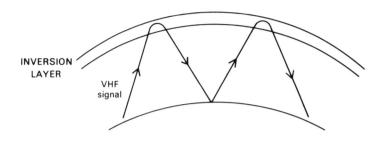

fig. 4.2

to clouds in the troposphere and drift with time. Sometimes they last for a few minutes, other times for a few hours. The signals up to about 150 MHz are scattered from the 'blobby' subsurface of the patches and may be received up to 1 000 to 1 500 nautical miles away. The phenomenon presents an ideal opportunity for long-range communication but for a DF application, due to its scattering effect the direction measured could be as much as 180° in error.

A scattering effect is also present in the troposphere in regions where air turbulence is prevailing. The eddies are found to contain discontinuous refractive indices, which results in abnormally strong signals on one occasion and equally strong interference on another.

Properties – miscellaneous

Static.   Static consists of amplitude-oriented spurious electromagnetic waves ranging in frequencies from a few hundred hertz to several thousand kilohertz. Atmospheric static is present in a cumulonimbus cloud, thunderstorms and all kinds of precipitations. Lightning discharge is a most common source of static.

Static also reaches us from interstellar space varying in frequency between 15 MHz and 100 MHz. It is high in field strength and fairly constant in amplitude. This is the very substance on which radio astronomers thrive.

Radio noise.   There are two sources of radio noise: avoidable and unavoidable.

Avoidable noise arises from use of poor-quality components, bad contacts and similar causes.

Unavoidable noise occurs both internally and externally. Internally, it is due to small thermal motions in the components. These are always present to a varying degree when the equipment operates at temperatures over absolute zero temperature. They show up as 'grass' on a radar screen or a hissing noise on a loudspeaker. The sight of grass on a radar screen is a source of delight to the operator who is thereby assured that at least the thing works up to that stage.

Externally, the source of noise is the electrical disturbance in the atmosphere and the outer space, in the form of static. Atmospheric static is important up to 30 MHz (end of HF band), extra-terrestrial noise may cause interference up to 100 MHz.

Seasonally, the effect of static is stronger in summer than in winter; geographically, it is stronger in the tropics than in temperate zones, and diurnally, it is stronger at night due to sky waves which travel a great distance picking up static en route.

Radio interference

Interference in reception may be caused by a variety of reasons. Due to congestion of radio frequencies, same and similar frequencies may be allotted to other stations which may cause direct interference. The remedy is that the propagation ranges of such stations are strictly regulated by the various States (protection range, altitude, see later chapters) and they determine the use of the station within its promulgated range altitude.

Stations are also given a fixed tolerance on transmission frequency and they must maintain the transmissions within these limits. Interference will be caused if the transmitter is allowed to drift beyond the limit, and if this comes to your notice the remedy is to report the matter to the authorities.

Man-made interference may exist where there are heavy industries in the vicinity of an aerodrome or a facility transmitter. Harmonics of 50 Hz a.c. can enter into ILS localiser radiation (150 Hz modulation), an overhead cable can affect an NDB radiation (Vanguard incident at Basle?) and even small components such as switches, motors and ignition systems can cause electrical noise resulting in interference. A moving vehicle can affect Cat II ILS directional characteristics. The remedy for this type of interference is to suppress it at the source. This type of interference does not affect high frequencies.

Signals/noise relationship

It will be apparent from the foregoing discussion that there is always some interference/noise present in the reception of radio signals. A receiver must be able to admit the selected frequency together with its sidebands. The bandwidth of a receiver may be too large. On other receivers it may be possible to select the bandwidth by means of a switch on the control box. If the interference is due to another more powerful transmitter on a nearby frequency, it may be cured by excluding interfering signals by narrowing down the reception bandwidth. Similarly, static interference may be minimised, but care must be taken not to exclude the wanted signal. Generally, do not select a bandwidth any higher than necessary.

The ultimate incoming signals (both wanted and unwanted) are expressed as signal/noise ratio. This ratio is given in decibels. A decibel (dB) is a unit which is extensively used in electronics to provide a measure of gain/loss in terms of power or voltage. In terms of voltage (in which the field strength is measured), the relationship is

$$\text{gain/loss in dB} = 20 \log (E_1/E_2).$$

Illustrating this: ICAO recommends that the States provide a protection to the NDB transmissions by ensuring a signal/noise ratio of at least 3 to 1. By means of the above formula we can work out what this means in terms of decibels.

$$\begin{aligned} \text{Gain} &= 20 \times \log 3 \\ &= 20 \times 0.4771 \\ &= 9.542 \text{ dB or } 10 \text{ dB.} \end{aligned}$$

Thus, the field strength of the wanted signal is 10 decibels higher than the unwanted signal.

Spurious noise may be reduced by such devices as wick dischargers and receiver filters.

Attenuation

Surface.   At low frequencies, the earth's surface acts as an absorber. Signals lose their strength as they travel forward. Attenuation also slows down a signal's velocity. The following velocities may be assumed for a 100 kHz signal:

299 750 000 metres/second over a good conducting surface (water),
299 250 000 metres/second over a poor conducting surface (sand).

At metric (VHF) and centimetric (SHF) wavelengths, the ground acts as a reflector.

Atmospheric.   Attenuation in the atmosphere occurs in two ways: by direct absorption in gases and by absorption and scattering by solid and liquid particles. Wavelengths of under 10 cm are affected by these elements and the effect progressively increases as the wavelength becomes shorter. Raindrops absorb signals at wavelengths immediately below 10 cm whereas signals of 5 mm wavelength are absorbed by oxygen molecules. The following are the typical losses as a signal travels a distance of one kilometre:

	Wavelength 5 cm	Wavelength 5 mm
Heavy rain	0.7 dB	7 dB
Fog, viz 100 ft	0.4 dB	3 dB

Summary

A summary of the frequency bands, characteristics of propagation and associated facilities is given in the following table.

Wavelength denomination	Frequency band	Characteristic	Application
myriametric	VLF	*Propagation:* ground and sky wave *Range:* 4 000 nm by surface wave *Static:* severe *Aerials:* very large	very long-range nav. aids Omega GPO long-range communicatic
kilometric	LF	*Propagation:* ground wave by day; ground wave and sky wave by night *Range:* 1 500 nm by surface wave *Static:* less, but still troublesome *Aerials:* large	Decca, NDB, Consol, Loran, Radio Range, Broadcast
hectometric	MF	*Propagation:* as LF *Range:* 300–500 nm, max. 1 000 nm over water by day; sky wave arrives a little beyond the ground wave, giving greater ranges at night *Static:* present and troublesome	NDB, Broadcast, Consol, Loran, Radio Range

Wavelength Denomination	Frequency band	Characteristic	Application
decametric	HF	*Propagation:* mainly by sky wave, day and night *Range:* ground wave approx. 100 nm; sky wave approx. 3 000 to 4 000 nm *Static:* still present but less troublesome	long-distance communication W/T, RT
metric	VHF	*Propagation:* space wave, giving line-of-sight ranges *Static:* negligible	VHF RT, ILS LOC, VDF, VOR, fan markers
decimetric	UHF	*Propagation:* line of sight *Attenuation:* attenuation from water vapour start above approx 1 000 MHz but not important	ILS GP, DME, surveillance radar, UHF RT
centimetric (also microwave)	SHF	as above, attenuation increase	PAR, surveillance radar, Doppler, airborne weather radar, radio altimeter
millimetric	EHF	as above, attenuation severe; very small aerials	airfield surface radar, experimental radar

Test questions
Check these out before going further — you won't regret it!
1. Explain the following terms
    (a) skip distance
    (b) ground (or surface) attenuation
    (c) duct propagation
    (d) ionospheric attenuation
    (e) atmospheric attenuation
    (f) tropospheric scatter.
2. By means of a suitable sketch, show the following
    (a) critical angle
    (b) skip distance
    (c) dead space
    (d) the wave giving the longest range by one hop.
3. Explain with the aid of a diagram the meaning of the term 'multi-hop refraction' and show the 1st, 2nd and 3rd hop on the diagram.
4. Discuss the advantages and disadvantages of sky waves to the present navigation aids.
5. Give the names and ranges of the frequency bands which lie between 30 kHz and 3 000 kHz inclusive, and give one example of a radio or radar facility appropriate to each band.

6. In which of the bands in question 5 would you expect to find
    (a)   the most complete freedom from static interference?
    (b)   sky waves reliable enough for use either by day or night?
    (c)   sky waves by night, but some or only weak ones by day?
7. When utilising sky wave propagation, what is the relationship between frequency and range? What factors affect this relationship?
8. Give a brief description of the ionosphere. What effect does it have on the reception of radio signals?
9. State briefly what you understand by 'atmospheric static'.
10. Comment briefly on the expression 'VHF line-of-sight transmission' used in radio.

5: Communication

Long range communication – choice of frequency band
To achieve communication on the basis of global distances, the choice must lie in the bands between VLF and HF, the frequency bands above HF being 'line-of-sight' propagation.

Starting at the lowest end, we could obtain very long ranges in the VLF and LF bands and settle for one of them without further ado, but there are some inherent disadvantages in the employment of these bands. Just two requirements, of aerial and power alone are sufficiently forbidding to spur the Marconis to investigate alternative possibilities.

And these possibilities are MF and HF. Of these two, HF is considered to be far superior:

(a)   aerials are shorter and less expensive to instal;
(b)   static noise is less than in MF and tolerable;
(c)   by using sky waves day and night, very long ranges are obtained for relatively less power;
(d)   higher frequencies suffer less attenuation in the ionosphere;
(e)   efficiency is further increased by beaming the radiation in the direction of the receiver.

In the early days of radio, experiments were made on the utilisation of long waves for communication purposes, but the benefits of the short waves soon became apparent and by the late twenties the rush was on for short waves.

HF communication
The principle of HF communication relies on choosing a frequency appropriate for a given set of ionospheric conditions that will produce the first return at the required skip distance from the transmitter. If the height of the reflecting layer is known, the ray's path from the transmitter to the receiver via the ionosphere can be plotted and, from this, the angle of incidence the ray makes at the ionosphere can be ascertained. The frequency to use, so that the ray travels along this path, is derived from the knowledge of the angle of incidence, θ, and the critical frequency, f_c. The critical frequency is that frequency which just starts to escape at vertical incidence to the ionosphere. The mathematical relationship between the two, $f_c \times$ secant θ, gives us what is called 'maximum usable frequency', MUF. This is the highest frequency available for that predetermined distance, prevailing density and height of penetration. If it is increased any further, the signal will escape. If it is lowered considerably, excessive attenuation will cause unacceptable power loss. When this limit is reached, it is called 'lowest usable high frequency', LUHF.

In practice, graphs and nomograms are made available to the radio stations from which this value is directly extracted. The graphs take into consideration such factors as the station's position in latitude and longitude, time of the day, season of the year, density of the ionosphere and any abnormal condition prevailing and the distance at which the first sky return is required.

It will be appreciated that because of the diurnal variation in the ionospheric density, if transmission is continued at night on day-time frequency, a wider skip distance will result, leaving the target receiver in the 'dead space'. This is because at night

(a)   the reflection height increases, and the wave is returned from a higher level, giving a greater skip distance

(b)   the density of the layer decreases which requires the same wave to travel still higher in denser density layers before being returned, giving the same consequence as (a).

For these reasons, the working frequency is lowered at night. This lowering of the frequency adjusts the skip distance because

(a)   lower frequencies reflect from lower levels

(b)   lower frequencies require a smaller critical angle.

It may be pointed out here that in lowering the frequency at night the signal is not being subjected to an increased attenuation since the density is less at night. In practice, the night frequencies are approximately half of the day-time values.

On the matter of the choice of frequency, if you are calling a station without success, but you are hearing another station which is at a greater distance in the same direction, you are operating on a frequency which is too high. The station you wish to contact is in the zone of skip distance. Lower the frequency.

The frequency band allotted to commercial aviation ranges from 2 MHz to 22 MHz – in practical use it is limited to around 18 MHz. The ground stations publish a number of frequencies for use, and the communication is generally addressed to the ATCC or ACC. The service range depends on the requirement (around 1 000 nm). The transmission is amplitude-modulated and a single sideband emission is used to economise in *power* and *channel space*.

In the early days when MF/HF W/T was in the forefront, the aircraft were equipped with a trailing aerial. It consisted of a coil of wire which was wound out and held downward by a weight. Normally it disappeared at the first sight of thunder or lightning. In another system a permanently fixed wire was used, stretching the length of the fuselage. These aerials have now been replaced by recessed aerials conveniently located to give an all-round reception.

Because of the expense of the initial installation, use of HF RT is limited at present to the airlines and other large aircraft. Power-wise, a mere 100-watt transmitter would provide transatlantic communication.

Factors affecting range

(a)   Transmission power.

(b)   Time of the day. This governs the density and height of refraction.

(c)   Season of the year. This has bearing on the density.

(d)   Any disturbances in the ionosphere.

(e)   Geographical location.

(f)   Frequency in use. This determines the critical angle and the penetration depth.

Short-range communication − choice of frequency band

The requirement here is to provide communication at 80 nm range at 5 000 ft and 200 nm at 20 000 ft. As these are very short ranges, frequency bands from VLF to HF may be ruled out.

Up the spectrum from VHF, it is best to choose the lowest frequency band from the aerial consideration. The aerial requirement gets more complicated as higher frequency bands are reached. Even in VHF, VOR employs a special aerial whereas VDF is a ground installation. For a simple aerial as used in RT, the signal strength received at a given range is proportional to the wavelength. Thus, a larger wavelength (i.e. lower frequency) would provide a better field strength.

VHF communication

The VHF band is chosen for RT communication at short ranges, the operative frequencies being kept at the lower end of the band, i.e., 118 MHz to 136 MHz. Within this band, 720 communication channels are or will soon be available at 25 kHz separation. The transmission is amplitude-modulated, the type of emission being A3. A transmitter producing 20 watt power would be considered quite adequate for maximum ranges.

VHF is practically free from static, but being vertically polarised, the signals do pick up some background noise. If absolute clarity of reception is required, the choice should be shifted to UHF where room may be available to accommodate FM sidebands.

Factors affecting range

(a)   Transmission power both at aircraft and ground station.

(b)   Height of the transmitter.

(c)   Height of the receiver.

(d)   Obstacles at or near the transmission site will block the signals or scatter them with inevitable attenuation.

(e)   Any upstanding obstruction in the line of sight between the aircraft and the ground station will have an effect similar to (d) above.

(f)   In certain circumstances the aircraft may receive both direct and ground reflected waves which may cause fading or even short term loss of communication.

Selective calling system (Selcal)

This system of communication relieves a pilot from the tiresome task of maintaining a continuous listening watch on the RT while in flight. It is most beneficial when an aircraft is flying in peaceful areas, e.g. on a long ocean crossing, where the only need for the RT is to make its periodic position reports. The advantage of the facility is taken by installing a selcal receiver in the aircraft. The Air Navigation Order prescribes rules with regard to its use.

(a)   The ground station is informed that you intend to use selcal

(b)   the ground station must not raise any objection, and

(c)   the particular ground station is notified as capable of transmitting selcal codes.

For its use outside of the U.K., ensure that the ground station concerned is designated as transmitting a signal suitable for the purpose.

The ATC must be informed of the codes carried in the aircraft and a preflight functional check must be carried out. If at this stage or at any stage en route it is thought that either the ground or the airborne equipment is unserviceable, listening watch must be resumed.

When on selcal, if the ground station wishes to contact you, it will transmit a group of two coded tone pulses. The decoder circuit will accept the signal if it is meant for it, and activate the cockpit call system by flashing a lamp or by ringing a bell or a combination of both.

Secondary surveillence radar (SSR)
Secondary surveillance radar is another method of communication from ATC to the aircraft. With the use of SSR, ATC derives an aircraft's ident, flight level and follows its track. For fuller information on SSR see chapter 25.

Legislation on the use of radio
The following provisions are prescribed in the Air Navigation Order:

'The radio station in an aircraft shall not be operated so as to cause interference with communication or navigational services and emissions shall not be made except as follows:

(a)   emission class and frequency must be appropriate to the airspace in which the aircraft is flying;
(b)   distress, urgency and safety messages;
(c)   messages and signals relating to the flight of the aircraft;
(d)   such public correspondence messages as permitted under the aircraft radio station licence.'

If the communication is made by wireless telegraphy, a telecommunication log must be maintained.

Test questions
1.   Give the main factors which affect the range of ground-to-air communication in (a) HF band; (b) VHF band.
2. Explain why day and night frequencies are different in HF.

6: Non-Directional Beacons (NDBs) and Direction Finding

From navigation plotting in connection with radio bearings, you will remember that great care was required in deciding who did the work; you in the aircraft or the chap on the ground. We will now deal with the aircraft getting a bearing on a ground-based radio station. Ground radio stations providing such a facility are known as non-directional beacons, NDBs for short.

Non-directional beacons (NDBs) transmit vertically polarised signals in the MF band. They are radiated equally in all directions, hence its name. An aircraft carrying associated radio compass equipment can tune in to a station on its published frequency and can measure the direction of the incoming waves. The datum for the direction measurement is taken from the nose of the aircraft and therefore, the radio compass indications are *relative bearings*. On modern equipment these bearings are displayed automatically (ADF) and when fed to a radio magnetic indicator (RMI), QDMs are indicated. Additionally, on some automatic equipment, a facility is provided to obtain bearings manually and to check the sense.

A loop aerial is used in the aircraft to determine the direction of the ground transmitter. It is rectangular in shape, is made up of a number of strands of wire (to give them an ideal aerial length) wound round the frame, and is mounted vertically in a most suitable position on the fuselage. The aerial itself may be rotatable or fixed, depending on the type of equipment.

Loop theory — rotatable loop

The vertical members of the loop are designed to pick up the signals. When the plane of the loop is parallel to the direction of the vertically polarised NDB radiation, signals will be picked up by the two vertical arms. There will be a phase difference between the signals arriving in the two arms because of the distance between them. This will cause a current to flow in both arms. These signals in the two arms are in opposition round the loop and therefore, the signals (or voltage) finally passed to the receiver will be the difference between the two, see fig. 6.1(a). Notice that with the

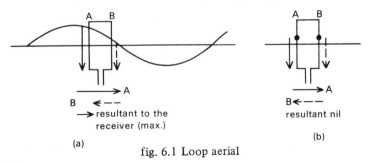

fig. 6.1 Loop aerial

loop in this position the distance between the two arms is at a maximum. Therefore the phase difference and the resultant current flow to the receiver is also at a maximum.

If the aerial is now rotated through 90°, both arms will face the transmitter together and the incoming wave will reach them at the same instant, that is, at the same phase (fig. 6.1(b)) and the resultant current flow is nil.

Thus, as the loop is rotated from position (a) to position (b) the current flow is reduced from maximum to nil. Therefore at any intermediate angle the current flow is a function of the cosine of the angle the aerial makes with the incoming wave.

If the loop is further rotated beyond 90°, current will start flowing again, but in the reverse direction. If a polar diagram is traced out showing the signal strength produced by the loop at different angles through 360°, the result is a *figure of eight*, see fig. 6.2.

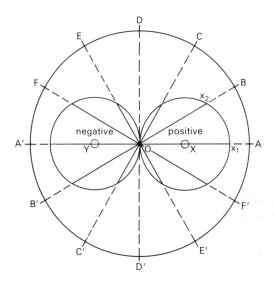

fig. 6.2

In fig. 6.2, XY is the loop, with its centre at O, and A to F and A′ to F′ are various positions of an NDB at 30° intervals. With the transmitter in position A, the loop is lying parallel to the incoming wave, X end leading, the current produced is at a maximum. Plot this as a vector, one unit in length, distance Ox_1 in fig. 6.2.

In position B, the current induced is shown by vector Ox_2 and its value is 0.86 vector units. In position D, cosine of 90° is 0, and when the transmitter is at E, cosine of 120° is −0.5. As you go through 360° you will have traced out a figure of eight, half of it will be positive and the other half, negative.

The polar diagram has two positions where maximum signals are being received (A and A′) and two positions where no signals are being received (D and D′). The zero strength positions are known as 'null' positions.

When establishing the direction of the ground station, the loop can be aligned so that the plane of the loop is parallel to the incoming signal, that is, the loop-transmitter relationship as in position A. This is done by turning the loop until maximum signal strength is heard, and calling that the direction of the station. The disadvantage of ascertaining the station direction from maximum signal is that the field strength on either side of the maximum falls very slowly and consequently the determined direction can be in error.

For this reason 'null' position is used to determine the transmitter direction. Nearer 90°, (loop-transmitter relationship as at D) the value of cosine falls rapidly and a total null is more easy to recognise than a total maximum. However, it should be noted that just as a total maximum may occur at A or A', the null may occur when the transmitter is in the D or D' position. In other words, there is a 180° ambiguity in the bearing indication.

This is resolved by the use of a sense aerial. It is an omni-directional aerial and its polar diagram is a circle, the radius of which is electronically adjusted to fit on top of the figure-of-eight polar diagram. To resolve the ambiguity these two fields are mixed together. The resultant polar diagram is a heart-shaped figure, called a 'cardioid' (fig. 6.3). It will be noticed that a cardioid has only one null position.

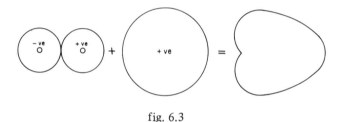

fig. 6.3

Loop theory — fixed loop

In the Bellini-Tosi method of direction finding, the system uses an omni-directional sense aerial and a pair of fixed loops at right angles to each other: one loop with its axis in the fore and aft plane, the other in the athwartships. These loops are connected to the field coils (stator) of a goniometer and the current in these coils sets up a field about a rotor. The direction of the field is related to the direction of the incoming signal.

If the rotor coil lies at 90° (null position) to the resultant magnetic field in the stator, the system is in balance. When the rotor is not at the null position, a current is induced in the rotor. This activates a motor which drives the rotor the shortest way to the null position.

Resolution of ambiguity

When the compass is functioning on ADF, 180° ambiguity is automatically resolved for you. In one system a pattern of 'switched' cardioids is produced by combining the output of an omni-directional sense aerial and alternating the connections rapidly.

The signal output from the cardioids governs the voltage applied to two uni-directional motors geared to the loop. The left-hand cardioid influences one motor, the right-hand cardioid the other. The motors turn in opposite directions and by means of the differential gear they rotate the loop in the appropriate direction.

When the loop is in the equi-signal position, the differential output is zero and the pointer is steadily indicating correct direction. This steady indication has a slight hunt about its mean position. This has two benefits. It ensures that the ambiguity cannot exist; if the pointer was indicating 180° out, as the needle departed from its mean position a voltage would be induced in one of the motors and would drive the needle through 180° to the correct null. The other benefit is that the steady movement of the needle about a mean position is an indication that the ADF is working and a good bearing is being displayed. Excessive hunt would develop when the incoming field strength is weak or the signal/noise ratio is low. With experience the operator is able to assess the degree of accuracy of the indications.

Occasionally, in conditions of heavy static or interference from a powerful transmitter on a nearby frequency it might be advantageous to operate on manual loop. The loop aerial is turned manually until it arrives at the null position, but the indication must then be checked for sense (see chapter 7 for the procedures).

Ambiguity may be resolved from knowledge of the DR position. You can also resolve it by observing changes in bearing with time. Unless you are homing directly to a station (or homing away from it) the bearings increase or decrease as the flight progresses. Study fig. 6.4 which is self-explanatory.

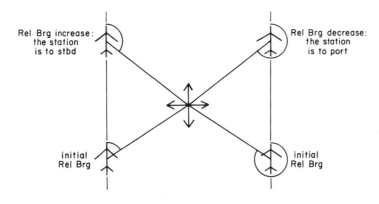

fig. 6.4

Coverage of NDB transmissions
The rated coverage of NDBs in the U.K. is noted in the Com section of the U.K. Air Pilot. Within this area the field strength of the wanted signals to unwanted signals exceeds the minimum value specified. ICAO recommends this value to be 15 dB but no less than 10 dB. This protection takes into consideration the average atmospheric noise in the geographical area concerned but not the presence of sky waves at night.

The rated coverage of an NDB depends on the frequency, transmission power and the conductivity of the path to the coverage boundary. These three factors, being measurable, enable the planners to establish the facilities by controlling the output power and allocating frequencies. The lowest field strength (ICAO recommendation is 70 microvolts/metre in Europe) will be received at the boundary.

Types of NDBs
Locators.   These are low powered NDBs in the LF/MF band, usually installed as a supplement to ILS and located at the sites of the outer and middle markers. A locator

has an average radius of rated coverage of between 10 and 25 nm. The type of emission is A0A2 and they identify by a two or three-letter morse group at 7 w.p.m. once very 10 seconds. During the ident period the carrier remains uninterrupted to ensure that the pointer does not wander away. The ident is effected by on/off keying of the amplitude-modulating tone.

Homing and holding NDBs.   These are intended primarily as approach and holding aids in the vicinity of aerodromes, with rated coverage of around 50 nm. The class of emission and method of ident are similar to the locators.

En-route and long range NDBs.   These provide en-route coverage along the airways and a long range bearing facility for ocean tracking and similar operations. The NDB at Cocos Island may be heard from several hundred miles.

The recommended type of emission is A0A2 unless the required rated coverage is not practicable because of interference from other radio stations or high atmospheric noise or other local conditions, in which case A0A1 emission may be used. With this type of emission the identification is effected by on/off keying of the carrier (during which period the pointer may wander away), and the NDB identifies at least once every minute.

The amplitude-modulating signal causing identification for A0A2 emission is either a 1020 Hz or a 400 Hz tone.

The choice of frequency band

The requirement is to produce surface ranges of intermediate order.

Frequency bands from VHF and above, being line-of-sight propagation, may be ruled out from consideration. HF would produce a very short ground wave, and the sky waves would interfere with the ADF operation day and night. VLF installation and running costs are high and require large aerials. Static noise is excessive.

The frequency bands chosen are upper LF and lower MF. In these ranges, aerial requirements are acceptable, static is less severe than VLF, there is no interference due to sky waves during the day time and the bands are ideally placed to produce the required ranges.

Frequencies

Although the frequencies are allotted from LF/MF, by convention an NDB is an MF aid. Frequencies assigned by ICAO are from 200 kHz to 1 750 kHz. In the U.K. and Europe, NDB frequencies are normally found between 255 kHz and 455 kHz.

Functional checks

ICAO provides for monitoring of NDBs for radiated carrier power (not allowed to fall below 50%), failure of identification signals, failure of the monitor itself or other malfunctioning. In the U.K. the NDBs are not regularly monitored but functional checks of NDB and locators are carried out at eight hour intervals during the period of service.

7: Automatic Direction Finding (ADF)

The automatic radio compass

The radio compass is a radio receiver that is able to identify the direction from which a signal is being received. It uses a loop aerial to determine the direction and a sense aerial to resolve the 180° ambiguity. An aircraft equipped with a radio compass may 'home' to the transmitter or use it as an aid to navigation. The relative bearings are displayed on the relative bearing indicator (RBI) and QDMs are indicated on an RMI.

Although there are many varieties of radio compasses on the market they are all basically the same. The main components of the system are:

(a) a radio receiver operating in the LF and MF bands;
(b) a control box;
(c) a shielded fixed or rotatable loop aerial;
(d) a non-directional aerial and
(e) one or more indicators.

Two typical control units are shown in figs. 7.1 and 7.2.

fig. 7.1 GEC radio compass

fig. 7.2 Marconi automatic direction finder

Controls

The two compasses illustrated in figs. 7.1 and 7.2 cover just about every type of control on ADF equipment. You should note here that not all compasses have all these facilities.

Function switch.   The number of positions for a function switch varies with the equipment. There are five positions on the GEC compass and four on the Marconi compass. The purpose of the various positions is as follows:

    (a)   Off position. This is the normal position when the compass is not in use.

    (b)   Tune RT. In this position the sense aerial is in the circuit and tuning of the station is carried out in association with the frequency band selector, the selectivity switch and the tuning meter. This switch is variously named as REC (receiver), ANT (antenna), OMNI or SENSE.

    (c)   Nav CW. This position is used when receiving Consol or Radio Range.

    (d)   ADF. In this position both sense and loop aerials are in operation and the compass gives a continuous indication of the bearing of the station to which the receiver is tuned. This position is also known by other names: VIS, COMP.

    (e)   Loop. In this position the equipment may be operated manually. The direction is indicated when the loop is turned to the aural null position. The sense aerial is not in the circuit.

BFO or CW/RT.   The need for this facility arises because the NDB emission may be A0A1 or A0A2. It will be recalled that in A0 and A1, parts of the emission are at a radio frequency which cannot be heard, being beyond human ear range. When the CW/RT switch is in the CW position or the BFO switch is in the 'ON' position, these emissions are made audible. This is done by the use of an oscillator inside the receiver which produces internally a frequency slightly different from the frequency being received from the NDB. For example, if the received frequency is 400 kHz, it may produce 399 kHz internally. It then takes the difference between the two (1 kHz in our example) which is an audio frequency. This difference is called the 'beat note' and hence the name BFO — beat frequency oscillator. Use the BFO switch as follows:

Emission type	When tuning the station	When identifying the station
A0A1	BFO ON; CW/RT to CW	BFO ON; CW/RT to CW
A0A2	BFO ON; CW/RT to CW	BFO OFF; CW/RT to RT

Commercial broadcasters may sometimes be used to take a bearing. In this case, since the transmission is in audio frequency, the BFO is not required and it is set to the 'OFF' position, CW/RT to CW.

In A0A1 emission, A0 is the carrier part and it is transmitted for about 10 seconds; it is then interrupted to give the A1 part, which is the ident and may last for around 5 seconds. During the ident breaks the pointer may wander away. For this reason A0A1 emission is not in favour with ICAO and the long range NDBs generally give idents at longer intervals to minimise breaks.

Similarly A0A2 emission is again an unmodulated carrier for about 10 seconds but the ident part, A2, is an amplitude-modulated carrier. The ident lasts a few seconds and generally the carrier is not broken during ident period.

Filter.   This position is used to reduce the amount of spurious background noise.

Sense.   The sense button when depressed introduces a sensing circuit in the receiver and is used to resolve ambiguity.

Bandpass selector.   There may be two/three positions shown by lines of varying thickness or simply two positions named broad and sharp. It allows the operator to reduce or narrow down the band of frequencies being fed to the receiver and exclude unwanted background noise.

Uses of the radio compass

(a)   As an en route navigation aid, position lines may be obtained. By taking two or three bearings on the same or different NDBs, fixes are obtained.

(b)   Flying airways — there are many airways in the world still marked by NDBs only.

(c)   A fix is obtained when overhead an NDB — useful on airways for position reporting.

(d)   An NDB can be used for holding at an en route point or at the destination aerodrome, for homing to the station and carrying out a let-down.

Procedures for obtaining bearings

(a)   Check that the aircraft is within the promulgated range of the station to be used.

(b)   Function switch to REC.

(c)   Select BFO for tuning.

(d)   Tune the station for maximum strength. Where available, a tuning meter may be used to give an indication of maximum strength.

(e)   BFO in appropriate position for identification of the station.

(f)   Function switch to ADF.

(g)   Note the bearing being indicated, and take the time. This is the time of your position line, and the bearing obtained is a relative bearing.

(h)   If the bearing is required on an RMI, select NDB on red (thin) needle and the bearing indicated is a QDM.

(j)   Unless planning to take a further bearing in a short space of time, return function switch to REC or even switch the compass off.

Manual determination of bearings

On occasions when excessive interference is present, the pilot may find it advantageous to obtain a bearing aurally by manual operation of the loop aerial. Not all radio compasses will have this facility but where the facility exists, the procedure is as follows:

(a)   Steps (a) to (e) as above.

(b)   Select LOOP position on function switch.

(c)   By operation of the loop L/R control, rotate the loop until the signal strength heard in the earphones is at a minimum (you are trying to locate the 'null' position).

(d)   The bearing is being indicated at this stage, but it is necessary to check the sense unless it can be resolved by one of the other methods. Press SENSE button and rotate the loop clockwise by holding the loop control to the right.

(e)   If the signal strength in the earphones decreases, the bearing is correct (cardioid's null is approaching you).

(f)   If the signal strength increases, swing the loop through 180° and repeat the sequence.

An illustration of relative bearings and indications on an RBI is shown in fig. 7.3.

fig. 7.3

Homing to a station

When homing to a station on the radio compass, the point to bear in mind is that the station is directly ahead of you (if not, you want it to be so) and therefore, the radio compass indication is 360° or around 360°. Similarly, if you are leaving a station on the radio compass, the station is directly behind you and the indication you are looking for is 180° or around 180°.

Theoretically, a station may be reached by maintaining 360° on the radio compass, but if there is any wind blowing (and when doesn't it blow?) you will fly a curved path to the station. Further, consequent upon wind, you will be continually altering heading to combat displacement caused by the wind and ultimately you will arrive overhead from a direction facing into the wind. See fig. 7.4.

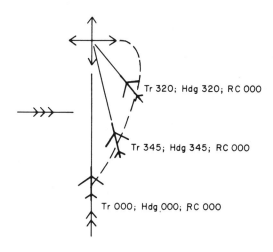

Tr 320; Hdg 320; RC 000

Tr 345; Hdg 345; RC 000

Tr 000; Hdg 000; RC 000

fig. 7.4

The above method of homing, apart from being time-wasting, may not be possible due to track maintenance requirements. In congested areas and on airways, when homing from beacon to beacon you are required to fly notified tracks. This may be done by simply making allowance for the wind velocity right at the start, adjusting as the flight progresses if a wind change is noticed.

In fig. 7.5, say, the drift is 10°S at the start. Steer 350° to allow for the drift. The radio compass will then read 010° (take away from the nose, add to the indication). As long as 010° remains indicating, you are maintaining the track, and you will arrive overhead. If the indication starts a gradual decrease, you are drifting to starboard, and you must allow for more than 10°S drift.

For the same reasons, if the reading starts to increase, you have allowed for too much drift and should alter the heading accordingly. After one or two such alterations you will hit on a heading which is right.

If while juggling with headings you managed to get off the track, or if you wish to join a given track, the technique employed is to intercept the desired track at a convenient angle, generally 30° — that is, at an angle of 30° between interception heading and the desired track. To calculate what bearing the radio compass will

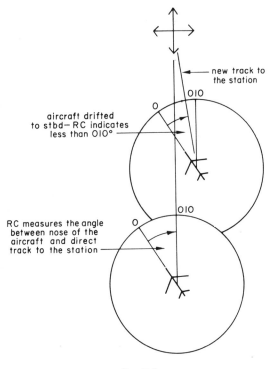

new track to the station

OIO

O

aircraft drifted to stbd—RC indicates less than OIO°

OIO

O

RC measures the angle between nose of the aircraft and direct track to the station

fig. 7.5

indicate when you arrive at the track, the rule is:

Add on the nose (i.e. heading), take away from 360;

Take away from the nose, add on 360.

Thus, if you intercept at an angle of 30° and your heading is smaller than your track (that is, you have taken away 30° from the nose) RC indication of 030 will tell you that you are crossing the track.

An aircraft in position 1 in fig. 7.6 wishes to intercept and follow a track of 070°; drift 5°P. Follow stages 1, 2 and 3.

Tracking away from the station

As the station approaches, a rapid build-up in volume is noticed; when passing the station, signals will momentarily fade, followed by another rapid increase in volume indicating station passage. The station passage is also indicated by increasing oscillations of the needle, subsequently settling down to an indication near 180°. When tracking away, the relative bearing indicated will be greater than 180° if starboard drift is being experienced (fig. 7.7), and less than 180° if port drift is being experienced. The procedure is to fly out with the drift applied to maintain the track. Then you know what ideal bearing you are looking for. As the flight progresses if the aircraft is not tracking correctly, the pointer will start drifting slowing to one direction or the other. If the readings are increasing, you are experiencing starboard drift; port drift if they are decreasing — the same rule as stated earlier.

fig. 7.6

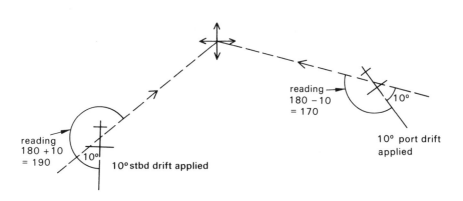

fig. 7.7

Holding patterns

Generally the holding patterns are race-track type patterns and all turns in the
pattern may be either right-hand (RH pattern) or left-hand (LH pattern). This is
indicated on terminal approach charts (TAPs) and they are studied carefully as a
matter of pre-flight preparation. Holding procedures are carried out in two phases:
entering the pattern and subsequently, holding in the pattern. To enter the pattern,
depending on the direction of approach to the NDB it may be necessary to carry out
a pre-entry manoeuvre. 360° approach directions round a holding NDB (as well as
any other holding facility) are divided into three approach sectors as shown in
fig. 7.8. Each sector has its own procedure to get you in the pattern.

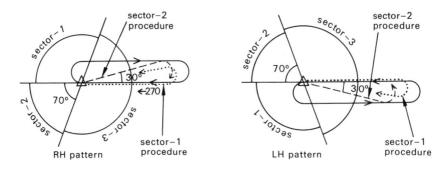

fig. 7.8

To clarify the sector arrangements, let us examine the RH pattern in fig. 7.8. The inbound track is 270°(M). The sector divisions based on this track are as follows:

Sector 1 when approaching NDB between 090°(M) and 200°(M).

Sector 2 when approaching NDB between 090°(M) and 020°(M).

Sector 3 when approaching NDB between 020°(M) and 200°(M).

If your approach track is one of the dividing lines you may choose either sector. Procedures to be adopted in individual sectors in an RH pattern, are as follows:

Sector 1

(a)   On arrival overhead, fly parallel to the reciprocal of the inbound leg for the appropriate time.

(b)   Then turn left and home back to the NDB.

(c)   On second arrival over the facility turn right and commence the pattern.

Sector 2

(a)   On arrival overhead, make good a track 30° to the reciprocal of the inbound leg towards the inside of the pattern.

(b)   At the appropriate time, turn right and join the pattern on the inbound leg, and home to the facility.

Sector 3

On arrival overhead, join the pattern directly.

Actual holding at the facility commences now. Turn right through 180° rate one and start timing when abeam the NDB. How do we know when we are abeam? Well, in zero wind conditions, an RBI (relative bearing indicator) pointer indicating 090°R indicates abeam position. To this figure add the amount of drift if it is starboard, subtract from it if it is port. In fig. 7.9 the aircraft having a 10°S drift would wait for its ADF to indicate 100°R.

fig. 7.9

The outbound track is parallel to the inbound track. Apply drift and adjust the leg timing for your ground speed to maintain the track. At end of the leg, turn right through 180°, rate one and fly inbound track by radio compass.

NDB let-down
On a terminal approach procedures chart, a typical let-down looks something like fig. 7.10. The let-down pattern is given in both plan and elevation and at the bottom

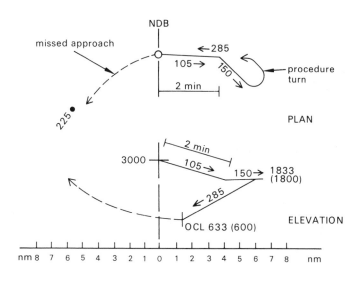

fig. 7.10

of the chart there is usually a scale showing distances in nautical miles from the NDB position. All bearings shown on the TAP are magnetic. A procedure turn may be a level turn or a descending turn. The outbound track may not be the reciprocal of the inbound track. In this case, a rate one turn through 180° generally brings the aircraft on to the inbound track. This turn, again, may be a level turn or a descending turn. Rate of descent on all approaches, unless otherwise shown on the TAP, is 650 ± 150 ft/min. At certain aerodromes 'shuttle' procedures are available permitting an aircraft to descend to the altitude from where a let-down may commence. Heights given on a TAP are related to aerodrome elevation with QFE equivalents in brackets.

During a let-down, maintain tracks by applying drift and flying with reference to ADF. Where a leg is time-controlled, adjust that time to compensate for your ground speed. A procedure turn is a 45 sec leg followed by a turn on to the inbound track.

A careful study of all possible destination and alternate let-down procedures should be made as part of the pre-flight preparation. As many details as possible are extracted in advance and arranged in a convenient form so that you are ready to commence the procedures at your destination with a minimum of work at that end. In case of any doubt in interpretation of information in TAP, AIP should be consulted. The following information is needed for an NDB let-down:

Height	TR	Drift	Ideal Brg on ADF	TAS	GS	Dist.	Time	ROD (rate of descent)

Finally, a pilot must not descend below his decision height unless the conditions are equal to or better than those specified in the operations manual.

Angle of lead

A turn on to the track must be commenced before the track is reached, otherwise the track will be overshot and a further alteration of heading in the opposite

fig. 7.11

direction will be necessary. This angular allowance that you will make for the turn is known as the 'angle of lead'. It is dependent upon various factors, e.g. aircraft's TAS which governs its radius of turn, its distance out from the station, wind velocity and the aircraft's rate of turn. Two points must be noted:

(a)   For a given airspeed, the angle of lead decreases as the distance from the station increases (fig. 7.11).

(b)   For a given time out from a station, the angle of lead is constant irrespective of aircraft speed (fig. 7.12).

fig. 7.12

8: ADF: Range and Accuracy

Now that we have learnt how omni-directional signals are converted by an aircraft's loop aerial to give direction of the station, and how to use the airborne equipment, we round up our studies by looking into the remaining, but very important aspect of this navigational aid — its operational limitations.

Factors affecting ranges

The undermentioned factors affect the useful ranges available from an NDB.

(a) *Transmission power.* The range at which an NDB may be successfully used depends on its power output. Being an MF transmission, an increase in power means an increase in the range available. The power requirements are, however, such that to double the range, the power must be increased fourfold (or, the range is proportional to the square root of the power output). It must also be remembered that the power output of a station is strictly limited to the value that will produce acceptable field strength at the rated coverage boundary. Associated with the power output, the radiation efficiency of the transmitter aerial (e.g. height and other characteristics of the radiating system) governs the field strength of the signals received from an NDB.

(b) *Frequency.* The operating radio frequency is a factor which also governs the field strength of a signal being received. As we learnt earlier, for a given transmission power, the lower the frequency, the lesser the attenuation and the greater the range.

(c) *Type of terrain.* This factor reduces the useful ranges in two ways: by affecting the field strength of the signal and by giving inaccurate information.

   (i) Type of surface. The conductivity of the path between the NDB and the receiver determines the attenuation of the signals, and the field strength. Longer ranges are always obtained over water than over dry soil.

   (ii) Mountains and other obstructions. Mountains and other obstructions may block the signals, or more likely the signals will be received after having been reflected from peaks and valleys or due to diffraction and scattering effect. These signals, not necessarily arriving from the direction of the station, will give erroneous indications. The effect is more pronounced at low levels; a gain in altitude is required to minimise the effect.

   (iii) Coastal refraction. In coastal areas the differing radio energy absorption properties of land and water cause refraction of radiated waves. The error in the indications is caused by what is called 'coastal refraction' If a wave does not leave the coast at $90°$, it will bend towards the medium of high density, that is, landmass (fig. 8.1). The amount of refraction depends on the angle between the signal and the coastline. Errors of the order of $20°$ may occur when the bearing is taken on a signal leaving the coast over $30°$. Thus, this factor reduces the effective ranges through giving

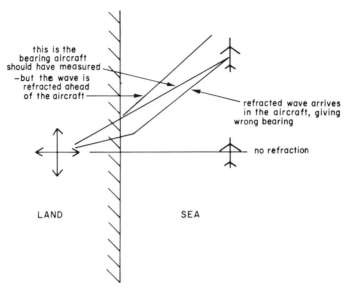

this is the
bearing aircraft
should have measured
—but the wave is
refracted ahead
of the aircraft

refracted wave arrives
in the aircraft, giving
wrong bearing

no refraction

LAND

SEA

fig. 8.1

erroneous readings. To minimise the error, use an NDB sited on the coastline or climb up to a higher flight level or use the signals which leave the coast around 90°. (This last one is a good one.)

(d) *Night effect.* The range of a long range beacon was given above as 200 nm by day, 70 nm by night. This serious cut-down in the range occurs due to the presence of sky waves in the MF band. In this band during the day time, sky waves are not present, but at night they affect the radio compass accuracy when they enter the horizontal members of the loop from above (fig. 8.2).

sky wave

phase
diff.

phase diff.

ground wave

null distorted

=

fig. 8.2

These waves will start coming from skyward from approximately 70 to 100 nm range upward. If the receiver is also within the range of the ground wave, the two signals will mix and distortion of the null will occur. On an automatic radio compass, this will be indicated by excessive oscillations of the needle. True null is masked and efforts to find a mean over a wavering area can lead to error since the mean is not necessarily the centre of a wavering needle. If the aircraft is only receiving sky waves, there will be a good null but that indication can again be erroneous since there is no guarantee that the reflecting plane is parallel to the earth's surface. In other words, the signal may not arrive from the station direction.

This effect on the radio compass is called 'night effect'. It is minimised when using a station in the lower section of the frequency band, thus reducing the incidence of the sky wave. Dusk and dawn are critical periods for radio compass operation — extreme care must be exercised. Also, use a more powerful beacon if you have a choice. Lastly, choose the station nearest to you.

The presence of sky waves is indicated to the operator in two ways: excessive oscillation of the needle, and fading of the signals.

(e)   *Protection range.* Irrespective of the range that an NDB is capable of producing, the use of an NDB in the U.K. is restricted to ranges promulgated in the UKAP. This is known as 'protection range' and this restriction is necessary in order to provide reception, free from interference from other NDBs transmitting on the same or similar frequencies.

The main reason for the interference is congestion in the MF band. In Europe (and in America) there is always a heavy demand for channel space in this band, which is already overcrowded with NDBs and broadcasters (not to mention the pirates). In LF and MF (lower end of the frequency spectrum) interference between two *similar* frequencies can take place quite easily (a common experience while tuning radio stations at night) and the protection is afforded by the CAA controlling the allocation of power and frequency to the stations. Protection ranges are based on providing a minimum protection ratio of 3. That is, the ratio of the field strength of the wanted signal to unwanted signal will be at least 3 to 1. Or, when translated in terms of noise, the level of wanted signal will be at least 10 decibels higher than that of unwanted signal within the promulgated range. In the U.K. the protection ensures that the errors in the service area will not exceed ±5°. But this protection is guaranteed only during day time. At night:

(i)   Sky waves seriously affect the operation of the radio compass due to night effect. Further, the E layer gains height at night, increasing the ranges where sky waves could be received. In other words, the sky wave from a distant NDB operating on a similar frequency will extend its range and produce interference within the protection range of your NDB.

(ii)   Broadcasters and other high-powered radio beacons will gain field strength at night. This means that at a given place, where during the day time you would receive wanted signals at a level of at least 10 decibels higher than the unwanted signals, the unwanted signals now increased in field strength will produce higher noise, and the protection minimum will fall.

(iii)   A forecast of interference-free ranges could not be made for night periods since the height of the ionospheric layer is variable and its density is also variable. Among others, these two factors decide the range of the return of the sky waves.

Therefore, the principle of protection ranges breaks down at night and the useful ranges are greatly reduced. Extreme caution should be exercised when using the radio compass at night and it is most important to ensure that correct tuning is done to the exclusion of any unwanted signals.

(f)   *Static.* All kinds of precipitation (including falling snow) and thunderstorms can cause static interference of varying intensity to ADF systems. Precipitation static reduces the effective range and accuracy of bearing information. Thunderstorms can give rise to bearing errors of considerable magnitude, even to the extent of indicating false 'station passage'.

It is not at all unusual for the pointer to point in the direction of a thundering cumulonimbus cloud.

The extent to which a receiver will admit the noise depends on:

     (i)   the bandwidth of the receiver;

     (ii)   the level of the atmospheric noise;

     (iii) the level of noise produced by other interference (e.g. other radio stations, industrial noise).

   (g)   *Type of emission.* For a given transmission power, the ranges produced by an A2 emission are shorter than A1 emission.

Factors affecting accuracy

Some of the factors mentioned above also affect the accuracy of the indications. There are other factors which affect accuracy without affecting range directly. Factors affecting accuracy are:

   (a)   *Night effect.* (Already discussed.)

   (b)   *Type of terrain.* Mountains, physical obstructions, refraction on leaving the coast.

   (c)   *Static interference.* The cause of static has already been discussed. Static can affect the accuracy of ADF at all ranges. At a comparatively short range, e.g. less than 50 nm, static and other noise is considered to be potentially dangerous and in these conditions the indications should be monitored on a VHF aid if available.

   (d)   *Station interference.* This is another potentially dangerous situation at short ranges. When two stations at different locations are transmitting on the same or similar frequency, the bearing needle will take up the position which is the resultant of the field strengths of the two transmissions. The indications may give large errors. To avoid this, use the facility when you are inside its promulgated service area.

   (e)   *Quadrantal error.* This error occurs because the fuselage reflects and re-radiates the signals hitting it. These signals mix with the signals entering the loop, giving an error in the indication. Signals arriving at the loop from the aircraft's relative cardinal points are not affected. Signals hitting the fuselage at any other angles are affected, the maximum effect is noticed when the signals arrive from the direction of the aircraft's relative quadrantal points. Hence the name 'quadrantal error'. These signals are bent towards the aircraft's major electrical axis, which is normally its fore-and-aft axis.

A radio compass is regularly calibrated and corrected and any remaining errors are recorded on a QE card. With modern equipment and improved techniques this error is of academic interest only.

   (f)   *Loop misalignment.* If the loop aerial is not exactly aligned with the fore-and-aft axis of the aircraft all bearings subsequently measured by the equipment will be in error by the amount of misalignment. This error is eliminated by careful fitting and aligning of the loop.

   (g)   *Lack of failure warning device.* Because there is no cockpit indication of a ground or airborne equipment failure, a serious situation can arise if the pilot continues to follow a steady indication when in fact no information is being fed to the pointer. This can occur for a variety of reasons: the pilot throwing the function switch to 'standby' position through habit or absentmindedness, the ground transmitter stopping radiation, airborne receiver going unserviceable and so forth. The only way to prevent such an incident, in the absence of a warning flag, is to constantly monitor the identification signals.

Effect of a/c height on range

NDBs transmit in the LF and MF bands. In these bands the radio waves curve with the surface of the earth. Because of this, an aircraft will receive signals, if otherwise within the range, no matter how low the aircraft is flying.

Since these waves also propagate in space, aircraft at higher altitudes will also receive the signals. Thus, the height of an aircraft has no significance as far as the range is concerned. Height, however, may become significant as pointed out earlier, when flying in mountainous areas or using coastal NDBs.

Signals/noise ratio

To improve signals/noise ratio,

(a)   narrow down receiver bandwidth ensuring that you do not cut out your own signals.

(b)   tune the wanted station carefully, and

(c)   if it is thought that the unwanted signal is the result of a more powerful beacon encroaching on your bandwidth, see if you can exclude it by off-tuning your own station.

Some interesting facts about ADF

(a)   If there are two NDBs, one on the coast and the other fairly inland, and if the coastal refraction for both propagations is the same when the bearings are taken, then when you plot the position lines, you will find that the NDB which is further inland gives greater error.

(b)   When flying over the water if you take two/three bearings to make a fix, and if errors due to coastal refraction are present, then the fix you make will put you coastward from your true position. Do a little plotting exercise and check it. First plot a fix from three position lines unaffected by coastal refraction; then plot another fix from the position lines in error.

(c)   In fig. 8.3 an aircraft is flying a track of 060°(T) in no wind conditions. When in position A it obtains a relative bearing of 050°R from NDB, C. Now if it waits until the bearing has changed to twice the original value, i.e. 100°R, its position at that time is at B. In this situation, we have a triangle ABC in which side AB equals side BC. This enables the pilot to calculate his distance from NDB, C, when at B. This distance is equal to distance AB which he can calculate from knowledge of his ground speed.

When there is wind, allowance must be made for the drift applied in the radio compass reading.

(d)   If an aircraft flies from one beacon to another and the relative bearing remains fairly steady, the wind velocity may be found on arrival over the second beacon. The time between the two beacons should not be too short. For example,

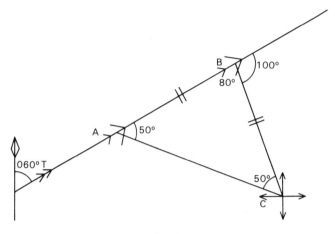

fig. 8.3

an aircraft passes over beacon A at 10.00 hrs, TAS 180, Hdg(M) 157°. Later the radio compass tuned to the NDB, A, gives a steady relative bearing of 186° and the aircraft passes over beacon B, 49 nm from A at 10.20 hrs. Var 8°W.

Aircraft's ground speed: 49 in 20 = 147 kt. Hdg(M) 157, Varn 8W; Hdg(T) 149, Drift 6°S, Tr(T) 155. Now the values of TR, HDG, TAS and GS are put on the computer to give wind velocity which is 123/37 in our illustration.

Test questions
1. List the factors that affect the accuracy of ADF indications.
2. Explain briefly 'night effect'.
3. List the factors that contribute to restricting useful NDB ranges.
4. List the factors that affect the field strength of the NDB radiation.
5. Explain briefly how station interference may affect ADF performance.
6. What minimum protection is provided when flying within protection range in the U.K.?
7. The emission of an NDB is listed as A0A2. Explain how you would use BFO before you are ready to take a bearing on it.
8. Describe the procedure to follow to obtain a QDM from an NDB.
9. Why is the promulgated range for an NDB valid only during the day time?
10. What is the guide line to be followed when deciding whether an NDB should have A0A1 or A0A2 emission?

9: VHF Omni-Directional Radio Range (VOR) – 1

An earlier navigation aid, Radio Range, operating in the LF/MF band served aviation for a period following the Second World War. It had its limitations inherent with lower frequencies and at best it could produce only four fixed tracks. A need for a more flexible and reliable aid soon became apparent with the expansion of aviation and VOR emerged as its successor. It was officially adopted by ICAO in 1960 as a standard short-range navigation aid.

VOR theoretically produces an infinite number of tracks, it is practically free from static and does not suffer from night effect. Consequently it could be used with confidence at any time of the day. The indications are in terms of deviation to the left or right from the selected track. Information may be fed to an RMI to give QDMs. When frequency is paired with DME, range and bearing information provides instantaneous fixes.

Principle of operation
The principle of VOR is bearing measurement by phase comparison. It will be remembered that an NDB transmits an omni-directional signal and the aircraft's loop aerial converts it to a directional one. A VOR transmitter does this work on the ground and the airborne receiver receives directional information. The ground station transmits two separate signals as follows:

Reference signal
The reference signal is an omni-directional continuous wave transmission on the station's allocated frequency. It carries a 9 960 Hz sub-carrier which is frequency-modulated at 30 Hz. Being an omni-directional radiation, its polar diagram is a circle. This means that at a given range from the transmitter, the same phase will be detected by an aircraft's receiver on all bearings around it. It will be noticed in fig. 9.1 that the phase pattern produced is independent of the receiver's bearing from the station. In the receiver, the 30 Hz component of this transmission is used as a reference (or datum) for the purpose of measuring the phase difference.

Variable or directional signal
This is again transmitted on the station frequency and the radiated pattern produces a polar diagram of a rotating figure of eight. And by rotating it 30 times per second the signal is given the character of a 30 Hz amplitude modulation. This simply means that the received signal will rise to a maximum and fall to zero value 30 times a second.

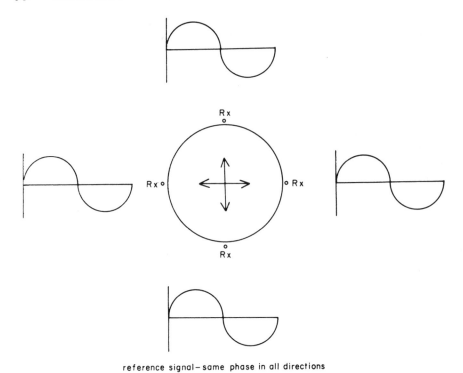

reference signal– same phase in all directions

fig. 9.1

Derivation of the phase difference
When the reference signal is combined with the directional signal, a rotating cardioid results. Unlike the cardioid of an ADF loop aerial, the VOR cardioid does not have a null position and in strict terms, a VOR cardioid is called a 'limacon' (see fig. 9.2). This absence of null is arranged at the transmitter by adjusting the power relationship between the reference and variable signals. The resulting field strength is in the ratios

fig. 9.2

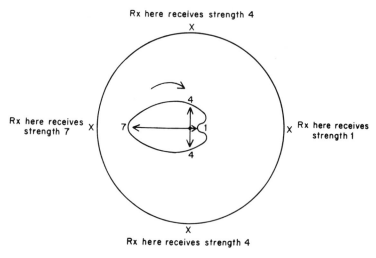

fig. 9.3

4 : 1 : 4 : 7 on four cardinal points. In fig. 9.3 the receivers are shown on four cardinal points, receiving signals of field strength in above ratios, and in fig. 9.4, when the amplitudes of the incoming signals are plotted on a time axis for the same four positions of the receiver, the signals' directional characteristic is revealed.

fig. 9.4

Rx MN: phase difference 0

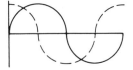

Rx 270(M): phase diff. 270

Rx 090 (M): phase diff. 90

Rx 180 (M): phase diff. 180

fig. 9.5

Now we have two signals in the receiver; the reference signal producing a constant phase as shown in fig. 9.1 and the variable signal giving a bearing-dependent phase, as shown in fig. 9.4. It will be seen in fig. 9.5 how the comparison between the two can yield the direction of the receiver. It will also be noted that the receiver north of the station receives both the signals at the same phase, that is, the phase difference between the two is zero. It is deliberately arranged that this zero difference should occur on the station's magnetic north to provide a measuring datum.

It will be observed from fig. 9.5 that an aircraft on a magnetic bearing of 090 receives a phase difference of 90° and when on 270, it receives a phase difference of 270°. Therefore, when on a bearing of 045, it will receive a phase difference of 45° and when on 227, it will receive a phase difference of 227° and so on. Conversely, when it receives a phase difference of 329°, its magnetic bearing from the station (QDR) is 329, and when it receives a phase difference of 063°, its QDR is 063.

Thus, a VOR transmitter continuously sends out 360 individual tracks. These tracks are oriented from the station's magnetic north (that is, the station's magnetic variation is applied) and the tracks radiating outward from the transmitter are called 'radials'. It is important to understand the strict meaning of this term so that it is not misused. Study fig. 9.6.

Airborne equipment
The basic airborne equipment consists of an aerial, a receiver and an indicator.
Aerial.   These are small, horizontal dipoles capable of accepting horizontally polarised signals in the frequency band 108 to 118 MHz. They should be installed so

fig. 9.6

that they offer omni-directional cover to VOR signals but receive no interference from the VHF aerial operating on RT communication channels. A VOR aerial also accepts ILS localiser signals which are in the same frequency band.

Receiver.   A VOR receiver compares the phases of the reference and variable signals and feeds the extracted phase difference in a suitable form to the various components of the indicator. The two signals are processed through two different channels, and their carriers are filtered out at appropriate stages. A 30 Hz FM reference signal is converted by a discriminator to a 30 Hz AM signal (see fig. 9.7) and it is then in phase compared with the 30 Hz AM variable signal in the phase detector unit.

fig. 9.7

If the two signals are in phase, the circuits are in balance and the indicator is indicating correct bearing. If the two signals are not in phase an error signal is produced in the phase detector which energises the servo motor. The servo motor is connected to a phase shifting circuit via a rotating shaft. On being energised, the servo motor turns the shaft in one or other direction to shift the phase. When the two phases are made alike in the phase detector, the error signal is cancelled and the system comes to rest. The angular rotation of the shaft is the measure of the phase difference.

Indicator.   The indicator consists of three basic components which may all be mounted in a single unit or installed separately or in combination. The three basic components are:

(a)   Omni-bearing selector (OBS),

(b)   TO/FROM indicator,

(c)   LEFT/RIGHT deviation indicator.

Two different types of indicators are shown in fig. 9.8. The function and the method of use of these components is explained in the following paragraphs.

fig. 9.8 VOR indicators

(a)   *Omni-bearing selector (OBS).* The OBS control knob is used by the pilot to select the *magnetic track* he wishes to fly to or from a VOR station. To home to the station he may select the track which will take him to the station (or the track he is required to follow) or its reciprocal, which is the radial from the station. For example, a VOR is to be reached on a magnetic track of 050°. The pilot may select 050° or 230° on the OBS. Similarly when flying away from the station on the same track, he may again use either of the above settings. As we will soon see, the selected track affects TO/FROM and L/R indications and so he chooses the best setting.

When the track is selected, the vertical left/right needle is displaced from its central position either to the left or to the right, unless the aircraft is on that selected radial at that time. Alternatively, a pilot may use his VOR just to obtain a bearing, in which case, he centralises the needle by use of the OBS control.

(b)   *TO/FROM indicator.* When the required magnetic track has been selected, the TO/FROM display will indicate either TO or FROM, according to whether the selected radial or its reciprocal is nearer to the aircraft's position. This indication will change when the aircraft crosses a line 90° to the selected track. The rate of change will depend upon the range of the aircraft from the ground station (when not flying overhead). In the following illustration, fig. 9.9, all aircraft have selected 010 on the OBS.

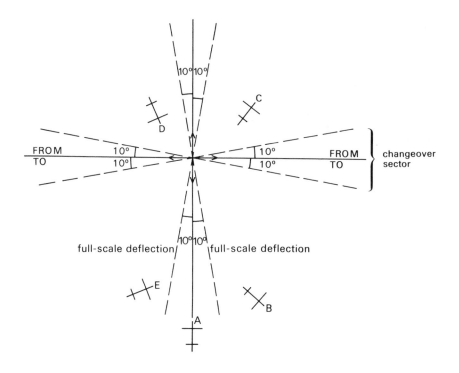

fig. 9.9 TO/FROM indications

Aircraft A, B and E will have TO displayed on the indicator since in all three cases if they wish to reach the station on magnetic track of either 010 or 190, then 010 is the nearer. For similar reasoning, aircraft C and D will indicate FROM suggesting that not the selected bearing 010 but its reciprocal 190 is the nearer radial to take him to the station.

There is another way of looking at it. In position A, B or E and having selected 010, ask yourself 'Does this setting take me to the station?' If the answer is 'yes', TO is indicated. In position C or D the answer is 'no' and FROM is indicated.

(c)   *LEFT/RIGHT deviation indicator.* The indicator consists of a vertical needle which moves left/right across the face from its central position to indicate deviations. The movement is against an angular scale shown by a number of dots. When the aircraft is on the radial the needle stays in its central position. When the aircraft is not on the selected radial, the needle indicates the difference between the selected radial and the radial the aircraft is actually on by moving out to left or right. The amount of deflection is the measure of the angular distance to the selected radial and is estimated from the dots scale.

A full-scale deflection occurs when the aircraft is $10°$ or more away from the selected radial. This means that no movement of the needle takes place from its maximum-deflection position until the aircraft is within $10°$ of the selected radial. The instrument may have either a 4-dot scale or a 5-dot scale. If it is a 4-dot instrument then one dot deflection indicates a deviation of $2\frac{1}{2}°$; similarly, on a 5-dot instrument it will equal $2°$.

Whether you would follow the needle by steering in the direction of the displaced needle or you would go against the needle depends on your physical position with regard to the selected radial, and is independent of the aircraft heading. However, since we must steer the aircraft to gain the radial we must translate this indication in terms of our present heading. The rule is: follow the needle to regain the radial if your heading and the selected bearing are in general agreement.

This rule immediately makes it clear that when homing to/from a station if the track set on OBS is the same as the track we want to follow then the L/R indications will be correct. When the aircraft deviates, say, to right of the track, the needle will move to the left, indicating that the pilot should turn to the left. To make this clear, say you are flying to a VOR on track 090 and you are going to continue on that track past the VOR, select 090 and not 270.

Going back to fig. 9.9 with this in mind:

Aircraft A will have its needle central.

Aircraft B will have a left turn indication as its heading is virtually the reciprocal of the selected radial.

Aircraft C has 010 selected and its heading is in general agreement and therefore, its indication is correct, that is, it should turn left to intercept the radial.

Aircraft D will have an incorrect indication of a right turn.

Aircraft E will also have a turn right indication.

Now study fig. 9.10 for further familiarisation with indications.

Failure warning flag.   All indicators employ a device to warn the pilot when the system has failed. An 'OFF' flag indicating a failure will appear on the face of the indicator in the event of any of the following occurring:

(a)   failure of the aircraft's receiving equipment;

(b)   failure of the ground station equipment;

(c)   failure of the indicator, or

(d)   where the signals being received are weak or the aircraft is out of range.

VOR frequencies

VOR operates in 108 to 117.95 MHz band as follows.

Band 108–112 MHz.   This is primarily an ILS frequency band but ICAO prescribes that it may be shared with VOR if it is not fully subscribed. Thus, normally this band is shared between ILS localiser and 'short range' (terminal) VORs. VOR uses frequencies on even decimals (108.2, 108.4, etc.) and ILS uses odd decimals (108.1, 108.3, etc.).

Band 112–117.95.   VOR (odd and even decimals).

ICAO's recommendation that the frequency spacing should be reduced to 50 kHz has been approved by the CAA and the future allocations will be based on this spacing. We will then have VORs operating on frequencies, for example, 112.30, 112.35 and so on.

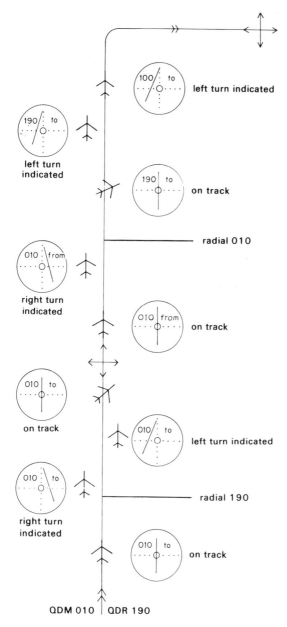

fig. 9.10

Exercises on use of VOR indicators and RBI

1.   An aircraft's VOR is tuned to station A. When 075 is selected on OBS the needle becomes central and the TO/FROM indicator indicates TO. At the same time, an NDB located on the VOR site gives a reading of 012° on ADF. What is the aircraft's heading, and what drift is being experienced?

Answer: the aircraft's magnetic track is 075, and as the ADF indicates 012, the aircraft's nose is offset by 12° to the left. Thus, its heading is (075 − 12) = 063 and the drift is 12° starboard.

2. An aircraft's heading is 050°(T), and is tracking on a VOR radial, with 068 set on the OBS and TO/FROM indicator indicating TO. The variation is 10°W. What should the aircraft's ADF read from an NDB sited at the VOR station?

Answer: 008°.

3. An aircraft bears 230°T, distance 15 nm from a VOR station. Local variation is 10°W.

(a)   What selected bearing should make the L/R needle central?

The aircraft's magnetic bearing from the station is (230 + 10W) = 240. Thus, the needle will be central when 240 is selected; it will also be central when its reciprocal, 060 is selected. Thus, the answer is: 240 FROM or 060 TO.

(b)   Would the L/R needle indicate left or right, if the bearing selected is 055?

Answer: turn right (if you draw a simple sketch you will notice that the radial 055 is to the right of the radial 060 when extended to the opposite side of the transmitter).

4. If an aircraft is on a true bearing of 216° from a VOR station, what is the phase difference between the reference and variable signals arriving in the aircraft's receiver? The variation is 10°E.

Answer: 206°.

5. An aircraft on a heading of 150°(M) tunes a VOR station, and selects 170 on the OBS. At that time the TO/FROM indicator reads TO and the L/R needle is displaced very close to the maximum deflection position, indicating a right-hand turn. What is the aircraft's approximate position in relation to the transmitter?

Answer: approximately to the magnetic north of the transmitter.

10: VHF Omni-Directional Radio Range (VOR) – 2

Use of VOR

VOR, like ADF, may be used in a variety of ways; it is more reliable and certainly easier to use once the principles are understood. You may home to your destination aerodrome from any direction. You may fly cross-country tracks from beacon to beacon, as on an airway. If your route does not take you over VOR stations, you may still make use of them in your navigation. You may carry out holding procedures and make an approach to let-down at your destination.

Before you actually use the VOR in the air for any of the above purposes it is important that you go through the following routine.

(a)   First check that you are within the DOC (designated operational coverage) of that station. This information is given in the commercial section of the U.K. AIP. Outside the U.K. you may find this information listed under 'range and altitude' or 'protection range and altitude'. If you are not within the DOC of the station you must not attempt to obtain the information even if the display units seem to give reliable indications. This is because the signals are not protected from interference from other beacons.

(b)   Having satisfied yourself that you are within the coverage, switch on the equipment. It may take a couple of minutes to warm up.

(c)   Select the station frequency, and if the indications are required on RMI, select VOR on the green pointer.

(d)   Check that the warning flag clears out of the window.

(e)   Identify the station.

You are now ready to use your VOR and we will discuss the procedures.

Homing on VOR

It is possible that you may be able to home to a station from any direction, that is, on any radial. In that case, as soon as you are receiving satisfactory signals you are on a VOR radial and ready to proceed.

But it is more likely that your approach direction is restricted for one reason or the other, e.g. a danger area in the way or presence of high ground and so forth. ATC imposes movement restriction to ensure a smooth traffic flow by prescribing inbound and outbound routes. These routes are defined by VOR radials and to home to the station you must use one of the routes most conveniently placed. Well, how do we get on this radial? With VOR it is relatively simple. In fig. 10.1, the aircraft in position 1 wishes to join radial 090 from VOR A. The inbound track is 270°(M). The pilot has some idea of his position in relation to the required radial. If he is not sure, his QDM to the station is quickly checked by turning the OBS control until the needle is central and TO is indicated. The following procedure is adopted.

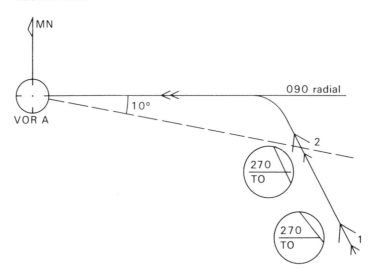

fig. 10.1

Set your track, 270 on the OBS counters. TO/FROM display will indicate TO (as this is your track to the station) and the L/R needle will swing to maximum deflection, indicating a right turn in our illustration. The indication of right turn is ignored as your own heading is not near 270°. With the knowledge of your position with regard to the selected radial, set a heading that will give you a comfortable angle of interception.

When in position 2, you are 10° away from the selected radial and the L/R needle will show an inward movement. Assess your angle of lead, taking into account your radius of turn, the angle through which you have to turn and the distance from the station. The movement of the L/R needle may give you an indication of how fast or slow you are approaching your radial. The further the distance from the station, the slower its inward movement.

If you have assessed your angle of lead correctly, on completion of the turn you should be on the radial, the L/R needle in the centre position and the TO/FROM indicator indicating TO. You are homing to the station.

Apply drift to fly 270 track. If the drift is correct, the needle will remain central. If the needle starts to ease to one or other side, follow the needle. One or two alterations in 5°/10° steps will give you the correct heading. Once on the correct heading, just monitor the needle for any indications of a wind change. The aircraft will arrive overhead VOR by keeping the needle central.

If the flight continues on the same track past the VOR beacon, the OBS setting remains unaltered. The TO/FROM indication will change to indicate FROM, and you follow the needle to correct for any deviations.

Taking a bearing

    (a)   Select a station within DOC;
    (b)   Switch on;
    (c)   Check the warning flag;

(d)   Identify the station;

(e)   Turn the OBS control until the needle is central;

(f)   Read off the radial indicated on the OBS counters and note the time;

(g)   Check the TO/FROM indication. If TO is indicated, it is QDM; if FROM is indicated, it is QDR.

Station passage and 'cone of confusion'

As the station is approached, radials get closer to each other and the needle becomes increasingly sensitive. Minor deviations are shown up calling for small adjustments of heading to keep the aircraft on the radial. When closer, the needle oscillates hard from side to side, the OFF flag may momentarily appear and TO/FROM display swings between TO and FROM, not being sure whether it is coming or going!

The cause of these erratic indications is the presence of what is called the 'cone of confusion' overhead the beacon.

The propagation specifications, as recommended by ICAO, require the signals to be transmitted up to 40° in elevation. In practice, the modern equipment is capable of radiating signals of up to 60° to 80° above the horizon. But it still leaves a gap overhead, in the form of a cone where no planned radiation takes place. While passing through this zone the receiver comes under influence of weak overspill, causing confusion to the indicators.

Once through the cone all indications settle down to indicate correctly, TO/FROM indication changing over to FROM. The time you will remain in the cone depends on your height and the ground speed.

Identification

In the U.K., VORs transmit a 3-letter aural morse group at a rate of approximately 7 words per minute, at least once every 10 seconds. This is the ICAO recommendation. Ident may also be given in speech form, e.g. 'This is Miami Omni Range', immediately followed by ident in morse. The voice channel may also be used to pass significant weather information to the aircraft.

Monitoring

All VOR ground stations' transmissions are monitored by an automatic monitor located in the radiation field near the station. The monitor will warn the control point and either remove the identification and navigation components from the carrier or switch off the radiation altogether in the event of any of the following circumstances:

(a)   a change in bearing information at the monitor site in excess of 1°;

(b)   a reduction of more than 15% in the signal strength of the two 30 Hz modulation components (or either one of them) or the RF carrier itself;

(c)   failure of the monitor itself.

When the main transmitter is switched off a standby transmitter is brought into operation. This takes a certain amount of time before its radiation stabilises. During this period the bearing information radiated can be incorrect, and as a warning to the users, no ident signals are transmitted until the changeover is complete.

When an approach to an airfield is being made using a short-range TVOR, it is vital that the pilot continuously monitors the ident signals in order to ensure that the bearing information being received is correct and the approach being made is safe.

Factors affecting VOR ranges

(a) *Transmission power.* The higher the power, the greater the range. En-route VORs with a power output of 200 watts achieve ranges of around 200 nm. Terminal VORs (TVORs) normally transmit at 50 watts.

(b) *Transmitter and aircraft height.* Because VOR transmissions are in the VHF frequency band, the theoretical maximum range depends on line-of-sight distance (in practice, slightly better due to atmospheric refraction). For calculating theoretical ranges for various heights, the VHF formula given in chapter 4 is used. This is repeated here for convenience.

$$\text{Max. range (in nm)} = 1.25 \sqrt{H_T} + 1.25 \sqrt{H_R}$$

where H_T is the height of the transmitter amsl, and H_R is the height of the receiver amsl.

The three factors involved in VHF formula are range, transmitter height (amsl) and the aircraft height (amsl). Knowing any two of these, the value of the third factor can be found.

Examples

1. If the transmitter's altitude is 100 ft and the aircraft's altitude 12 500 ft, at what maximum range would the aircraft receive the VOR signals?

$$\begin{aligned}
\text{Range} &= 1.25 \sqrt{H_T} + 1.25 \sqrt{H_R} \\
&= 1.25 \sqrt{(100)} + 1.25 \sqrt{(12\,500)} \\
&= (1.25 \times 10) + (1.25 \times 112) \\
&= 12.5 + 140 \\
&= 152 \text{ nm} \quad \text{(near enough).}
\end{aligned}$$

2. At what altitude should an aircraft be to receive VOR signals at a range of 130 nm if the VOR transmitter is 500 ft amsl?

$$\begin{aligned}
\text{Range} &= 1.25 \sqrt{H_T} + 1.25 \sqrt{H_R} \\
130 &= 1.25 \sqrt{(500)} + 1.25 \sqrt{H_R} \\
130 &= 1.25 (\sqrt{(500)} + \sqrt{H_R}) \\
\frac{130}{1.25} &= \sqrt{(500)} + \sqrt{H_R} \\
104 &= 22 + \sqrt{H_R} \\
\sqrt{H_R} &= 104 - 22 = 82 \\
H_R &= 82^2 \\
H_R &= 6\,725 \text{ ft}
\end{aligned}$$

(c) *Protection range and altitude.* At present there are only 20 channels in the 108–112 MHz band and a further 60 channels in 112–117.95 MHz band. Thus, the VOR band is very limited in channel space and like NDBs it is necessary to protect the wanted signals from interference due to unwanted signals. The protection is given not only in range but in altitude as well. Protection in altitude is possible because the signals travel in straight lines.

This need for protection becomes apparent when one looks at the problem from the planner's point of view. Suppose it is required to establish a VOR to give interference-free reception at 25 000 ft. First the distance the wave must travel to gain that altitude due to the earth's curvature is calculated; the TX is at sea level.

$$\begin{aligned}
\text{Range} &= 1.25 \sqrt{(25\,000)} \\
&= 1.25 \times 158 \\
&= 198 \text{ nm.}
\end{aligned}$$

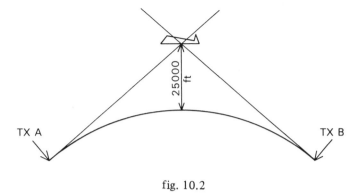

fig. 10.2

(See fig. 10.2.) Based on this calculation, another station, operating on the same frequency channel must be at least another 198 nm further away so as not to produce interfering radiation. This gives a geographical separation distance of 396 nm.

But this figure is derived from consideration of only one factor, that is, the line-of-sight propagation. There are other calculable factors which must be considered, e.g. the relative radiation strength of the two transmitters, attenuation of the signals due to range and altitude and the degree of protection required. The planners normally work on providing a protection of 20 dB. At a fair estimate these factors would add another 100 nm. Thus, to establish this VOR, the planners must ensure that no other VOR within a radius of 500 nm transmits on the same channel.

In a practical approach, a transmission is protected only to the extent necessary, in range and altitude, and not necessarily to the maximum line-of-sight range. Further, by increasing the radiation power of one transmitter, the separation distance from other co-channel transmitters may be reduced. Fig. 10.3 illustrates the practical scheme of providing protection. In the U.K. these values are published under the term 'designated operational coverage' (DOC).

In fig. 10.3 let us say that the protection range and altitude for VOR 1 is given as 50/25 000. An aircraft at a range of 50 nm from the transmitter is protected from interference to an altitude of 25 000 feet. Another aircraft, say at 30 000 feet will pass over the protected volume of airspace, when not at 50 nm but less than 50 nm (observe the diagram) and it has a fair chance of receiving interference-free signals. These should not be used.

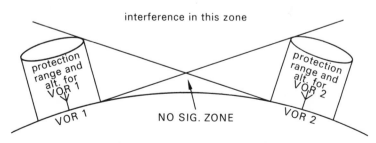

fig. 10.3 Protection range and altitude

(d)   *Nature of terrain.*   Uneven terrain, intervening high ground, mountains, valleys, man-made obstacles: all these features affect VOR propagation. The signals are stopped, reflected, bent, split and so forth, giving erroneous information. Where such effects have been known to exist, sectors giving errors are marked out and noted in the AIP. Typical information reads: 'errors up to 5½° may be experienced in sector radials 315° to 345°'. You may also find VORs in respect of which more than one protection altitude and range are prescribed.

Factors affecting accuracy

(a)   *Site error.*   Irregular or uneven terrain, physical obstacles, etc. in the vicinity of a VOR transmitter affect its directional propagation. Stringent requirements are laid down by ICAO regarding site contours, presence of structures, trees, wire fences, etc. Even the overgrowth of grass affects the signals. Error introduced in radiated directions by these features is called 'VOR course displacement error'. As we learnt earlier, VORs are ground-monitored to an accuracy of ±1°.

(b)   *Propagation error.*   The signals having left the transmitter giving an accuracy of ±1°, suffer further inaccuracies as they travel forward. Uneven terrain and other features which affect the signals at the site, continue to affect them throughout their passage to the receiver.

(c)   *Airborne equipment error.*   Airborne equipment is required to translate one degree of phase difference to one degree of change of direction. Inaccuracy is introduced in the process to which the indicator makes its contribution when the signals finally arrive for the display.

The above three errors in combination are called VOR aggregate errors; errors listed under (a) and (b) being due to ground propagation and those under (c) due to airborne equipment.

These errors are easily calculable by taking the square root of the sum of the squares of the two types of errors. For example, if the error due to ground propagation is 3.5°, and the error in the airborne equipment is 3°, then

$$\text{aggregate error} = \sqrt{(3.5^2 + 3^2)}$$
$$= \sqrt{(12.25 + 9)}$$
$$= \sqrt{(21.25)}$$
$$= 4.6°$$

In addition to the above we must consider a further two causes of errors as follows.

(d)   *Pilotage error.*   As the VOR station is approached, the signal strength increases rapidly and the radials get closer. The needle becomes sensitive to minor deviations and the pilot cannot or may not keep his aircraft precisely on the radial. However, because at this stage the radials are very close to each other the lateral displacement of the aircraft from its intended track is small. In planning calculations, this error is given a fixed value of ±2.5°.

(e)   *Interference error.*   This is an avoidable error which affects the indications when using a VOR outside the DOC or when below the line-of-sight altitude. When below the line of sight, if the signals are being received it is obvious that they must be weak signals arriving in the receiver due to reflections and other scatter effects.

The overall accuracy of the information displayed is ±5°; in the worst case due to other random variable errors this may deteriorate to ±7½°.

On the basis of a worst accuracy of ±7½° on an airway where the navigational information error should be limited to ±5° (to keep the aircraft within the airway limits), two VORs should not be further apart than 80 nm, as can be seen in the following calculations using 1 : 60 rule.

$$\text{Track error} = \frac{60 \times \text{dist. off}}{\text{dist. to go}}$$

$$7.5 = \frac{60 \times 5}{\text{dist. to go}}$$

$$\text{dist. to go} = \frac{60 \times 5}{7.5}$$

$$= \frac{300}{7.5}$$

$$= 40 \text{ nm}$$

Thus a 5° error occurs at a distance of 40 nm from the transmitter, setting the limit to its use.

Test VORs

These are installed at certain aerodromes to enable the pilots to test the airborne VOR equipment during preflight checks. The transmitters are called VOTs and the frequencies are published in the States' AIPs. To test the airborne equipment from any position on the aerodrome, just tune in to the channel and centralise the needle. OBS counters should indicate 000 FROM or 180 TO. If they do not indicate within ±4°, the equipment requires servicing.

Advantages of VOR as a navigational aid

(a)   In comparison with the system it replaced, VOR gives its indications in a form which is easy to see and follow.
(b)   In theory it provides an infinite number of tracks.
(c)   It is free from night effect and practically free from static.
(d)   Being a VHF aid its ranges can be accurately forecast before the beacons are sited, thus avoiding interference.
(e)   Its left/right deviation indicator can also display ILS signals.
(f)   It can be frequency-paired with DME to give fixes.
(g)   It incorporates an equipment-failure warning device.
(h)   Its channel spacing is much better than NDB's.
(i)   Being in the VHF band, its aerials are smaller.

Disadvantages of VOR as a navigational aid

(a)   Its left/right indications do not point to the beacon; thus, for a continuous indication of QDMs an RMI must be used.
(b)   Only position lines are available.
(c)   High ground and man-made obstructions can cut off, reflect and attenuate the signals.
(d)   Numerous beacons are required to give a large area coverage.
(e)   It gives line-of-sight ranges only.

Doppler VORs

Doppler VORs are the second generation VORs, the main aim being to improve the accuracy of the signals.

Conventional transmitters suffer from reflections from objects in the vicinity of the site. It was found that the errors due to this could be reduced if the horizontal dimensions of the aerial system were increased. However, this could not be achieved with the conventional method of transmission and a new approach was necessary.

In the DVOR (Doppler VOR) system the reference (or constant phase) signal is transmitted from a central aerial and it is amplitude-modulated. The variable signal is transmitted from a system of 50 aerials encircling the central aerial and it is frequency-modulated. Thus the modulations are employed in reverse roles. The resultant propagation is much less sensitive to obstructions in the vicinity.

Otherwise, the transmission frequencies are the same, the same airborne equipment can receive and process the signals and, as far as the airborne operation is concerned, there is no difference.

11: Radio Magnetic Indicator (RMI)

RMI, as the name suggests, is only an indicator and not an independent navigational aid. It accepts relative bearings from the ADF receiver and phase differences from the VOR to indicate QDMs in both cases. It employs a rotating scale card calibrated in number of degrees and positioned by the aircraft's remote indicating compass. Thus, on the indicator at the 12 o'clock position the aircraft's magnetic heading is read off against a heading index. QDMs are indicated by two concentric pointers, differently shaped, each of which may be energised simultaneously by two like or unlike aids. Fig. 11.1 shows a typical RMI. The thin pointer is coloured red and the wide pointer

fig. 11.1 Radio magnetic indicator

green. By convention the red pointer is called 'number one' needle and the green pointer 'number two'. And again, by convention, number one needle is used for ADF, and number two for VOR indications.

RBI relative bearings
In the following illustration, fig. 11.2, an aircraft on heading 030°(M) has tuned to NDB, X. The ADF gives a relative bearing of 090°R. The measuring datum on the indicator is 000, that is, the fore-and-aft axis of the aircraft. From fig. 11.2 we can see that the QDM to the NDB is 120° and thus, the relationship between a relative bearing and a QDM is the aircraft's heading. Or,

$$
\begin{array}{ll}
\text{Rel brg} & 090 \\
+ \text{ Hdg(M)} & 030 \\
\hline
\text{QDM} & 120 \\
\end{array}
$$

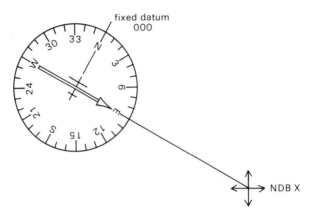

fig. 11.2

In an RMI, this addition of the heading to the relative bearing is automatically carried out by adjusting the measuring datum. By measuring the pointer's indications from the aircraft's magnetic heading for datum (fig. 11.3), the aircraft's QDM is read off. It will be noted that as the aircraft measures ADF relative directions with

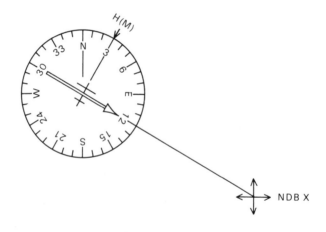

fig. 11.3

reference to its magnetic heading, when this QDM is converted to a true bearing for plotting from the station, the aircraft's magnetic variation (*not* the station's) must be applied.

VOR phases

VOR airborne equipment receives phases of two different signals (reference and variable) and derives QDR by taking the difference between the two. Its reciprocal is QDM. An RMI accepts relative bearings and not QDMs. Therefore the VOR phase difference giving QDM is first converted to give relative bearing. This is achieved by use of a differential synchro in the VOR navigation unit which subtracts the aircraft's magnetic heading to give relative bearing before the information is fed to the RMI. The RMI subsequently adds the aircraft's heading to give the QDM. In the following illustration (fig. 11.4) the aircraft is heading 030°(M) and the RMI indicates 120° QDM from VOR, Y. The magnetic variations at the VOR station and the aircraft position are different. The process of indication is as follows.

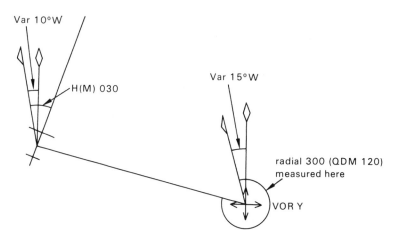

fig. 11.4

QDM received from VOR	120	
− Aircraft H(M)	030	− aircraft variation
Rel Brg	090	
+ Aircraft H(M)	030	− RMI card, aircraft variation
Indicated QDM	120	− Station variation

Thus, first the magnetic heading is subtracted, and then the same value is added. These two operations mutually cancel each other out and the resultant indication is affected only by the variation at the VOR station. Therefore, when converting QDM to true values for plotting, variation at the station position is applied.

For reasons of mutual cancellation, the use of the aircraft's heading introduces no error in the indication of VOR QDM. What would be in error is the calculation as above to the stage where the relative bearing is found. This is because the aircraft is using a variation which is different from the station variation. We will look into this in detail.

Discrepancies in indications

(a)   If the aircraft's variation is different from the station's variation, the indication of the relative bearing is incorrect but the QDM indicated is still correct.

In fig. 11.5, aircraft A and B are on a magnetic heading of 030°. The variation at A's position is 20°W, the variation at both B's and the station's position is 10°W. Both aircraft are on a QDM of 100° from VOR, X. From the figure it will be apparent that the relative bearing of the VOR transmitter from aircraft A is 080°R and from aircraft B, 070°R. Both aircraft calculate a QDM of 100° as follows.

fig. 11.5

A/c A: QDM   100
        −Hdg(M) 030
        RB   070   — This is what will be read off against a fixed RB scale; its
                             true relative bearing is 080°

        +Hdg(M) 030
        QDM   100

A/c B: QDM   100
        −Hdg(M) 030
        RB   070   — Indicates correct relative bearing (same variation)
        +Hdg(M) 030
        QDM   100

    (b)   If an NDB is located on the VOR site, QDMs from the VOR and the NDB
as displayed by an RMI will be different, if the variation between the aircraft and the
station positions is different.
    In fig. 11.5, the VOR gives a QDM of 100°. This is measured at the VOR site.
An NDB on the same site would give a relative bearing of 080°R to the aircraft, using
local variation. An RMI adds relative bearing to the heading to give the QDM. Thus
the QDM displayed is (080° + 030°) = 110°. Simultaneously, the VOR pointer will
indicate a QDM of 100°.
    Similar discrepancies in the indications will be observed due to convergency
between aircraft and the station positions. This is because, like variation effect, the
aircraft's true north (from which it derives its magnetic heading) is different from the
true north direction of the station. When QDM from a VOR is displayed, the
relative bearing indication will be approximate and when QDMs from VOR/NDB are
displayed, the two QDMs will show a difference. The discrepancy will be the value of
convergency.
    Thus, variation and convergency affect the indications as explained above. How-
ever, these considerations are more of academic nature than practical. In practical use
of the equipment, an aircraft not too far from the transmitters will experience only
minor discrepancies and these may be disregarded. And the QDMs from VORs are
always shown correct.
    However, if these two QDMs are required to be reduced to plotting values, the
procedure should be as follows:
    QDM derived from an NDB: apply variation at the aircraft and plot the reciprocal;

QDM derived from a VOR, apply station variation and plot the reciprocal. For fuller explanations on plotting techniques, the student should consult volume 2 'Plotting and Flight Planning'.

Advantages of RMI
(a)   QDM/QDR are indicated continuously and read off directly. The tail end of the pointers indicate QDRs.
(b)   Using two beacons, instantaneous fixes are obtained.
(c)   RMI indications provide a very useful guide when initially joining a radial for VOR homing.
(d)   The indicator itself can be used for homing.
(e)   Magnetic headings can be read off together with QDMs.
(f)   Approximate relative bearings may be read off against a fixed RBI scale or assessed visually.

Homing to/from a station
Fig. 11.6 shows the indications on RMI and RBI and fig. 11.7 shows indications on the VOR L/R deviation indicator and RMI when homing to/from a station.

VOR – NDB – RMI exercises
1.   An aircraft bears 220°(T) distance 20 nm from a VOR beacon. Its heading is 055°(M) and variation is 20°W.
(a)   What selected bearing should make the L/R needle central?
(b)   Would the L/R needle indicate turn to left or right if the selected radial was 055?

(a)   Brg Mag = 220°(T) + 20°W (Var)
              = 240
      ∴ QDM = 240 − 180
              = 060 which, when selected will make L/R needle central.
Also, its reciprocal, 240 will make the needle central.

      ∴ 060 TO and 240 FROM
(b)   If 055 was selected, the indication will be turn right (see fig. 11.8).
2.   An aircraft is heading 060°(T), tracking on a VOR radial 078 TO the station. Variation 10°W. What should ADF read on beacon sited at VOR station?
              Hdg(M) = 060°(T) + 10°W
                      = 070°(M)
              A/c's track is 078°(M) ∴ aircraft has 8° starboard drift.
              ∴ NDB will read 360 + 8 = 008°
3.   An aircraft is heading 060°(T). Variation is 10°E. An NDB bears 200°(R). Show by means of a sketch how this information would appear on the face of RMI.
              RB   = 200
              Hdg(M) = 050
              QDM   = 250 (See fig. 11.9)

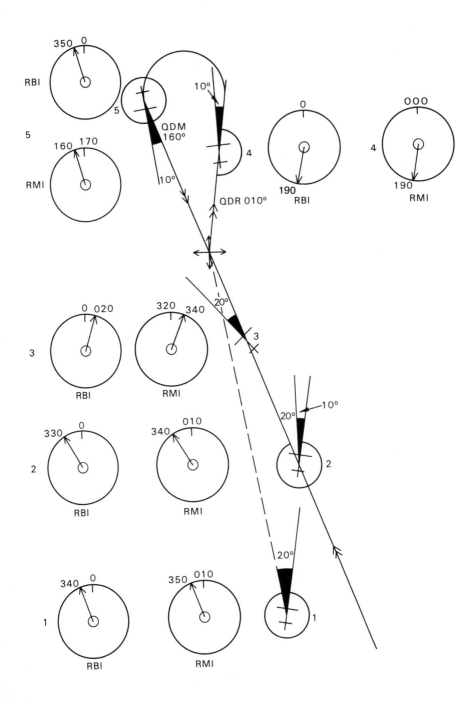

fig. 11.6 Homing procedures using RBI and RMI

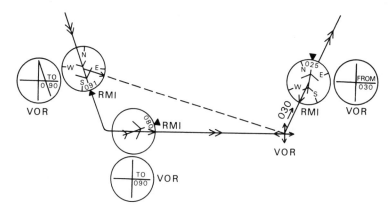

fig. 11.7 Homing procedures using VOR L/R deviation indicator and RMI

fig. 11.8

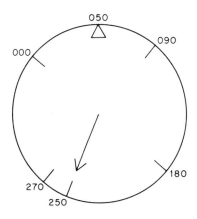

fig. 11.9

4.   An aircraft is flying a constant heading with 8°P drift and is making good a track parallel to the centre line of an airway, but 5 nm off to the left of the centre line. Estimate the ADF reading of an NDB sited on the centre line of the airway, but 30 nm ahead.

fig. 11.10

In fig. 11.10, the angle between the aircraft's track and the radio station is worked out using the one in sixty rule.

$$\text{Tr Error} = \frac{\text{Dist. off} \times 60}{\text{dist. to go}} = \frac{5 \times 60}{30}$$
$$= 10°$$

The nose of the aircraft is offset to the right (to compensate for port drift) by 8°. Therefore, the angle between the nose of the aircraft and the NDB

$$= 10 - 8$$
$$= 2°$$

The radio compass will read 002°.

5.   An aircraft is heading towards VOR, A, maintaining radial 130°, drift 10°P. NDB, B is due east of VOR, A and when it is abeam present track, heading will be altered for B. Drift will then be 5°S.

   On an RMI show the approximate indications of A and B as they would appear

   (a)   shortly before altering heading for B and
   (b)   shortly after the heading has been altered.

See fig. 11.11.

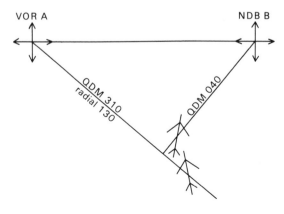

fig. 11.11

Indications will be as follows:
(a)   Just before altering heading:
RMI heading – 320(M)
VOR pointer – 310 (QDM to VOR)
NDB pointer – 035° (QDM from abeam position is 040°).
(b)   After altering heading:
RMI heading – 035°(M)
NDB pointer – 040 (QDM to NDB, B)
VOR pointer – 300.
6.   Complete the following table:

	Hdg(M)	Rel Brg	RMI indication
(a)	210	182	–
(b)	130	–	160
(c)	040	–	160
(d)	–	240	038
(e)	–	193	026

Answers: (a) 032; (b) 030; (c) 120; (d) 158; (e) 193.
7.   An aircraft is homing to a VOR. Drift is 8°P, variation at VOR is 5°W, variation at the aircraft position is 4°W. Give the initial heading to maintain a radial of 253°.
Answer: 065°(M).
8.   An aircraft's RMI is being fed with information from a VOR and an NDB. The aircraft is tracking to VOR on radial 228°. Drift is 5°P. An NDB bears 060°R from the aircraft. Give the two indications on an RMI.
Answer: VOR pointer 048°; NDB pointer 113°; RMI heading 053°(M).
9.   An aircraft is heading 041°(M). It is 20 nm from a VOR and on a bearing of 215°(M) from the station. The pilot has selected 212° on OBS and the TO/FROM indicator is indicating FROM. What information is displayed on (a) RMI; (b) ILS/VOR indicator?
Answer: On the RMI, the heading is 041°(M) and the VOR pointer indicates its present QDM which is (215° – 180°) = 035°.
On the L/R indicator, the selected bearing is 3° off from his own radial, and to his right. Therefore the indications are: 1½ dots in 5 dots or slightly over 1 dot in 4 dots. As the aircraft is heading against the selected radial and FROM is indicated, the left/right display will give him a left turn.

12: Ground DF: Fan Markers

A ground station can be equipped for taking a bearing of an aircraft on that aircraft's transmission. In earlier days such a service operated in MF, HF and VHF bands. In the U.K. this service now only operates in the VHF band, that is, the normal communication band of 118 to 136 MHz. Service in other bands still exists in certain parts of the world and, where applicable, relevant information such as frequency in use, range, accuracy is found in the Aerad Flight Guide.

When the service is required, the procedure is to call up the station on the appropriate RT channel. Frequencies are given in the section of the AIP.

Services

A ground DF station can give true or magnetic bearings as follows:

QTE – aircraft's true bearing from the station
QUJ – aircraft's true track to the station
QDR – aircraft's magnetic bearing from the station
QDM – aircraft's magnetic heading to steer in zero wind to reach the station.

QTEs and QDRs are normally used in en route navigation for plotting as position lines. QDMs are requested when the pilot wishes to home to the station. QUJ is generally only known to academics and examiners.

In addition to the above, if you want a series of bearings or headings to steer (as for example you are homing to a station), the service you request is QDL. Where a three-station triangulation service exists (none in the U.K. at present, except on your MAYDAY or PAN calls), you may request a QTF. The station will take a fix on you and pass it to you in lat. and long. co-ordinates or bearing and distance from a recognisable landmark, town, facility, etc.

DF stations can refuse to give bearings if the conditions are poor or the bearings do not fall within the classified limits of the station. In this case, the controller will give his reason for the refusal.

Classification of bearings

According to the judgment of the operator the bearings are classified as follows. When the controller passes the bearing to the pilot he adds this classification to it, e.g. 'your true bearing 247°, class alpha'.

Class A – accurate to within ±2°.
Class B – accurate to within ±5°.
Class C – accurate to within ±10°.

Scope of the service

There are many automatic VDF stations whose purpose is purely to assist in radar identification for ATC purposes. These stations are not listed in the AIP for the obvious reason that they do not provide a normal DF service to the aircraft. The stations that are listed in the AIP provide normal 'homer' service and they are listed as such. Generally the class of bearing is not better than class B. Automatic VDF stations are not to be used as en route navigation aids but their service is available to the fullest extent in case of emergency or where other essential navigation aids have failed.

Automatic stations (homers as well as those established for radar ident purposes) utilise a cathode ray tube for bearing measurements. With this type of equipment, the aerial is rotated in response to the incoming transmission and the direction of the received wave is displayed on the tube instantaneously. On the tube, the transmission appears as a trace and the bearing is read off against a scale. The main advantage here is that only a very short transmission is required — just long enough to read off the bearing.

Ranges available
Being VHF transmission, the range will primarily depend on the height of the transmitter and the receiver, that is, the line-of-sight range. Other factors e.g. power of the ground and airborne transmitters, intervening high ground, etc., will also affect the range. Further, as explained in an earlier chapter, the aircraft may receive both the direct wave and the ground reflected wave in which case fading might be experienced or even the signals may be lost completely. But this situation would not linger too long and a satisfactory two-way communication would soon be restored.

Factors affecting accuracy
Earlier, we studied the factors that affect VOR bearings. The same factors will affect the VDF bearing, only the process of transmission being reversed. If an aircraft's transmission for a true bearing has been reflected by either uneven terrain or obstacles through its travel or by objects on the site, the aerial will read a wrong direction. Thus, propagation error and site error will affect the accuracy. Poor accuracy is also obtained when nearly overhead the station, as there is a 'cone of no bearing'.

The aircraft's attitude when transmitting signals may also affect the results. As you will remember, in general aviation, VHF communication transmission is vertically polarised. Best results are obtained when the transmission arriving at the ground DF aerial is vertically polarised. When an aircraft is in an attitude such that its transmission aerial is in the horizontal plane, the transmitted signals will be horizontally polarised and no signals will be received. In between the two extremes, poor reception on the ground may give poor results.

The effect due to coastal refraction on VHF is negligible.

VHF let-down service
The VHF let-down service, available throughout the world, has the primary advantage that the aircraft does not require any specialist equipment to carry out a let-down. The stations which provide this service are listed in the Com section of the AIP where you also extract frequency and the callsign. Details of the procedures are published by Aeradio and other aviation publishers. These details are also found in

the RAC section of the AIP and it should be consulted whenever any details on TAP are not clear.

Two types of procedure are in current use: the VDF procedure and the QGH procedure. Generally, the VDF procedure is available and the AIP annotates in the remarks column against the station where QGH may be carried out. Where both procedures are available at the same station, the let-down pattern is usually the same.

For a VDF let-down, the pilot calls the station and 'requests VDF'. The pilot is subsequently given a series of QDMs which he uses to achieve the approach pattern for landing, as published in the aerodrome landing chart.

With the QGH procedure the pilot is given headings to steer instead of QDMs. Based on the pilot's frequent transmission, the aircraft is first homed to the overhead (aerial) position at correct height. This height is the lowest available flight level or the safety altitude. When overhead the pilot will be given instructions for descent on the timed outbound leg. The aircraft will turn inbound on completion of this leg and further instructions to decision height will follow. Heading corrections will be given on the inbound leg until the pilot is in visual contact.

Fan markers

Fan markers transmit a narrow vertical fan-shaped beam of horizontally polarised radiation. All markers operate on a single frequency, 75 MHz. Because of the shape of the transmission, they cannot be heard unless the aircraft is in the fan, and therefore, they cannot be used as directional aids.

Fan markers have two main uses: they are used to mark reporting points on airways and they are also used in conjunction with ILS to provide a precision approach facility.

On airways, Fan is identified by a high-pitched (3 000 Hz) audio signal giving out identification in morse, 6 to 10 words per minute A2 emission. Further, the white light in the airborne installation flashes to identify visually. The vertical coverage of the fan is limited to the operational requirements: there are low power fan marker beacons and high power beacons. Because in the horizontal plane the area of coverage increases with height, if accurate navigation is required, the time of entering and leaving the fan should be noted and the mean time taken for the fix. On some equipment a high/low switch is fitted which may be used to reduce the coverage area inside the fan.

The use of fan markers in conjunction with ILS is described in chapter 14.

13: Consol

Consol is a long range navigation aid which operates in the MF band. Ground installation consists of a transmitter and three aerials sited in a straight line. Transmitted
signals are received in the receiver and heard in the earphones as dots and dashes. The
type of emission is A1 and to receive such signals the aircraft only requires a CW
receiver, operating in 200–400 kHz frequency band. The bearing resultant from dot
and dash count is plotted on a special consol chart which has these counts printed on
it. There will be more than one position line on the chart representing the same
count, but if the aircraft is a reasonable distance away from the transmitter this will
cause no ambiguity. Should any ambiguity arise (due to closeness to the station, un-
certainty of position, etc) it is resolved by taking a loop bearing on the transmitter.
As an alternative to the printed chart, CAP 59 gives several tables from which possible
great circle bearings for a given count may be extracted. When using these tables, if
the bearings are plotted on a Mercator's projection, conversion angle must be applied.

Principle
Current from a common transmitter is fed to three aerials, installed in a straight line
and three wavelengths apart from each other. At the start, with reference to the
transmission phase of the centre aerial B (fig. 13.1), aerial A transmits a signal which

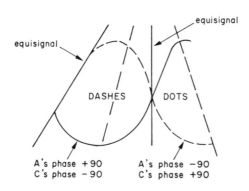

fig. 13.1

is +90° in phase, and aerial C −90° in phase. The phases of the outer aerials are then reversed, that is, A transmits at −90° and C at +90° with reference to B. This interchanging of phase between outer aerials and centre aerial produces a transmission lobe pattern as shown in fig. 13.1.

The resultant pattern of the equisignals produced right round the transmitter is shown in fig. 13.2.

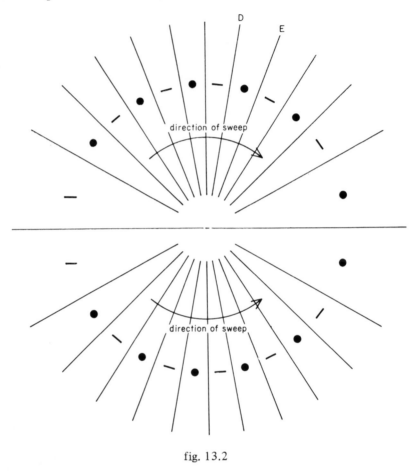

fig. 13.2

The pattern is made up of sectors of alternating dots and dashes, separated by lines of equisignals, that is, the bearing where the operator would hear a continuous signal instead of dot or dash. There are eleven such equisignals on either side of the base line. Sectors normal to the base line are approximately 10° wide and they open up to approximately 15°–20° in direction along the base line. Two sectors on either side of the base line where continuous dots or dashes are received cannot be used.

These equisignal lines lie on known bearings from the station. Therefore, whenever an aircraft passes through one of these equisignals, it can obtain a bearing. It would, however, be most inconvenient if the aircraft had to wait until the next equisignal line is crossed, which in some cases may be as far as 200 miles away. Therefore, instead of moving the aircraft to an equisignal line, the equisignal lines are made to move to the aircraft. The direction in which the equisignals move is called the direction of sweep and is shown in fig. 13.2.

As the sweep takes place, all lines of equisignals progressively move in the direction shown until they occupy the position previously occupied by their immediate neighbours. For example, D in fig. 13.2 will progressively move towards E and will occupy E's position in a given time, usually 30 or 60 seconds. The transmission stops at this stage, and all equisignal lines are brought back to their original positions to start a new cycle.

How does this all help us to get a bearing? Follow this illustration:

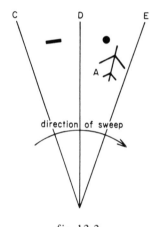

fig. 13.3

As the cycle commences, D will progressively move in the direction of E to occupy E's position in say, 60 seconds. During that time, 60 dot characters will be transmitted, DE being a dot sector. If an aircraft A was say two thirds of the way from D, then there are 40 dots between the aircraft and equisignal D, which the operator will count as the sweep progresses. Equisignal will then arrive. As the equisignal goes past the aircraft (to reach E) characters from sector C–D (dashes) will be heard. When the operator has counted 20 such dashes, the equisignal will have reached E and the cycle stops.

Aircraft's count of 40 dots and 20 dashes tells that:
1.   It is in dots sectors, since dots were heard first.
2.   That it is two thirds of the way (40 : 60) from D to E.

A bearing which is two thirds of the way; thus a bearing of any proportion of 60 is determinable, since the bearings of two equisignals are known. Therefore, the system can be used to provide bearing information.

Taking a consol count
1.   Tune the receiver to correct frequency. CW/RT switch to CW (BFO on). A narrow band receiver is advantageous from the accuracy and range point of view, since the frequency band occupied by a consol signal is small.
2.   Automatic Gain Control – off.
3.   Identify the station.

4. If necessary, take an ADF bearing on a long dash which is transmitted prior to the sweep cycle for this purpose.
5. Start counting as soon as the signals are heard.
6. Note time when equisignal is heard. This is the time of the position line.
7. Add up both the counts (of dots and dashes). These, in normal circumstances will not add up to 60, since some characters are invariably lost in the equisignal. Suppose the count was as follows:

40 dots, equisignal, 16 dashes. 4 symbols were lost in the count during the equisignal. Here we will presume that of these 4, the number of dots lost was 2, and the number of dashes 2. The dot count is then 42 dots, which is plotted.

Example: equisignal, 56 dots.

Here, 4 characters are lost – attribute 2 to dots and 2 to dashes. Therefore, the count to plot is 2 dashes.

Example: 54 dots, equisignal.

Six characters are lost, 3 dots and 3 dashes. Therefore, the count to plot is 54 + 3 = 57 dots.

Usable sectors
1. Very close to the station, that is 15–20 nm, the consol count is not clearly defined and therefore cannot be used.
2. Approximately 15 to 20° either side of the base line there is a continuous dot or dash pattern, and consol cannot be used in these areas.
3. When close to the station – 30 to 40 miles – the pattern is clear but the sector width is very small. Hence an aircraft travelling in direction normal to the equisignal line may race the count.
4. Between 350 and 450 miles from the station both ground and sky waves are received at night. These give erroneous readings. Beyond that range, sky waves only are received, and the count is correct again.

Range

	Flat Land	Sea	
Day	700	1 000	on 90% of occasions
Night	1 200	1 200	on 95% of occasions

Accuracy
1. Accuracy depends on the bearing of the aircraft from the station. The error is minimum on the normal to the line of the aerials, twice the minimum value at 60° to normal and 20 times the value of the minimum in the direction of the line of the aerials.
2. *Minimum errors at normal*

Day: Land – 4 characters or 2/3°;
       Sea – 2 characters or 1/3°

Night: Land and Sea – between range 350 and 450 miles: 15 characters or 2½°
                      Beyond 600 miles – 4 to 6 characters or 2/3° to 1°
       (Thus, accuracy improves as range increases.)

Checking accuracy
If the total count is more than 59 or less than 52, the accuracy of the count is suspect, and the count should be discarded.

Advantages of the system
1.   No special equipment required in the aircraft.
2.   Simple to use.
3.   Very long ranges available.
4.   Ground equipment easy to maintain.

Disadvantages
1.   Simultaneous fixes cannot be obtained.
2.   Taking a position line is a slow process – takes about a minute to identify and count, and further time wasted if you tuned in in the middle of a sweep when you should wait for a new sweep to start.
3.   Counting of signal requires concentrated effort – when you see your navigator tapping his pencil on the table you would know what he is doing.
4.   Not suitable as a homing aid.
5.   Being an MF aid, it suffers from static.

Extract from consol tables – CAP 59
Bushmills Consol station – DOT SECTORS

Count of dots	True Bearing from Station								
21	027.0	053.4	098.5	125.7	151.9	185.0	255.4	288.6	314.7	341.9
	*	*	*	*	*	*	*	*	*
30	–	–	096.2	123.8	149.8	181.8	258.7	290.6	316.6	344.2

Where the bearing is not available, the count is not plottable. In other cases, a bearing nearest to the aircraft's DR bearing (or bearing given by radio compass) is selected and plotted from the station. Appendix III in CAP 59 gives the values of conversion angles for aircraft in different positions, very handy indeed when using a Mercator Chart.

14: Instrument Landing System (ILS)

ILS is a pilot interpreted runway approach aid, developed by the RAF during the Second World War and is now in world-wide use. The system provides the pilot with visual instructions enabling the aircraft to be flown along a predetermined flight path to the threshold of the runway being served by the system. In practice, the pilot descends to his decision/critical height and then by visual reference makes his final decision to land or overshoot. With this system the ground transmissions are continuous and no assistance from the ground control is required.

The runway being served by the ILS or precision approach radar (PAR) is called 'precision instrument runway'.

The ILS ground installation consists of the following three components:

(a)   Localiser transmitter, together with its aerial system. This transmitter supplies approach guidance in azimuth along the extended runway centre line.

(b)   Glide path transmitter, together with its aerial system. This transmitter provides approach guidance in the vertical plane.

(c)   Two or three marker beacons, each with its own aerial. They provide range check points.

A layout of the ground system is shown in fig. 14.1 below.

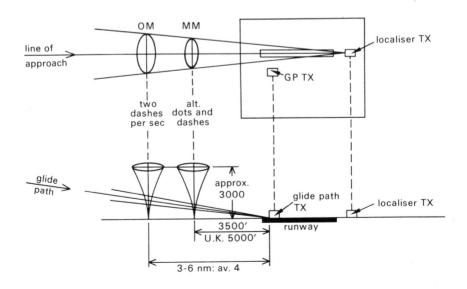

fig. 14.1

The localiser transmitter

The radio signals transmitted by the localiser antenna produce a composite field pattern along the approach direction, consisting of two overlapping lobes. The transmitter aerial is located in line with the runway centre line, approximately 300 m from the up-wind end of the runway. The two lobes are transmitted on a single ILS frequency in VHF and in order that the receiver can distinguish between them, they are differently modulated. That lobe on the right-hand side of the runway as seen by the pilot making an approach is modulated by a 150 Hz signal and the sector it forms is called 'blue' sector (see fig. 14.2). The lobe on the left-hand side is

fig. 14.2

modulated by a 90 Hz note and the sector formed by it is called 'yellow' sector. An aircraft approaching the runway in the landing direction will detect more of the 90 Hz modulation note and relatively less of the 150 Hz modulation note if it is to the *left* of the centre line. This excess of 90 Hz modulation (DDM: difference in depth of modulation) will energise the vertical needle of the ILS meter (or VOR/ILS indicator) to indicate a right-hand turn. Similarly, an aircraft flying to the right-hand side of the centre line will have an excess of the 150 Hz modulation note and the needle will indicate a left-hand turn. The line along which the DDM is 0 defines the runway centre line. When flying along this line there will be no deflection of the needle, indicating that the aircraft is on the centre line.

Localiser coverage – cat. I

The localiser coverage extends from the transmitter to 25 nm, 10° either side of the centre line. However, it widens to 35° from the centre line to a range of 17 nm (see fig. 14.3). These dimensions may be reduced where it is necessary for topographical reasons. The vertical coverage in the areas already described is 7°. In this volume of airspace the radiation field strength is sufficient to permit satisfactory operational use of the localiser. (The minimum prescribed is 40 microvolts per metre.) Signal strength reduces rapidly outside this airspace: similarly, the maximum field strength is directed on the centre line, to a distance of 10 nm.

If the localiser centre line is being used for navigational purposes (e.g. taking a position line) it should be noted that the localiser signals are protected from interference out to a range of 25 nm at an altitude of 6 250 feet along the on-course line. As for the accuracy, they are checked up to 10 nm.

The glide path transmitter

Ideally this transmitter and its aerial should be located at the touch-down point on the runway. But in the early experimental days the RAF found that the airmen

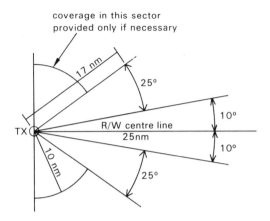

fig. 14.3 Localiser coverage

manning the transmitter did not run fast enough to get out of way and consequently, kept damaging the landing aircraft. Hence it is located to one side of the runway, approximately 150 m from the centre line, 300 m upwind from the threshold. The transmission is beamed in the vertical plane in two lobes similar to the localiser transmission. The upper lobe has a 90 Hz modulation, the lower lobe has a 150 Hz modulation. The line along which the two modulations are equal in depth defines the centre line of the glide slope. It is generally 3° from the horizontal but it could be adjusted to between 2° and 4° to suit the particular local conditions (see fig. 14.4).

fig. 14.4 Glide slope pattern

The glide path coverage – cat. I
The coverage in azimuth extends 8° on either side of the GP centre line, to a distance of 10 nm (see fig. 14.5). In the vertical plane the coverage begins from 0.45 x GP angle (θ) above the surface to 1.75 x GP angle (θ) above the surface. This means that for a 3° GP angle the coverage is from 1.35° to 5.25° above the surface. (Note: The coverage and field strength data given above for localiser and glide path transmissions are appropriate for Cat I, ILS.)

ILS indicator
ILS uses the VOR's left/right deviation indicator, incorporating an additional horizontal needle. This needle is inoperative when the indicator is displaying VOR

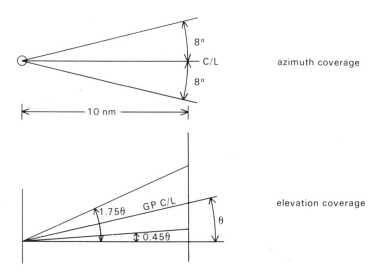

fig. 14.5 GP coverage

information. The indicator is also described as the VOR/ILS meter (fig. 14.6). The indicator illustrated in fig. 14.6 is a five-dot indicator, dot one being the outer edge of the centre circle.

When used with ILS, the vertical pointer indicates the aircraft's deviations in azimuth, and the horizontal needle indicates its position with regard to the glide slope centre line. Both needles remain in the central position when

(a)   the receiver is switched off or no signals are being received, or

(b)   the aircraft is on the centre line of the localiser and the glide path.

The bottom of the dial is coloured blue to the left and yellow to the right. This indicates to the pilot the localiser sector he is in, e.g. if the vertical needle has swung to the left, the aircraft is in the blue sector.

All ILS indicators employ two failure warning flags; one operating in association with localiser signals (this flag also operates in association with VOR), the other with

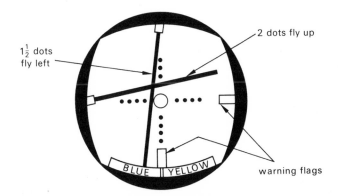

fig. 14.6 ILS indicator

the glide path signals. They fall into view in the windows and the needles return to the central position when:

(a)   ground or airborne equipment has failed or is switched off, and

(b)   out of the service area or the signals being received are too weak. (The signal strength falls off quickly once outside the service area.)

Monitoring of ILS transmissions

Both localiser and glide path transmitters are automatically monitored by monitoring equipment located in an area of guaranteed reception within the normal service sector. It will act in one of the following circumstances:

(a)   a localiser shift of more than 35 feet from the centre line;

(b)   a glide slope angle change of more than 0.075 x basic glide path angle, e.g. $3 \times 0.075° = 0.225°$;

(c)   a reduction in power output of 50% or more of any of the transmitters.

In any of the above circumstances, the monitoring unit will provide warning to a designated control point and cause any of the following to occur before a stand-by transmitter is brought into use:

(a)   the cessation of all radiations;

(b)   the removal of the ident signal and/or the navigational component (i.e. localiser and glide path);

(c)   if the ILS is category II or III, the monitor may permit operation to a lower category, i.e. I or II. (See later reference to ILS categories.)

Localiser indications

The vertical pointer is used for localiser indications. The needle tells you which way to turn and the horizontal deflection scale gives you an estimate of the angular displacement from the centre line. The coloured sectors at the bottom tell you which sector you are in. Follow the illustration in fig. 14.7.

Aircraft A is in the blue sector, and the needle indicates left turn. Aircraft B is in the blue sector, and the needle indicates left turn. Thus, the indication is given according to the sector the aircraft is in, not according to its heading. In this case aircraft B is on the right-hand side of the centre line and on reciprocal heading, there-fore it will have to *reverse* the indication. The same applies to aircraft D which is on the left-hand side (or yellow sector) with reciprocal heading. Its turn right indication is reversed if it wishes to regain the centre line. In all cases notice that the needle indicates the sector the aircraft is in and 'follow the needle' rule applies when making an approach. Reverse the indication if going away on the QDR.

As for the deviation scale the centre line beam is 5° wide, that is, 2½° on either side of the centre line. Maximum deflection of the needle occurs when the aircraft is 2½° or more from the centre line. On a 4-dot indicator, one dot represents a deviation of approximately 0.6°, on a 5-dot indicator, 0.5°. (Remember that the same needle will give a full deflection when a 10° deviation from a VOR radial occurs.)

Glide path indications

The horizontal needle is used in conjunction with the glide path transmissions. If the aircraft is below the glide path the needle moves upwards, indicating that the aircraft

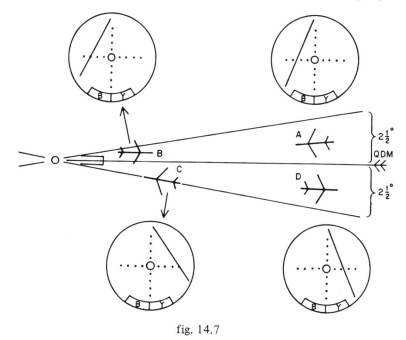

fig. 14.7

should fly up to regain the glide slope. This indication will occur irrespective of the heading, that is, whether the aircraft is on QDM or QDR. Therefore, a departing aircraft wishing to climb along the glide slope will obey the needle. If an aircraft (approaching or departing) is above the glide path the needle will move downward, indicating that the pilot should come down (see fig. 14.8).

Full deflection of the needle occurs when the aircraft is 0.7° or more above or below the glide path. A 2-dot fly-up indication out of four dots or 2½ dots out of five dots (in other words, half full deflection) is to be regarded as the maximum safe deviation below the glide path. On seeing any indications below this, an immediate climb must be instituted: remember this at all costs.

In fig. 14.6, the indicator gives the combined indications of localiser and glide path deviations. The interpretation depends on whether you are approaching the runway (on QDM) or going away from the runway (QDR):

if on QDM, the indications in fig. 14.6 instruct you to turn left and climb;

if on QDR, the instructions are to turn right and climb.

Marker beacons

Usually two, sometimes three marker beacons are installed along the extended centre line to give range indications on approach. This enables the pilot to check his height as he passes each marker. All markers transmit on a single frequency of 75 MHz and radiate a fan pattern upward to a calibrated height of approximately 3 000 feet. The marker farthest from the touch-down point is placed approximately 3 to 6 nm, average 4 nm, from the touch-down point and is known as the 'outer marker'. It transmits a low-pitched 400 Hz modulation signal and identifies itself in morse as well as visually. When crossing the beacon, a series of dashes is heard in the earphone,

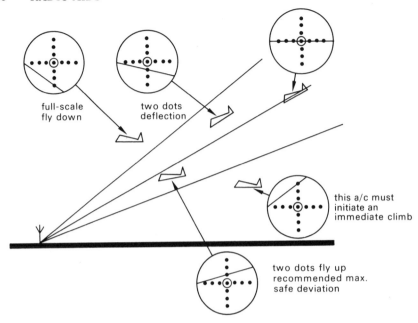

full-scale
fly down

two dots
deflection

this a/c must
initiate an
immediate climb

two dots fly up
recommended max.
safe deviation

fig. 14.8 Glide path indications

the rate being *two dashes* per second. Simultaneously the *blue* marker light will flash dashes at the same rate.

The next marker on the approach path is called the 'middle marker', placed approximately 3 500 feet (5 000 ± 500 ft in the U.K.) from the touch-down point. It transmits a series of alternate dots and dashes at a higher pitch, 1 300 Hz, which are heard in the earphones and also seen flashing on the *amber* marker light.

The marker nearest to the beginning of the runway is called the 'inner marker'. It transmits six high-pitched (3 000 Hz) dots per second and the *white* light flashes. *When installed*, it is located between 250 and 1 500 ft.

Summary of the markers associated with ILS

Designation	Distance from the R/W threshold	Signal characteristics
Outer marker	3–6 nm, average 4 nm	Transmission modulated by 400 Hz, 2 low-pitched dashes per second — blue light flashes
Middle marker	3 500 ft (5 000 ± 500 ft in the U.K.)	1 300 Hz signal keyed to form alternate dots and dashes — amber light flashes
Inner marker	250–1 500 ft	3 000 Hz signal, 6 high-pitched dots per second — white light flashes

Thus the markers are identified in three ways: by audio signals, visual signals and the transmission pitch.

One or two locators may be used to supplement the ILS. These locators are low-powered NDBs and share the sites of the outer and middle markers. If only one locator is used, it is usually installed on the site of the outer marker. The transmission frequencies of these locators (where two are being used) should not be closer than 15 kHz, otherwise mutual interference may result. Also, they should not be further apart than 25 kHz to permit a quick tuning shift when operating on a single radio compass. These locators serve a three-fold purpose:

(a)   they assist the pilot to home to the station and subsequently join the ILS pattern;

(b)   they may be used for holding purposes;

(c)   they provide a double check when passing over the markers.

On approach charts they are indicated by a standard abbreviation LOM (locator, outer marker) and LMM (locator, middle marker).

A DME may be used as an alternative to the markers. Its radiation is then so adjusted as to give zero range at or near the touch-down point. It may be frequency-paired with the ILS localiser so that when the ILS is switched on, the DME automatically starts functioning.

Airborne equipment

The airborne equipment consists of:

    channel control box

    VHF localiser receiver

    UHF glide path receiver

    75 MHz marker beacon receiver

    ILS meter or VOR/ILS indicator

    Three separate aerials for the three receivers.

A block schematic diagram of the airborne equipment is shown in fig. 14.9.

fig. 14.9 Airborne equipment

Frequencies

Localiser.   Frequencies allocated to ILS in the VHF band are: 108 to 112 MHz at odd decimals. e.g. 108.1, 109.3. In the U.K. the military uses some even decimals as well. Future ILS frequency assignments will be on frequencies ending in odd tenths plus a twentieth of a MHz.

Glide path.   Transmission takes place in the UHF band on 20 spot frequencies from 329.3 MHz to 335 MHz at 300 kHz spacing, e.g. 329.3, 329.6, 329.9, etc. The use of UHF is to produce more accurate beams. In the future, glide path channel spacing will be reduced from 300 kHz to 150 kHz.

Frequency pairing.   Localiser and glide path transmissions are frequency-paired. This means that for each one of the twenty localiser spot frequencies there is one glide path frequency allocated to it. For example, frequency of 109.3 is paired with 332.0 and 111.5 is paired with 332.9. (You need not memorise these paired figures — they are for illustration only.)

The advantages of frequency pairing are as follows:

(a)   By means of one switch, two receivers are activated — this reduces the workload.

(b)   Frequency selection is quicker and easier. There is no need to look up the glide path frequency in the flight information documents.

(c)   A potential error in frequency selection is prevented.

(d)   Separate identifications are not necessary.

Type of emission

The type of emission is A2 for localiser, glide path and marker transmissions.

Identification

As localiser and glide path frequencies are paired, whenever the localiser frequency is selected, the glide path receiver circuits corresponding to the paired frequency are automatically energised. Therefore, if you are subsequently receiving glide path signals, they can only be from the correct transmitter. Hence it is unnecessary for both localiser and glide path transmitters to identify themselves separately.

The ident takes place on the localiser transmission. Its carrier is amplitude-modulated by a horizontally-polarised 1 020 Hz tone to give the ident. The ident itself is by two or three letters in morse, seven words per minute. Where it is neces-sary to distinguish an ILS quickly from other facilities, the ident may be preceded by the letter 'I'. And since the localiser carries the ident, if it becomes unserviceable or it is withdrawn from service for any reason, the ident will be automatically suppressed.

Ground-to-air voice communication may be conducted on category I and category II ILS localiser carriers provided it does not interfere in any way with the navigational or ident function of the localiser.

ILS reference datum

This is defined as a point at a specified height (usually around 50 ft) located vertically above the intersection of the runway centre line and the ILS landing threshold through which the downward extended path portion of the ILS glide path extends.

ILS categories

Background.   The ILS project, originally conceived to develop a blind landing system, did not quite reach its objective and turned out to be an instrument 'approach to landing' aid. But still it was a great step forward in those days, its faults were forgiven by the operators and it received ICAO's blessing in 1946.

As civil aviation developed, the operators became increasingly more weather-conscious. They disliked the thought of delaying a flight or wasting time and fuel while holding overhead an aerodrome waiting for the weather to clear. The ILS had its faults, the main one being production of bends in the beam. These were produced by reflections from obstacles on and around the aerodrome, e.g. airport structures, vehicles, aircraft flying overhead the localiser aerial, and so forth. The airborne equipment, similarly, was just adequate to handle the existing system.

In 1958 British Airways (then BOAC) announced its intention to go for all weather operation and a positive move in that direction began. Improvement had to come to both the ground and the airborne equipment. As for the ground equipment, it was decided to develop an entirely new landing system based on modern technology, but in the meantime to retain and improve the present system. For an improvement, new transmission data were prescribed, course structures and course bends were tightly defined, the forward beam was narrowed down to reduce the reflections and to assist in the overall advancement, the airport and environment needed to be 'cleaned up' from interference. As the improvement progressed, a system of categories was established to define the capability of a particular ILS. As a matter of interest in the U.K., ILS serving runway 10L at London Heathrow was the first one to be up-graded to Cat II. These categories are called 'ILS facility performance categories', and they are defined as follows.

ILS facility performance categories

Category I   — an ILS capable of providing accurate guidance from the coverage limit down to a height of 200 feet above the ILS reference point.

Category II   — an ILS capable of providing accurate guidance from the coverage limit down to a height of 50 feet above the ILS reference point.

Category III   — an ILS capable of providing accurate guidance from the coverage limit down to the surface of the runway.

Operational performance categories

We saw from the above that with an improved ground equipment, guidance down to the surface became possible. The operational objective of establishing the above categories is defined by ICAO in terms of 'operational performance categories' (also known as 'operational approach categories' or 'weather categories'). The criterion here is the corresponding improvement in the airborne equipment.

Although the transmitted signals might be absolutely correct, a receiver with out-of-balance components can produce an indication of false centre line, both in elevation and in the azimuth. Consequently, a pilot descending with his ILS needles perfectly centralised, on being visual, may find himself displaced to one side or the other or too high/too low. The improvement had to start from here; the search for the components that would reproduce information faithfully and reliably was on. In fact, the improvement in airborne equipment went ahead side by side with ground equip-

ment and full 'hands off' landing tests were being carried out as far back as 1961.
Now with super, complex, computer-controlled equipment on board, an aircraft may
be certificated to an appropriate category from the following classification.

Category I   —   operation down to 200 feet decision height with RVR 800 metres.
Category II   —   operation down to minima between 200 and 100 feet decision
                     height with RVR between 800 and 400 metres.
Category IIIA   —   operation down to the surface of the runway with RVR
                     200 metres.
Category IIIB   —   operation down to the surface of the runway and taxiways with
                     RVR 50 metres.
Category IIIC   —   operation down to the surface of the runway and taxiways
                     without external visual reference.

Back beam

The localiser transmission is normally directed in the direction of the approach area
to provide azimuth guidance to the approaching aircraft. But usually there is a certain
amount of overspill of radiation behind the localiser aerial and the signals would be
received when flying in this area. This beam is not to be used. Some transmitters are,
however, designed to radiate a back beam. Where this facility exists, it can be used
when overshooting the precision runway. It can also provide a back course approach
to the reciprocal runway. It must be noted that when using a back course there is no
benefit of a glide path. Usually, they are less accurate than the front beams, there
are no range-check markers and they are not checked for accuracy. The needle sense
is reversed.

ILS offset localiser signals

Occasionally for technical reasons a localiser aerial has to be temporarily offset to one
side of the centre line. On these occasions the relevant information is published in
NOTAMS. If the need for an offset aerial is to extend over a period, the information
is published in the RAC section of the UKAP.

   Under the early system, with an offset localiser the decision height occurred at
that height at which an aircraft on the glide path would transit the middle marker.
Under the present system, when the offset does not exceed 2°, the decision height is
calculated from the published OCL or 200 feet above the runway threshold, whichever is higher.

False glide paths

These are defined as those loci of points in the vertical plane containing the runway
centre line at which the DDM (difference in the depth of modulation) is zero, other
than that locus of points forming the ILS glide path.

   What all this means is that, in the process of producing the glide path, due to the
inherent metallic structures at the point of transmission, and the aerial's propagation
characteristics, the radiated twin lobes are repeated several times above the true
centre line. These produce several other equisignals (see fig. 14.10). The number of
such false glide paths produced at any ILS site depends on several factors such as the
design of the transmitting aerials, obstructions around the transmitter, transmission

power and such like. These false glide paths, however, are not a danger to the pilot for the following reasons.

(a)   The first false glide path does not occur until above 6°. Thus, if you caught it, you would soon appreciate the mistake.

(b)   False glide paths always occur above the true glide path, and therefore cannot bring the aircraft dangerously low.

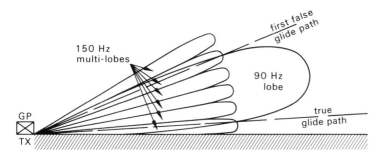

fig. 14.10 False glide path

(c)   It is a normal practice, when intending to carry out an ILS approach, to establish on the localiser first and then to meet the glide slope from underneath. It is most unlikely that a pilot would miss the true glide slope and continue flying level until the next equisignal is reached.

(d)   With the recommended localiser coverage in elevation of 7° and the glide path coverage of 1.75 x GP angle, the signals being received on the false glide path will be weak and the warning flags may operate.

(e)   It is a recommended practice that establishment on the promulgated glide path be confirmed by.the relationship between aircraft height and the distance to the runway threshold.

Pilot's serviceability checks

During an approach the localiser and glide path serviceability may be checked by the pilot in two ways:

(a)   The failure warning flags should remain clear of the window. The warning flags are actuated by the sum of the two modulation depths, and as we saw earlier, in the case of total unserviceability, the monitor removes a navigational component. As soon as this happens, the flag will appear in the window.

(b)   A pilot monitoring the identification signals will soon be warned if the ident signals stop coming.

As a further precaution, where a ground precision approach radar is available, it is mandatory for the radar to monitor ILS approaches in certain weather conditions.

Extract from U.K. AIP

This is an illustration of the type of information usually given in any AIP on ILS, and this particular illustration is from the U.K. AIP. The information is in 13 columns:

Station	Service	C/s or ident	EM	Transmits		Receives		Hours of service
				kHz	MHz	kHz	MHz	
1	2	3	4	5	6	7	8	9
Belfast/ Aldergrove	ILS	I–AG	A2	–	109.7 333.2	–	–	HO

Co-ordinates	To Aerodrome		Operating authority and remarks
	Mag	NM	
10	11	12	13
–	256	–	ICAO facility performance Cat II. Glide path 3°. Localiser 417.4 m from THR 08. MM 1649 m OM 4.29 nm from THR 26. ILS ref. datum ht. 52 ft.

Some of the above columns need decoding. In column 3, the ident is given as I–AG. The dash after I indicates a slight pause. In column 4, A2 is the type of emission. In column 6, 109.7 is the localiser frequency to which you actually tune. The glide path frequency is 333.2, which will be automatically activated. In column 9, HO means 'operates during times to meet operational requirements'. In column 11, 256 is the final magnetic track to the runway. In the remarks column, localiser is 417.4 metres from threshold of runway 08, middle marker is 1649 metres and outer marker is 4.29 nm from the threshold of runway 26.

From the information given above we can draw a sketch of the ILS layout as shown in fig. 14.11.

fig. 14.11

Rate of descent and other calculations

While carrying out an ILS let-down, it will be necessary to calculate the rate of descent for the glide path angle. This is calculated from the following formula:

$$ROD = GP \text{ angle} \times \frac{GS}{60} \times 100$$

Example: calculate the rate of descent for a glide path angle of 2.9° and a ground speed of 112 kt.

$$ROD = 2.9 \times \frac{112}{60} \times 100$$

$$= 541 \text{ ft/min.}$$

With ILS, the aircraft height, the ground distance to go and the glide slope angle make a right-angled triangle. Consequently, if two of the above factors are known, the third one can be calculated. In the absence of math tables, and in any case for the practical usage, the 1 : 60 rule may be used to solve the problems.

Examples

1. What is the approximate height of an aircraft at 2 nm range on a glide slope of 2.7°?

$$\text{TE (track error is our GP angle)} = \frac{60 \times \text{ht. (ft)}}{\text{dist. to go (ft)}}$$

$$2.7 = \frac{60 \times \text{ht. (ft)}}{2 \times 6\,080}$$

$$\therefore \qquad \text{Height} = \frac{2.7 \times 2 \times 6\,080}{60} \text{ ft}$$

$$= 547 \text{ ft}$$

2. At a distance of 3 nm from the threshold a pilot receives a full deflection on the glide path pointer, indicating fly up. Approximately how many feet below the glide path is the aircraft at this time?

The maximum deflection occurs when the pilot is 0.7° below the glide path. Therefore,

$$\text{vertical distance from the centre line} = \frac{0.7 \times 6\,080 \times 3}{60} \text{ ft}$$

$$= 213 \text{ ft.}$$

3. An aircraft on an ILS approach indicates half full-scale deflection on the glide slope pointer, giving fly-up indication. At 2.2 nm range from the threshold there is an obstruction, 285 feet above threshold level. What will be the vertical clearance from the obstacle when the aircraft passes over it on a 3° glide slope?

Half full-scale deflection occurs when the aircraft is 0.35° below the glide path. Thus, the aircraft is $(3° - 0.35°) = 2.65°$ above the surface at 2.2 nm range. At this point

$$\text{height of aircraft} = \frac{2.65 \times 2.2 \times 6\,080}{60}$$

$$= 590.8 \text{ ft.}$$

The vertical clearance of the aircraft from the obstacle $= (590.8 - 285) \text{ ft}$

$$= 305.8 \text{ ft.}$$

Limitations of ILS

ILS has the following limitations:

(a)   Unpredictable bends in localiser and glide slope beams may occur. The pilot must always remain on the alert and particularly so when making a fully automatic landing. This is the reason for the prescription that half full-scale deflection is the maximum safe deviation below the glide path.

(b)   The cost of installation is high, and particularly so in mountainous and other difficult areas.

(c)   It is a permanent fixture and cannot be moved from runway to runway. Hence very few runways are equipped with this facility.

(d)   For reasons of minimising interference, the landing rate is kept low, and there may also be restrictions of vehicle movement on the ground.

15: Basic Radar

When the word 'radar' was coined, it expressed precisely the function it performed, that is, radio detection and ranging. The use of the pulse technique clearly distinguished it from 'radio' which used continuous waves. With the subsequent advance in the technology, what we would have originally described as 'radio' (a continuous wave) can now perform the tasks of radar — detecting and ranging (for example, a radio altimeter). Radar, in its turn, now performs a variety of tasks not included in its original definition. These tasks include turbulence indication by weather radar, navigational assistance from hyperbolic systems such as Loran, and ground speed and drift from Doppler. Radar may now perhaps be described as radio systems performing particular functions inside the range of the radio spectrum.

Radar frequencies
Radar occupies frequencies from VHF upwards. The reasons for the choice of higher frequencies are as follows:
(a)   It gives freedom from external noise and ionospheric scatter.
(b)   Radar using the beam technique operates efficiently with narrow beams. These can be produced at shorter wavelengths.
(c)   Similarly, shorter pulses can be produced with shorter wavelengths.
(d)   The efficiency of reflection from an object depends on the size of the object in relation to the wavelength. At shorter wavelengths the signals will be reflected more efficiently by the reflecting objects.

Timing in radar
It will be appreciated that where timing is required to be carried out for radar operation, these times must be essentially very small, considering that a radio wave travels 300 000 kilometres in one second. Fortunately, radar can measure these small time intervals very accurately. The times are measured in microseconds, occasionally in milliseconds.

$$1 \text{ second} = 1\,000 \text{ milliseconds or } 1\,000\,000 \text{ microseconds } (\mu s)$$

$$1\,\mu s = \frac{1}{1\,000\,000} \text{ second} = \frac{1}{1\,000} \text{ millisecond.}$$

Radar systems work by a variety of techniques. Two such techniques that interest us are (a) the pulse technique and (b) the continuous wave technique. Of these two, the pulse technique is far more widely used and we will discuss this first.

Pulse technique
Primary radar, secondary radar and Doppler radar all employ the pulse technique although performing vastly different tasks. The technique involves transmission of

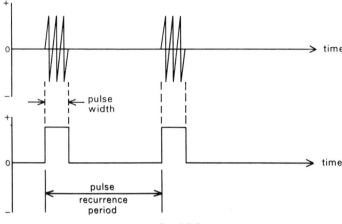

fig. 15.1

energy not in the form of a continuous wave but in very short bursts. Each tiny
burst of this CW is given a predetermined shape and radiates in the form of a pulse.
The mechanism of pulse transmission is shown in fig. 15.1. The duration or size of
the pulse is called the 'pulse width' or 'pulse length'. Although the pulse width is
very small it can contain many radio frequency cycles. For example, a radar pulse is
transmitted on a carrier frequency of 1 000 MHz (DME). If the pulse length is
3.5 μs, the number of cycles of the carrier frequency that occur in each transmitted
pulse may be calculated as follows:

number of cycles occurring in 1 second = 1 000 000 000
number of cycles occurring in 1 μs   = 1 000

and   number of cycles occurring in 3.5 μs   = 1 000 x 3.5 = 3 500.

Thus, each burst contains 3 500 complete cycles and if the transmission was at
10 000 MHz, each pulse would contain 35 000 cycles. These figures give us some
idea of the dimensions and magnitudes we are talking about.

The distance between two pulses *in time* is called 'pulse recurrence period' (PRP)
and the number of pulses transmitted in one second is called 'pulse recurrence
frequency' (PRF). The relationship between these two terms is

$$PRP = \frac{1}{PRF} \text{ seconds}$$

Example: If the PRF is 250, what is the PRP of the transmission?

$$PRP = \frac{1}{250} = \frac{1\,000\,000}{250} \ \mu s$$

$$= 4\,000 \ \mu s$$

Pulse shape.   A pulse is given its shape by the process of pulse modulation and it
is a design consideration. Although rectangular pulses can be produced by applying
an instantaneous rise in the voltage, followed by an instantaneous collapse to zero,
a practical pulse has a finite build-up time and decay time. The amplitude, pulse
width, rise and decay times (all these factors defining a pulse) are subject to ICAO
approval in respect of individual systems. A typical ICAO approved pulse as used in
DME is shown in fig. 15.2.

We are now ready to discuss the various systems operating on pulse technique.

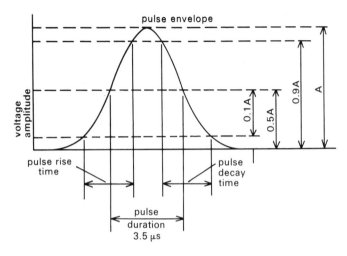

fig. 15.2

Primary radar

This is the original radar and uses the principle of pulse technique to determine range and bearing of an object. Working on 'echo' and 'search light' principle, a transmitter transmits a train of beamed pulses either in a fixed direction or omni-directionally by a rotating scan in azimuth (surveillance radar). The beam may also scan in elevation according to the purpose of the equipment. All objects in the path of the pulses which are of a size commensurate with the wavelength, will reflect and scatter the energy. Some of this reflected energy will reach the receiver, but it will be greatly weakened. The strength of these echoes depends on several factors:

    (a)   power of the transmitter
    (b)   range of the reflecting object
    (c)   shape, material and attitude of the reflecting object
    (d)   size of the object in relation to the wavelength.

This reflected energy will be processed through the receiver and fed to the indicator in an appropriate form to give the information. In this process the object's co-operation is not required.

Distance measurement – echo principle.   Radar finds the distance of an object by timing the interval between the pulse's despatch and its return as an echo. This timing is done electronically (we will see later in this chapter how a CRT could be utilised to do this) and knowing the speed of the electromagnetic waves, the formula, distance = speed x time, can be solved. It will be noticed that the distance found in this formula is the one-way distance to an object. As the pulse has travelled out and back, the distance of the object is half the distance so found, or, distance = (speed x time)/2.

Example: An echo registers a time of 500 microseconds. What is the distance in kilometres of the object reflecting it?

$$\text{Distance} = 300\,000\,000 \times \frac{500}{1\,000\,000 \times 2} \text{ metres}$$

$$= 75\,000 \text{ metres}$$

$$= 75 \text{ km.}$$

In implementing the above principle, two assumptions are made: that the speed of the electromagnetic waves is constant and that the waves travel in straight lines. Neither assumption is valid in the earth environment but the variations are so small that they can be ignored without incurring sizeable penalty.

Determination of direction.   The search light principle utilises transmission of radio pulses concentrated into a very narrow beam. The beam width should be kept as narrow as possible for accurate bearing discrimination. Narrow beams can be produced either by shortening the wavelength or by increasing the aerial size. With advanced techniques an aerial can be adjusted electronically to give a beam of the required width. The beam is made to scan through azimuth or elevation, starting from a fixed datum point. The direction of the object then is the direction in which the beam is pointing at the time when the echo is received. It is read from a scale, calibrated from the starting point.

Ranges of primary radar.   The ranges available depend on numerous factors; of particular interest to us are the following:

(a)   Transmission power. It is obvious that an increase in power will increase the range. However, with radar, the signal not only has to travel to its destination (reflecting object) but must travel an equal distance back to the receiver with sufficient strength to predominate the internal receiver noise. Thus, the power/range relationship for primary radar is given in the expression, max. range = $\sqrt[4]{(power)}$. This means that the power must be increased 16 times to double the range.

(b)   Characteristics of the reflecting object. The size and shape of the object, the reflecting material (metal will reflect more efficiently than wood), aspect of the target: these factors determine the strength of the echoes coming back. An aircraft reflecting from the length of the fuselage will give a better echo than when its nose and tail are in line with the incoming wave. Further, an aircraft in an unusual attitude may shift polarisation of the waves, causing polarisation fading at the receiver.

(c)   Pulse recurrence frequency (PRF). This determines the *maximum range* of the equipment. Each pulse must be given time to travel out to the most distant reflecting object as planned, and return, before the next pulse goes out. Otherwise it will not be possible to relate a particular echo to a particular pulse.

Suppose we wish to have the equipment capable of measuring distances up to 185 km. The pulse must travel 185 km x 2 = 370 km before the next pulse can be sent out.

$$\text{Time to travel} = \frac{370 \times 1\,000 \times 1\,000\,000}{300\,000\,000} \mu s$$

$$= \frac{3\,700}{3} \mu s$$

$$= 1\,233\ \mu s.$$

(Note: in the above fraction, 1 000 converts kilometres to metres and 1 000 000 is used to give us an answer in microseconds.)

The second pulse can only go out 1 233 μs after the first pulse. The number of pulses that can be transmitted in one second is given by

$$\text{PRF} = \frac{1\,000\,000}{1\,233}\ \text{pulses}$$

$$= 811\ \text{pulses}.$$

Taking the problem in reverse, let us say that the PRF of the equipment is 1 000 and it is required to find the maximum range.

$$PRP = \frac{1}{PRF} = \frac{1\,000\,000}{1\,000} = 1\,000\,\mu s$$

Now we need to calculate distance covered by 1 000 μs.

$$Distance = \frac{300\,000\,000 \times 1\,000}{1\,000\,000 \times 2}\,metres$$

$$= 150\,000 \text{ metres or } 150 \text{ km.}$$

In the above problems, 811 pulses gave us the range of 185 km whereas a PRF of 1 000 reduced the range to 150 km. Thus, an increase in PRF results in a decrease in the operational range.

(d)   Pulse width. The pulse width decides the *minimum range* of the equipment. Radio waves travel 300 metres in one microsecond. Therefore, for an example, a pulse one microsecond wide would extend that distance along the line of propagation. If an object at a distance of 150 metres was reflecting the pulse, it would arrive in the receiver at the instant that the tail end of the same pulse was leaving the transmitter. Any object closer than 150 metres reflecting the pulse will not be received as the transmitter would still be transmitting. Further, two objects in line and 150 metres or less apart will appear as a single echo. Thus, if short range operation is required, for resolution and accuracy short pulses are employed, e.g. 0.1 microsecond. Larger pulses are generally employed on long range work as they carry relatively more energy in them. In practice, 1 or 2 microsecond pulses are used in medium range radar and about 5 microsecond ones for long range work.

(e)   Aircraft height. Radar waves in the frequency bands we are discussing travel in straight lines. Because of the curvature of the earth, a considerable proportion of the surface will remain in the shadow no matter what maximum range is possible at height. The VHF formula given earlier gives an approximation of the expected ranges for given heights.

(f)   Elevation of radar head. As you will recall, this is another factor in the VHF formula.

(g)   Precipitation and cloud returns. At wavelengths of 3 cm and below one cannot neglect the absorption and scattering of radiation by droplets of water in clouds and falling precipitation. Cloud returns can have a most damaging effect on the performance of 10 cm and 3 cm radars and the scatter from rain drops and other weather can clutter up the display areas. Various suppression devices (e.g. circular polarisation having a rotating field) are now available to reduce rain clutter, but most work at the expense of power or range.

(h)   Intervening high ground. If there is no clear line of sight between the transmitter and the target, radar signals will be stopped by the intervening object and that will limit the effective range in that particular direction.

Other factors, such as receiver sensitivity, bandwidth used, aerial gain in the direction of propagation, also affect the range but these are mainly equipment design considerations.

Basic elements of primary radar
Of the main components of basic radar, the master timer or trigger unit is the brain

of the equipment. Its function is to trigger off a series of short electrical pulses at regular intervals. These pulses are delivered to the modulator (fig. 15.3) and at the same time, the time base unit is advised to start timing.

The modulator's task is to generate pulses of predetermined width and sharpness. The very high voltage content of these pulses triggers off the oscillator working at the radar frequency. It is so arranged that the beginning of each pulse switches on the oscillator and the end of each pulse switches it off. Thus, the modulator acts as an on/off switch for the oscillator. The oscillator, in its turn, generates pulses of high power but short duration. The output of the oscillator is fed to the aerial.

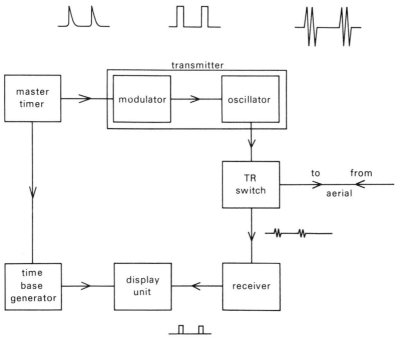

fig. 15.3

Normally a single aerial is employed to act as transmitter and receiver aerial. A TR (transmit-receive) switch isolates the aerial from the receiver when transmission is taking place; and when the transmission is complete it switches on to the receiver to receive the pulses. Thus when the echoes are received in the aerial they are delivered to the receiver unit which, after appropriate treatment presents them to the display unit. Here they are displayed on a trace which commenced at the start of the operation under instruction from the master timer.

Advantages of primary radar
Primary radar has the following advantages:
   (a)   It is a self-contained system, requiring no external assistance.

(b)   Peak power of the transmitter can be made very high owing to the relatively short time of actual transmission.

(c)   A common aerial may be used for both the transmission and the reception.

(d)   For a ground installation, sharp accurate narrow beams can be produced by increasing the aerial size.

Secondary radar
In this system, a transmitter (called 'interrogator') transmits a group of pulses on a given carrier frequency. The transmission is either omni-directional (DME) or directed towards an object (scanner sweep of SSR). An aerial in the path of these pulses receives the signals and passes them on to the receiver. If the signals are recognised at the receiver, it instructs its transmitter (called 'transponder') to give a reply. The reply then goes out on a different carrier frequency.

The differences between primary and secondary radar are as follows:

(a)   Unlike primary radar, the operation of secondary radar depends on the active co-operation of the other object.

(b)   In secondary radar the information is exchanged in the form of groups of pulses and not by individual pulses.

(c)   A secondary radar system requires a transmitter and a receiver, both in the aircraft and on the ground.

Advantages of secondary radar
There are various advantages of using a secondary radar over primary radar.

(a)   The important advantage is the power requirement. With this type of radar it is possible to work with much lower power. There are two reasons for it: (i) the signals are only doing a one-way journey, and (ii) there is no double scattering to combat, as with primary radar.

(b)   Because of the use of different frequencies, the ground transmitter will not pick up ground reflections on transmission frequency. Similarly, the airborne transmitter will not pick up its own ground reflection.

(c)   Interference through weather is reduced (see chapter on DME).

(d)   The system is independent of such considerations as reflecting area, shape, material, etc.

Uses of secondary radar
Distance Measuring Equipment (DME) works on the secondary radar principle. The Air Traffic Control uses secondary surveillance radar (SSR) in a variety of ways. Both these systems are covered in later chapters.

Doppler radar
This topic is fully dealt with in a separate chapter.

Continuous wave radar
As the title suggests, in this type of radar, both the transmission and the reception take place continuously. Consequently, two aerials are used: one for transmission and one for reception. These aerials must be suitably screened from each other,

otherwise the receiving aerial will receive signals direct from the neighbouring transmitting aerial.

Unmodulated CW may be used in the Doppler role. In this case, the transmitted and reflected signals will differ in frequency due to Doppler effect and will produce the airborne transmitter's velocity. For range measurement, the transmitted carrier is progressively frequency-modulated. The received frequency is then compared with the frequency actually being transmitted at the instance of reception, and knowing the rate of change of frequency, the range is worked out. The radio altimeter uses this principle.

The CW technique is eminently suitable for short range work. Unlike pulse radar where the minimum range is controlled by the pulse width, CW radar can work from zero range upwards. Speed detecting radar used by the police works on CW.

Advantages of CW radar
The advantages of CW radar are as follows:

(a)   Because in modulated or unmodulated form, the receiver operates on a frequency different from the transmission frequency, it is fairly free from ground clutter and other permanent echoes.

(b)   It has no minimum range limitations, in altitude or azimuth.

(c)   The system is less complex than pulse radar systems.

Cathode ray tube (CRT)
The purpose of the CRT is to display visually the radar signals that are reflected by the objects. Further, by incorporating a time base, distance and bearing (or other data for which the CRT is being used) can be determined. The CRTs are classified according to the way in which focussing and deflection are achieved. There are three such classes: electrostatic CRT having electrostatic focussing and deflection devices, electromagnetic CRT having electromagnetic focussing and deflection, and lastly a

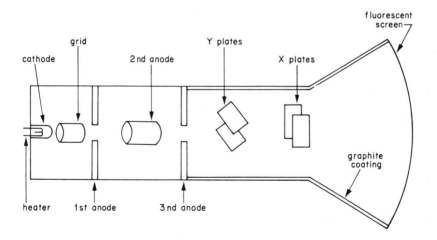

fig. 15.4

combined CRT which has electrostatic focussing and electromagnetic deflection. For the purpose of the present study the electrostatic CRT is described below.

The main components of a CRT are: a cathode, a grid, three anodes and two pairs of deflecting plates (fig. 15.4).

Cathode

The cathode consists of a small cylinder, one end of which is coated with a small quantity of barium or other similar oxide. The cylinder covers a low voltage heater which heats the barium oxide. Barium oxide when heated emits electrons.

Grid

The grid is a metal cylinder and surrounds the cathode. Its purpose is to catch as many electrons as possible emitting from the cathode and direct them in a narrow beam towards the anodes. This is done by applying a potential which is negative with respect to the potential of the cathode. Electrons are negative charges and when they find that the walls of the grid are more negative than they are, they tend to be repelled from the wall and pass through the grid in a narrow beam at the centre. By varying the grid potential we can control the number of electrons passing through the grid. This is the brilliance control.

Anode system

As soon as the electrons are emitted from the cathode, the cathode becomes positive relative to the electrons and the most natural thing would be for the electrons to return to the cathode. This must be prevented; the electrons are in fact encouraged to travel forward to the screen by means of three anodes. First and third anodes have the shapes of plates while the second anode has the shape of a cylinder (fig. 15.5).

fig. 15.5

The first and third anodes are positive, the second anode is negative. The first anode attracts the electrons which pass through its centre and then start diverging. This tendency to diverge is checked at the second anode (being negative) and the electrons deflect back and pass through the third anode under the attraction of positive potential. When they hit the fluorescent coated screen they show up as a glow. How sharp the glow is depends on how much divergence took place at the second anode. The potential of the second anode can be varied to give different sharpness – this is the focussing control. As to where on the screen the electrons will hit depends on the potential of the X and Y plates.

X and Y plates

The set of plates nearest to the third anode is called the Y plates. As the electrons pass through the pair of Y plates, if, say, the top plate is positive and the bottom plate is negative, the beam will be deflected upward towards the top of the plates. This means that the beam will hit at the top of the tube, the Y axis. If we had the bottom plate positive initially and varied the potential gradually until the top plate became positive, the beam hitting the screen during this time would appear to move from the bottom of the tube towards the top. If the potential was varied quickly enough we would only be able to see a continuous vertical trace.

Similarly, X plates produce a trace in the X axis or horizontally. These traces are the basis for forming time bases to measure distances. For example, earlier in the chapter we calculated that a radio wave will travel 370 km in 1 233 μs. If we move the spot on the CRT so that it takes 1 233 μs to travel from one end of the tube to the other, what we have done is to produce a scale along which the distance of the echo could be measured (fig. 15.6).

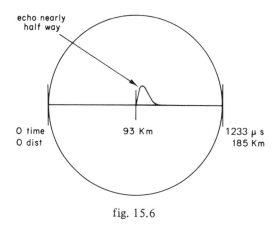

fig. 15.6

In fig. 15.6 the time base is produced by the X plates, and the echo is presented through the Y plates. The time base so produced may be calibrated to read in terms of microseconds or distance, knowing that the distance from one end of the tube to another in this case is 185 km. The time base may then be calibrated by pips at convenient distances. Further, for more accurate reading, a small portion of the time base where the signal appears may be exploded to a larger scale. This is done by 'strobing' the signal, a process you will read about later in the chapter on Loran.

It will be appreciated that in order to produce the time base, the voltage (that is, potential) to the plates must be varied progressively and systematically. The voltage that has this effect is called 'saw-tooth' voltage or waveform. This is shown in fig. 15.7.

In fig. 15.7, the voltage starting at A is increased progressively and steadily to the value of B in time T. In this example, the value of T is 1 233 μs. The voltage AB is called the sweep voltage and the trace is visible. Once the beam reaches the opposite end, it must be brought back to the other end to start a new cycle. Certain time is

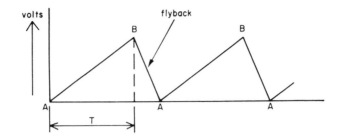

fig. 15.7

lost as the voltage falls back to the original value. This part of the voltage change is called the 'flyback' voltage, and it is, in general, not visible.

In practice, radar transmitters incorporate a master circuit. As the master instructs the transmitter to transmit, it simultaneously triggers the time base and the cycle commences. So the time base and echo remain in synchronism.

Gain control
Atmospherics and noises set up by electrical disturbances within the receiver or caused by nearby equipment manage to get on to the radar screen. These tiny signals travel on to the CRT via the Y plates and show up on the screen as multitudes of small blips in the vertical axis. These blips are known as 'grass' because of their appearance. Their presence is an essential check that the CRT is serviceable to a stage beyond producing the time base. The size of the grass is controlled by the gain control'.

Problems
1.   A particular radar equipment operates on a PRF of 1 000 per second. Two-fifths of the cycle is used in the flyback. What is the maximum range possible in statute miles?
Answer: 55.8 sm.
2.   If a radio signal takes 400 μs to travel from A to B, what is the distance of B from A in nautical miles?
Answer: 64.8 nm.

16: Radio Altimeters

Frequency modulation altimeters

Radio altimeters are designed to give indication of actual height above the ground. Those operating on the principle of frequency modulation are mostly used for low level flying where a high degree of accuracy is required. They are otherwise unsuitable for level flight since they indicate the contour of the ground below instead of a constant level. When installed, however, they may be used to check the accuracy of a pressure altimeter if the elevation of the ground below is known. In the past much use was made of them in flying 'pressure pattern'. In the latest development, they can be used to feed 'height' information to an automatic landing system.

Principle

The principle of frequency modulation is utilised to measure time (and thereby, height) taken by a radio wave to travel to the ground directly beneath, and to return.

The frequency band allocated is 1 600 MHz to 1 700 MHz and one complete burst of transmission covers a space of 60 MHz.

The aircraft transmits radio signals vertically downward. The transmission frequency, however, is not constant but it is varied progressively and *at a known rate* from its start frequency to 'start + 60' MHz, and then back to the start frequency. This constitutes one complete cycle of modulation.

Some of these transmitted signals will be reflected and return to the aircraft. The frequency of these returning signals, however, will be different from the frequency actually being transmitted at that instant. Further, the higher the aircraft, the greater the difference between the two. Since the rate of change of frequency is constant when flying at a constant height, this difference must be proportional to the time taken, that is, the height of the aircraft, as the speed of the radio propagation is known.

Change of freq. = rate of change of freq. × time taken

This frequency difference is measured and is registered on the indicator as height.

Equipment

Transmitter/receiver.   These generally work in conjunction with separate transmitter/receiver aerials.

Indicator.   Several different types of indicators are available, one of them, shown in fig. 16.1, has a pointer on the face of the dial calibrated in hundreds of feet. Thousands of feet indication is given on a counter in the window at the 6 o'clock position. The instrument shown reads 4 350 feet.

The indication is not limited to one single indicator in one position. As many repeater indicators as necessary may be installed to cater for various crew positions.

fig. 16.1

Limit height indicator

This indicator works in conjunction with a limit switch and is used when flying below 1 000 feet. The height the pilot wishes to fly is selected on the limit switch (which has the facility to select 50 feet, 100 feet and intervals of 100 feet until 1 000 feet) which operates a system of lights on the height indicator as follows:

Amber: flight is being made above the height selected.
Green: flight is made ± 15 feet of the selected height.
Red: flight below the selected height.

Uses

Mainly low-level flying. Most instruments cater for height up to 4 000 to 5 000 feet.

Accuracy

Fixed error.   This error arises in the method of transforming frequency difference into height and feeding the current to the indicator. The indicator pointer moves in steps of 5 feet, which means an error up to 2½ feet may be present any time.
Mushing error.   This occurs where transmitter and receiver aerials are not at the same height. Generally ignored.

Overall accuracy is of the order of 5 feet ± 3% of the indicated height.

Pulse modulation altimeters

These altimeters also operate in the frequency band of 1 600 MHz and are generally designed for high level operation, the upper limit being 50 000 feet. The height is indicated by a blip on a circular time base, and is read off in terms of its distance from the start of the time base which also appears as a blip.

Principle

Principle utilised is the echo. The time taken by a radio pulse to travel out and back is the direct measure of the distance (height in this case) on the assumption that the speed of the radio wave is constant. This assumption is not an unfair one, since the speed of a radio wave is known to a considerable degree of accuracy. The timing, of course, must be done electronically.

The master circuit instructs the transmitter to transmit, and at the same instant, instructs the time base circuits to start timing. The transmission takes place vertically downward in the form of a series of pulses. On the CRT the start of the time base is indicated by a blip in approximately the 12 o'clock position and the time base itself is a greenish, circular glow.

Signals reflected from the ground underneath will be picked up by the receiver aerial. These will be fed to the CRT via the receiver and other components such as the rectifier and video amplifier. On the CRT these will appear in the form of a blip on the time base.

The distance of this received pulse along the time base from the start point of the time base is the measure of the time taken by the pulse to return. This distance is read off against a scale in terms of height of the aircraft.

Formation of the time base

If the distance between two blips (start of the time blip and the echo received) is to represent the height, the total length of the time base must relate directly with the total height it measures. In other words height and time taken by a radio pulse out and back must correspond.

On this equipment, the operator has the choice of selecting 0–50 000 or 0–5 000 feet scale. Say, 0–50 000 feet scale is selected; this means that the pulse tracing out the time base must complete one full circuit in exactly the time the radio wave takes to travel 100 000 feet. Time base is then complete, new pulse goes out and new time base begins. To the naked eye, these breaks are not visible; the time base and both the blips are continuously visible. Now, if the aircraft is flying at 50 000 feet, the time base start blip and the echo will be coincident. If the return blip appears at, say, the 6 o'clock position, it has travelled only half of the time base, that is, 50 000 feet. The aircraft height then is 25 000 feet which is read off against the scale.

Similarly, when 0– 5 000 feet scale is selected, the length of the time base represents 10 000 feet and the next pulse is timed to go out in the revised time.

Indicator

The indicator consists of a CRT with a radial scale and two circles printed on the face of it. The inner circle defines the radius of the 0–50 000 feet time base; the outer circle defines the radius of 0–5 000 feet time base.

Controls

A simple control on the indicator is used to adjust the radius of the time base so that it coincides with the appropriate circle. This ensures that a correct time base is formed.

Two zero knobs (one for 0–5 000 feet time base and the other for 0–50 000 feet time base) are used to zero the start of the time base, where the leading edge of the start blip is not at 0 position. If this is not done, wrong heights will be read.

Reading the indicator

Read the height on the scale at the leading edge of the received blip. As the time base moves clockwise, the leading edge is the edge in anti-clockwise direction, or, it is that edge which is earlier in time. Make sure the leading edge of the start blip is at zero.

fig. 16.2(a)

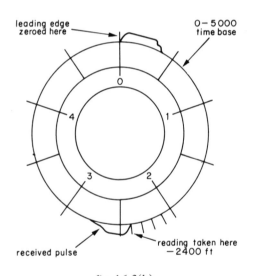

fig. 16.2(b)

When flying below 5 000 feet, use 0–5 000 feet scale for accuracy. When flying above 5 000 feet, on this scale, the indication will be inside the 5 000 feet band and therefore there will be a height ambiguity. Say you are flying at 22 400 feet, the height indication on this scale will be 2 400 feet, fig. 16.2(b). Now select scale 0–50 000 feet to resolve the ambiguity and to determine the true height. The indication in our case is 'slightly over' 22 000 feet, fig. 16.2(a). We are only interested in the figure 22 000; that 'slightly over' bit is actually 2 400 feet displayed on the expanded scale. On interpretation, the aircraft height indicated is 22 400 feet.

Aerials
Two separate aerials are used, one for transmission and one for reception.

Limitations
Minimum range is limited by the pulse width. The equipment is inaccurate below 500 feet.

Accuracy
The main cause of inaccuracy is the instability of the transmitter. Any deviation from the correct frequency will result in an incorrect time base. In the worst situation, the time base may not even form a true circle.

Accuracy of the equipment below 10 000 feet is ±100 feet. Above 10 000 feet, 150 feet or ½% of the height, whichever is the greater.

Advantages of radio/radar altimeters
The radio/radar altimeter has the following advantages:

(a)   It gives actual height above the ground — a very useful piece of information when flying low level.

(b)   It provides a cross check capability with the pressure altimeter for terrain clearance purposes.

(c)   Later improved models working in a frequency band of 4 200–4 400 MHz produce very high accuracy (2 ft or 2% from 500 ft to touch-down). Developed for operation with Cats II and III ILS, they provide a tie-in with flight director/auto-pilot to initiate initial flare during approach and landing. A warning signal at decision height may be given.

17: Distance Measuring Equipment (DME)

DME is a secondary radar system which provides accurate and continuous indications in the cockpit of the slant distance between an aircraft and the ground transmitter. The use of primary radar is unsuitable for DME operation for a variety of reasons. The power requirements for a secondary radar are relatively low. For example, in order to cover a range of 200 nm (present limit of our DMEs) 1.5 kilowatt power output of pulses would be considered adequate (peak power output of modern equipment varies from 1 kW to 2.5 kW) using secondary radar. With primary radar, a power output of the order 1.5 megawatt would be necessary to cover a similar area.

A primary radar scanner sweeping through $360°$ produces a picture of the whole surface beneath the aircraft, rather than giving a range from a designated reporting point. With this radar it is impossible to create a system of positive reference points on the ground, say along an airway. Further when flying over certain types of territory (e.g. flat lands, mountainous territory), primary radar echoes may not be identified whereas with secondary radar, the ground stations can and do identify themselves.

The basic airborne system consists of:
an interrogator (a combined receiver and a transmitter),
an indicator, and
an omni-directional blade aerial, able to pick up vertically polarised signals.

Principle of operation
The system on the ground is called the 'transponder'. It also consists of a receiver and a transmitter. The aircraft interrogator interrogates the transponder on a given carrier frequency by sending out a continuous series of pulses in pairs. The distance between two pulses of a pair is 12 μs and the time interval between the pairs is varied at random — a technique called transmission at random PRF. At the same time that the interrogation goes out, the aircraft's receiver starts timing and commences a search for the transponder's replies.

The transponder replies to the interrogation by sending out pairs of pulses on a carrier frequency 63 MHz removed from the interrogation frequency. The receiver receives all the responses that the transponder is sending out to different aircraft but only accepts those responses which match its own PRF.

The receiver searches the responses through the maximum range of 200 nm in a matter of a few seconds (4 or 5 seconds in newer models, 25–30 seconds with older models). During this time the pointer or counters on the indicator revolve rapidly. If no response is achieved by the time the search reaches the maximum range, the pointer (or counters) swiftly return to zero range and the search starts again. Once the response is found the receiver 'locks on' to it and tracking commences. This is the condition which exists when the interrogator has acquired replies in response to its own interrogations and is continually displaying the slant range distance to the ground station. This distance is computed from the knowledge of the speed of the radio waves and the time taken for the pulses to travel out and back.

During the search period, the interrogator transmits at a high rate (150 pulses per second, pps) to achieve a quick lock-on condition. But if the lock-on is not acquired after 15 000 pairs of pulses have been transmitted, the PRF is lowered to 60 pps and maintained at this rate until the search is successfully completed. The system then operates on a PRF between 25 and 30 pps.

Illustration of random PRF technique
Random PRF was mentioned above. This random variation in time between successive pairs of interrogation pulses prevents locking on to responses meant for some other aircraft. We will now take a closer look and see how it is done.

To keep the arithmetic simple, let us say that our equipment's PRF is 25 pps. This gives us the pulse recurrence period of

$$\frac{1\,000\,000}{25} = 40\,000 \text{ microseconds.}$$

This means that if this was the PRF of a primary radar, one pulse after another would be despatched exactly at 40 000 microsecond intervals. With the DME, this time interval is intentionally varied, and it is a random variation. A pulse may be sent out 39 956 μs behind the previous one, and it may be followed by another pulse at 40 115 μs distance. The transmission pattern would look like fig. 17.1(a). In the meantime the transponder is replying to all aircraft triggering it. Since all these

(a) Interrogation pattern

fig. 17.1(a)

responses are on the same carrier frequency, they all arrive in the receiver. The transponder's transmissions arriving in the receiver would look as in fig. 17.1(b). Some of these responses must belong to us and they are the ones which arrive with a regular delay from the interrogation pulses. A narrow gate in the receiver admits

(b) Transponder responses

fig. 17.1(b)

only those pulses which fall inside it, and the delay or the distance between the two pulses is the measure of the aircraft's range from the transponder. This arrangement is shown in fig. 17.1(c). It will be seen in the figure how the pulses arriving after a regular time interval 't' (shaded dark for easy recognition) enter through the gate

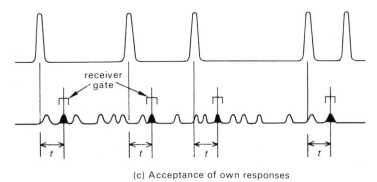

(c) Acceptance of own responses

fig. 17.1(c)

whereas the other responses are excluded. Of course it will be appreciated that this regular distance '*t*' is only momentary because unless the aircraft is circling round the beacon at a constant range, its range relationship with the station is changing all the time. However, on the microsecond timing scale this change is only minute but progressive. The gate is wide enough to accommodate these changes and it in fact moves along with the progressively changing time delays so as to keep its own responses in the lock. This technique is called the 'lock-follow' technique. This movement is shown in fig. 17.1(c), the last pulse arriving at *t* time delay.

Indicators
The varieties are legion; presentation of information is either by pointer or by digital counters (fig. 17.2). In most installations the DME is channelled by the VHF navigation frequency selection and both pieces of equipment become active together. Alternatively a separate frequency selector may be available which enables the pilot to select VOR and DME (or TACAN) as required.

fig. 17.2

The basic information is slant range from the selected station up to a distance of 199 nm. To this, an additional small computer can add the luxury of rate of change of distance display, indicate instantaneous ground speed, give time in minutes to the station and so forth. The advent of the course-line computer opened up the prospect of area navigation. The indications are in the form of left/right deviation from your track and distance to your destination. This is in spite of the fact that your destination is not the VOR/DME station you are tuned to.

Failure indications

If the transponder reply detected by the aircraft is below a pre-set value the equipment will go on 'memory mode' for a period of around 8 to 10 seconds (depending on the equipment) and continue to indicate the ranges based on the last known change of range. If no signals of acceptable strength are received after this, the equipment will unlock and commence a fresh search. It will only lock on when correct signals of sufficient strength are again detected.

The unlock condition will be indicated to the pilot by an 'off' warning flag on the rotary types of indicators and a bar falling across the face of the digital types. In addition the needle of the rotary indicator will rotate continuously and the numbers on the digital indicator will run up to the maximum value. Failure indication will be displayed when the equipment is switched on and:

(a)   no signal is being received, or

(b)   the received signals are below the minimum strength (just entering the DME coverage), or

(c)   the aircraft is out of range of the transponder.

And of course the flag is in view when the equipment is not switched on.

Frequency and channel spacing

As we noted earlier, DME using secondary radar technique transmits and receives on different frequencies. This is a matter of necessity, because if both transmitters operated on the same frequency, assuming that this was possible and that all aircraft radiated individually coded transmissions, we would have confusion and chaos in our hands, since

(a)   the transponder's response, while arriving at the aircraft receiver, will be swamped by the ground reflections of the original transmission,

(b)   the transponder's transmission will be reflected by the objects and obstacles in the vicinity of the transmitter and some of these will arrive back at the transponder. The transponder, not being able to discern between these ground reflections and the aircraft interrogations (being the same frequency), will start dishing out ranges to the reflecting objects as well. This process is called 'self-triggering'.

With the use of different frequencies, the airborne receiver will not accept its own reflections and the ground transponder will not be activated by its transmission frequency.

DME operates in the UHF (1 000 MHz) band in the frequency range of 962 MHz to 1 212 MHz. The frequency allocation is divided into two bands, low and high, as follows:

Low: A/c transmits from 1 025 to 1 087 MHz; ground replies from 962 to 1 024 MHz (at minus 63 MHz difference)

High: A/c transmits from 1 088 to 1 150 MHz; ground replies from 1 151 to 1 213 MHz (at plus 63 MHz difference).

For example, for an interrogation frequency of 1 100 MHz, the response will come on 1 163 MHz. Under this arrangement 63 channels are formed in each band. Channels in the low band are numbered from 1 to 63 and those in the high band from 64 to 126. These 126 channels are collectively called X channels. There is a provision for expansion into another 126 channels, to be called Y channels. We will then have, for example, a 22X channel and a 22Y channel. The channels 1 to 16 are reserved for national allocation and channels 17 to 56 are paired with VOR/ILS frequencies, as shown in the following illustration.

20X frequency paired with 108.3; 21X frequency paired with 108.4
20Y frequency paired with 108.35; 21Y frequency paired with 108.45.

Range and coverage

DME is a short range navigation aid providing a maximum coverage of 200 nm at 30 000 ft. The ranges indicated are slant ranges and the conversion to ground distances is by use of Pythagoras.

Example 1:   An aircraft at 40 000 feet reads a DME distance of 80 nm to the station. What is its ground distance from the station?

As the distance required is in nautical miles, we must convert 40 000 ft into nautical miles before applying it to the Pythagoras formula.

$$(\text{Ground distance})^2 = (\text{slant range})^2 - ht^2$$
$$= 80^2 - \left(\frac{40\,000}{6\,080}\right)^2$$
$$= 80^2 - 6.58^2 \text{ (approx.)}$$
$$= 6\,400 - 43 \text{ (approx.)}$$
$$= 6\,357$$

$$\therefore \qquad \text{ground distance} = \sqrt{(6\,357)}$$
$$= 79.7 \text{ nm}$$

Example 2:   An aircraft at 24 320 feet is 30 nm ground range from the station. What is its DME range? See fig. 17.3.

Ht
4 nm

30·26 nm

30 nm

fig. 17.3

$$4^2 + 30^2 = (\text{slant range})^2$$
$$916 = (\text{slant range})^2$$
$$\text{slant range} = \sqrt{916}$$
$$= 30.26 \text{ nm}$$

From the above two examples it will be noticed that the slant range errors at long distances are practically negligible. But the inaccuracy does exist which is revealed at closer range.

When directly overhead the beacon, the DME will indicate the aircraft height in nm above the beacon and not zero range. For example an aircraft overflying a beacon at a height of 30 400 feet will indicate

$$\frac{30\,400}{6\,080} = 5 \text{ nm.}$$

(When overhead, there is a small cone of silence but the range indications will continue to operate on 'memory'.)

The actual ranges available depend on

(a)   the aircraft height;

(b)   the transmitter height;

(c)   any intervening high ground; this will cut off the signals and reduce the range in that direction.

The ranges for various heights are worked out using the VHF formula.

$$\text{Range} = 1.25\,\sqrt{H_R} + 1.25\,\sqrt{H_T}.$$

We are familiar with this formula but we will give you one more example of its employment.

Example: Give the approximate theoretical maximum range that an aircraft at 26 000 feet may expect if the DME transponder is 81 feet amsl.

$$\text{Range} = 1.25\,\sqrt{(26\,000)} + 1.25\,\sqrt{(81)} \text{ nm}$$
$$= (1.25 \times 161) + (1.25 \times 9) \text{ nm}$$
$$= 200 + 11.25 \text{ nm}$$
$$= 211.25 \text{ nm}$$

Accuracy of the equipment

The receiver computes the elapsed time between transmission of the interrogating signals and the receipt of the reply signals, and determines the distance. The accuracy is of very high order. Between a slant range of 0 and 200 nm the total system error is designed to be no greater than ±½ nm or ±3% of the distance measured, whichever is greater. Thus, the worst case is 6 nm at a range of 200 nm. In practice a modern DME system is considered to be inherently capable of providing an indicated range accuracy equal to ±0.2 nm or 0.25% of the slant range measured, whichever is greater. This is ½ nm in the worst case and the figures are valid on 95% of the occasions.

Uses of DME

(a)   It provides a circular position line when a single DME is used. Fixes are obtained when it is used in conjunction with VOR.

(b)   Its range indication is very useful when carrying out an instrument approach.

(c)   It eases the task of the ATC in identifying for radar when an aircraft reports its position in terms of range and bearing from a VOR/DME station.

(d)   When two aircraft are using DME and flying on the same track, the positive ranges from these aircraft enables the ATC to maintain accurate separation.

(e)   Accurate ranges to touch-down are read off when a transponder is operating in conjunction with ILS.

(f)   It provides a basis for more accurate holding patterns.

(g)   With an additional computer, area navigation may be carried out with accuracy.

Advantages of DME as secondary radar

It will be appreciated from the earlier chapter on radar that DME uses the principle of secondary radar. The advantages of secondary radar are as follows:

    (a)   Interference due to weather is reduced, as seen in fig. 17.4 below.

fig. 17.4

It will be seen in fig. 17.4 that an active cloud not directly in line between the aircraft and the ground beacon will have little effect in causing interference or clutter.

    (b)   Transmission power required is only that which is sufficient to carry the signal up to the station. In other words, the signals need not be strong enough to survive a two-way journey.

    (c)   The ground beacon uses a different frequency from that used by the aircraft. Therefore, self-triggering will not occur.

Beacon saturation

Like a shopkeeper who opens the doors of his shop in the morning and makes available any and all of his wares to the customers, once he is sold out, he puts the shutters down; the ground equipment, when switched on, does likewise. The transponder transmits 2 700 pulses per second at random whether or not it is being triggered for information. These pulses are available to its customers. When an aircraft interrogates the transponder it replies by using some of these random pulses. Now, unless an aircraft is in search mode, its normal operating PRF is 25–30 pps, average 27. One aircraft triggering a transponder and in lock-on condition replaces 27 transmitter random pulses. At this rate if 100 aircraft are simultaneously triggering a station, the transponder's capacity will be exhausted and the beacon would become saturated.

    We said above that 100 aircraft will saturate the beacon. In arriving at that figure we did not consider those aircraft which are operating on higher PRF in the search mode. They would put excessive loading on the transponder's capability. However, the search mode at higher PRF runs for such a short time that it can be discarded for practical purposes, and the search at 60 PRF is not normally continued for a long time because if it is not locking, it is very likely that you are still out of range.

When the beacon becomes saturated it adjusts itself to cope with the situation by reducing receiver gain, fig. 17.5. If you are receiving strong music on your wireless

fig. 17.5

which is accompanied by strong background noise, you turn the volume down. In doing so, you aim to exclude the weaker, unwanted noise. The transponder, by reducing its receiver gain excludes interrogations from more distant aircraft whose pulses reaching the transponder are relatively weaker. In fig. 17.5, in normal operation all aircraft from A to G would be receiving ranges from the transponder (aircraft B is just entering the coverage and might start receiving soon). When the beacon gets saturated and the receiver gain is reduced, aircrafts A, B, D, and possibly F will be excluded from service and an unlock will occur in the airborne equipment. The purpose of the system is to give preference to the nearest aircraft. In any case, the transponder will not reduce the number of aircraft obtaining service to below 70.

VOR/DME planning

A VOR provides magnetic bearing information. A DME provides slant ranges from the station. When these two equipments are used together, we can have instantaneous fixes in the form of a bearing position line and a circular range position line. Further, if the two transmitters are co-located, these two position lines may be plotted from a single point.

To achieve speed in selecting the facilities in the cockpit and to reduce the workload on the flight crew, VORs may be frequency paired with DME or TACAN (military installations) stations. This means that when a VOR frequency is selected, the DME circuits would be activated automatically. Ideally, VOR and DME meant for use in conjunction with each other should be co-located, that is, both the transmissions made from the same geographical point. However, this is not always possible and where VOR and DME stations are not widely separated they may still be used in conjunction with each other. The pilot will know the relationship between the two stations by noting the ident signals and frequency pairing arrangements as explained below.

(a)   Where both VOR and DME/TACAN transmit the same callsign and in synchronism, the stations are called 'associated' and they are always frequency paired. The term 'associated' means that

(i)   the two transmitters are co-located (i.e. the two antennae are co-axial), or

(ii)   they are a maximum distance of 100 feet apart where the facilities are used in the terminal areas for approach purposes, or

(iii)   they are at a maximum distance of 2 000 feet apart where their purpose is other than (ii) above but where the highest position fixing accuracy is required.

Synchronised idents are transmitted every 7½ seconds, that is, each 30-second period is divided into 4 equal parts. The DME transponder transmits its ident during one of these four periods, and the VOR in the other three.

(b)   Those VOR and DME stations which are not associated but serve the same station and which may be used in conjunction with each other are also frequency paired. But in this case, both VOR and DME will identify separately and one of the two will have a letter Z in the callsign, e.g. STN–STZ.

(c)   Where VOR and DME stations are at entirely different locations, they may or may not be frequency paired. Both facilities will have independent idents. Note that when a VOR is frequency paired with military TACAN the system is called VORTAC.

DME ident is made up of a series of paired pulses at PRF of 1 350 pps. A decoder in the receiver converts the information and feeds it into the earphone as morse letters.

Miscellaneous

The type of emission is 'P'. A typical AIP entry records transmission and reception frequencies, e.g. transmit 1 174, receive 1 111. These apply at the station and mean that the aircraft transmits at 1 111 and receives at 1 174. In any case you select a channel number which in this case is 87X.

18: Ground Controlled Approach (GCA)

The popularity of this aid is in direct proportion to the reputation of the airfield's controllers. It is a radar search system in the airfield areas; the controller gives instruction on the R/T to the pilot all the way down to visual contact.

There are two separate systems: 'approach surveillance radar' (RAD) and 'precision approach radar' (PAR). Surveillance radar is a 10 cm or 50 cm unit and identifies the aircraft in the approach zone and vectors it on to the final approach path. This is the responsibility of the traffic director. Precision approach radar, a 3 cm radar, scans the final approach path of the aircraft and talks it down to visual contact. The responsibility is the precision controller's. A lower wavelength is used in order to produce an accurate narrow beam.

RAD

It is common, to ensure firm identification, to call on the aircraft to perform a simple manoeuvre (e.g. a procedure turn) and follow its blip on the radar screen. Other methods of identification acceptable are a VOR/DME fix, a response from the aircraft's SSR transponder or a direct handover from one radar unit to another. Once identified, the aircraft is guided verbally to the approach path at 1 500 feet and is handed over to the precision controller. ICAO lays down a minimum specification of being able to identify a small single-engined aircraft at a distance of 20 nm at 8 000 feet. The equipment must give a position accuracy of $\pm 2°$ of the true position and be able to see two aircraft separately when $4°$ apart from each other in azimuth. This is achieved by radiating a beam $2°$ in azimuth to an elevation of $30°$. The scanner rotates at 10, 15 or 20 rpm and the system is duplicated. The display face is switchable to scales of 10, 20, 40 or 60 nm range.

The use of a relatively long wave produces only weaker rain echoes and when working on a 50 cm (600 MHz) band it is completely clear of the rain clutter and therefore no suppression device is necessary.

PAR

Precise information must be readily visible for immediate instructions to the aircraft, so two discriminators of 3 cm wavelength are available. The beam sweeps both in azimuth and in elevation along the approach line. The antennae are sited to one side of the runway near the touch-down point. The system requirements are that it should be capable of detecting and indicating the position of an aircraft of 15 square metres (165 square feet) echoing area (or larger) which is within a space bounded by a 20 degree azimuth sector and a 7 degree elevation sector to a distance of at least 9 nm. The maximum permissible error from on-course indication is 0.6% of the distance from antenna plus 10% of deviation from the on-course line or 30 feet whichever is greater. Similarly, elevation accuracy is 0.4% of the distance from the antenna plus 10% of the actual linear displacement or 20 feet, whichever is greater.

The information is displayed on two screens mounted one on top of the other and the controller is able to pass instructions to the pilot by watching two blips in relation to the centre lines on the screens.

General notes

It is important that when PAR is on a location also served by ILS that glide path and azimuth indications are coincident inbound from the outer marker. Two pilots in CAVOK will practise the two approaches, one monitoring the other. In certain weather conditions it is mandatory for the GCA to monitor ILS approaches. In this case the precision controller will advise the pilot that his approach is being monitored by GCA, but the controller will take no action as long as the pilot remains inside the ILS funnel (½° above/below the glide path and 2° either side of the centre line). The pilot will be warned if he goes outside the funnel and the PAR will take over if the pilot requests.

The procedures are precisely laid down in the AIP, and the pilot doing the GCA is on airfield QFE, azimuth and elevation information is given absolutely and in relation to the on-course and glide path line.

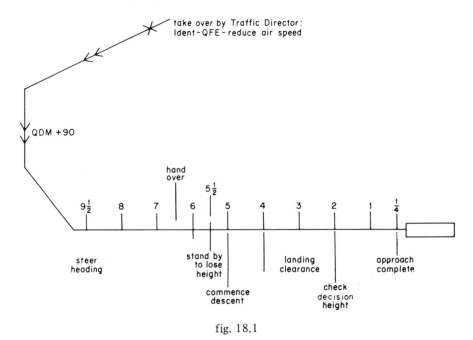

fig. 18.1

At 7–6 miles, the traffic director hands over to the precision controller. Satisfactory RT contact, then do not acknowledge further instructions. Prepare to descend, and commence descent to maintain a $x°$ glide path.

Azimuth instructions and information as to position with regard to centre line from hand-over to completion.

Elevation instructions and information as regards glide path from start of descent to completion.

4 miles out — 'clear to land, surface wind so and so'

2 miles out — 'check decision height'

¼ mile out — 'approach completed'

After landing contact tower on frequency . . . for taxying instructions.

It is the pilot's obligation to break off if not in visual contact at decision height. The controller throughout gives definite headings (M) to fly, so he has made wind adjustments for the QDM to make good. He usually, too, gives the range every mile until 4 miles off, every ½ mile thereafter — sometimes every ¼ mile after 2½ miles off. The last range given is ½ mile, when all the crew are searching for the approach lights.

Surveillance radar approaches

At airfields where either PAR is not available or the glide path element of the PAR has gone unserviceable, approaches may be made on surveillance radar without the benefit of the glide path. The instructions passed to the pilot are similar to PAR except that in the absence of glide slope, check heights are passed, e.g. 'your range is 4 nm, your height should be 1 200 feet'. Depending on the accuracy of the surveillance radar, the approaches are terminated either when ½ nm from the threshold or 2 nm. These terminal distances are also given in the AIP.

The frequencies given in the AIP are the actual RT frequencies and not the frequencies on which the radar operates.

Range of the surveillance radar

The range that a primary radar produces depends on

(a)   transmission power

(b)   PRF used

(c)   type of suppressor in use.

The range at which an aircraft will be detected depends on

(a)   the aircraft height

(b)   intervening high ground

(c)   the aircraft shape, size and material

(d)   the weather conditions.

Accuracy

Within the limitations of the radar, the accuracy of the approach depends primarily on the skill of the controller and also the ability of the pilot to rigidly follow the instructions.

Advantages/disadvantages

The advantages are clear: no special gear is required in the aircraft, the pilot has only to obey RT instructions, no interpretation of meters is involved and the search system provides a means of partial traffic control. Above all, the system is movable from runway to runway to be operational within half an hour.

The disadvantages are: several RT channels are needed at busy airfields, landing rate is limited, ground controllers must be highly skilled (as well as pretty durable), identification of blips can be difficult and there will be some clutter in rain or snow (remember that a pulse is reflected from objects of comparable wavelength — PAR is 3 cm).

Break off
The pilot must break off the approach at the decision height unless a visual landing can be made. The controller has authority to order an overshoot.

19: Airborne Search Radar (ASR)

'Airborne search radar', also called 'weather radar' primarily provides a pictorial representation of turbulent and dangerous clouds located along the flight path and warns the pilot well in advance. The information is displayed on a cathode ray tube and the picture can indicate the best route of penetration through bad weather.

As a secondary function the equipment also provides the pilot with the facility of map-painting radar for the purpose of navigation and avoidance of high ground.

Principle
ASR is a primary radar. In both mapping and cloud detecting roles, the requirements are to find the range and bearing of the objects. The range is found by the echo principle and the direction is found by use of the searchlight principle. Both these techniques have been discussed in the chapter on radar.

Weather radar
The requirement is to detect turbulent cloud, provide information on weather severity and indicate safe routes round, if any. The efficiency of the equipment in discharging the above functions depends on the following two factors.

(a) Wavelength (or frequency). As noted earlier in the text, the efficiency of the reflection depends on the wavelength in relation to the reflecting object. For ASR radar, the wavelengths considered appropriate for satisfactory operation lie between 10 cm and 3 cm in the SHF band. At these wavelengths fine mist, haze, clouds of tiny water droplets do not reflect energy whereas water droplets in a cumulonimbus will have reached sufficient dimensions to give an echo. In this way a harmless stratus is prevented from cluttering up the screen.

If the wavelength is increased above 10 cm the waves will be too large and no reflections will occur. On the other hand if it is reduced too much below 3 cm, a relatively large amount of energy will be absorbed instead of being reflected, although some radar does work on a 2 cm wavelength.

Thus, the choice being limited between 10 cm and 3 cm, for a given power output, the energy on a 3 cm wavelength will give a better range and a more comprehensive picture of the situation. On the other hand, at a shorter wavelength it will possibly not look behind a reflecting cloud. A 3.2 cm radar is quite popular with commercial transport aircraft.

(b) Beamwidth. The beamwidth must be kept as narrow as possible for good target resolution. Two targets less than a beamwidth distance apart will appear as one single target, see fig. 19.1. The beam widens with range. Therefore, for example, two objects at 100 nm distance may appear as a single target, but as the range is closed and the beam narrowed, each will establish a separate identity. To an operator this

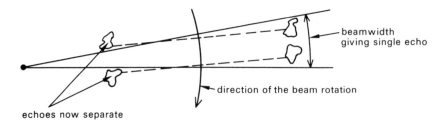

fig. 19.1

may give a false impression of fresh activity being developed at a close range. There-fore, the narrower the beam, the better the resolution; and for airborne equipment this again means the use of shorter wavelengths.

From the above study we can conclude that the factors which determine whether or not a cloud within the equipment's range will be detected or not are:

(a)   the size of the water drops, and

(b)   the wavelength or frequency in use.

The accuracy of resolution will depend on the beamwidth. A conical pencil beam is considered to be the most suitable for use with ASR.

Map-painting radar

Mapping, again, should be done on a narrow beam in the interest of resolution (the beamwidth used is around 3½°). It should be broad enough to cover a maximum possible horizontal distance. Such a beam would be a fan-shaped beam, see fig. 19.2.

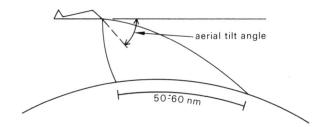

fig. 19.2 Cosecant (mapping) beam

It will be appreciated that with this type of beam the surface illuminated below and closer to the aircraft will give stronger (and thus brighter) reflections than the ground further away. The picture on the PPI will appear progressively fading away with distance. This in itself may not be an inconvenience but radar maps are essentially read from the differing brightness of the dissimilar objects. Some objects come up very bright, others not so much, and yet others which do not reflect at all. For a reliable interpretation we would like all similar objects to produce similar brilliance. This difficulty is overcome by adjusting the power spread so that maximum power is directed to the farthest point to be covered. The power is progressively reduced as distances decrease so that the power directed to the closest object is minimum. This reduction in power with decreasing range is the function of cosecant of the depression angle and the beam so produced is called a 'cosecant' (or mapping) beam.

Theoretically, for the maximum range the upper edge of the fan should radiate horizontally ahead of the aircraft, that is, at a depression angle of 0 degree. This cannot be achieved in practice as the cosecant of 0 is infinity. A practical beam is tilted down by about 5°. In flight the aerial tilt angle can be adjusted to give a most advantageous display.

As the cosecant beam is more widely spread out than the pencil beam used for weather detecting, and as the power available to both is the same, the distance of coverage available using a cosecant beam will be much more restricted. The actual range available depends on the power, the aircraft's altitude, the reflecting property of the surface and the angle of depression in use. Around 50 to 65 nm is just about the limit. Use a pencil beam where distances beyond the cosecant beam's range are required to be scanned.

The shapes that you will see on the PPI, such as a coastline, or the contours of a hill or the outline of a town, will not be identical to what you would see with your naked eye for the following reasons.

(a)   Radar measures slant ranges. At larger distances the difference between slant range and ground range is only slight and will not be conspicuous on the picture. At closer ranges, however, the picture will be distorted. This effect is further aggravated by the fact that at short ranges the scale itself is slightly distorted on purpose to improve bearing accuracy. Fig. 19.3 shows the picture of a straight coastline, six

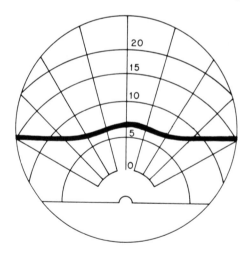

fig. 19.3

miles ahead. The amount of distortion depends on the range of the object and the aircraft height. If a very high degree of accuracy is required, this distortion may be removed by the employment of a non-linear time base. This is not called for in normal operation.

(b)   Effect of beamwidth on the picture. We noted above that the beamwidth determines the equipment's capability of resolution. In fig. 19.4 we can see how an object becomes distorted in size. On the picture, the beam adds one half of the beamwidth distance on either side of the object. This effect is maximum when the object is farthest away — the beam is widest.

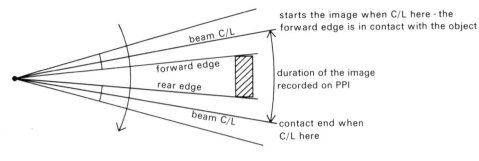

starts the image when C/L here - the
forward edge is in contact with the object

duration of the image
recorded on PPI

contact end when
C/L here

fig. 19.4

(c)   Effect of the pulse length on the picture. An object reflects a pulse for the
same time-duration as the length of the pulse itself. It is presented on the screen
against a time base, measuring ranges. Now, this time scale is halved in order to display
target ranges. Therefore on such a time base the pulse length extends the PPI image
in range by a distance equivalent to one half the pulse length.

These factors distort the shapes and the operator needs a degree of skill for a
quick recognition of the features.

Interpretation of the display
The next thing in radar map reading is to be able to tell a town from a coastline,
that is, to differentiate between features. To do this, it is important to understand
the principles of reflection. Radar reflections occur as follows.

(a)   Reflections from smooth, plane surfaces. Smooth surfaces reflect like
mirrors. That is, the angle of incidence is equal to the angle of reflection, fig. 19.5(a).
Therefore, unless the angle of incidence is very small, there will be no returns.

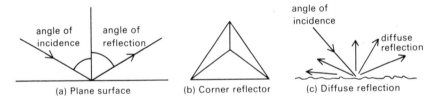

(a) Plane surface   (b) Corner reflector   (c) Diffuse reflection

fig. 19.5

(b)   Corner reflectors. If there are three corners to a structure, which are
mutually perpendicular to each other (as would happen in built-up areas), the
reflection from one surface to another would be such that ultimately the energy will
be reflected back to the source (fig. 19.5(b)).

(c)   Diffuse reflections. Between the above two extremes, rough surfaces will
cause reflections scattered in all directions, fig. 19.5(c). The roughness or irregularities
only need to be comparable to the wavelength, and there can be no shortage of these
on the landmass.

Keeping the above principles in mind, we summarise that little or no energy will
come back from a calm sea. This would make a coastline easily separable from the

hill shadow (may give a
false impression of water)

fig. 19.6

landmass. Similarly fine sand or flat terrain will not give reflections. Brighter echoes
will occur in built-up areas, taller buildings showing up brighter still. Hills and man-
made structures cast shadows behind them, fig. 19.6, sometimes giving a false
impression of water or a lake. If you are used to a route and seeing the same picture,
it is worth bearing in mind that the picture can change substantially with seasons in
the middle and higher latitudes. For example, rivers and lakes show up nicely in
normal circumstances and also when iced up (ice has jagged edges which reflect), but
will not show at all when covered with snow. The same is true for landmasses. Snow
reduces the detection range of the equipment and the responses from the features are
toned down, irregularities being removed by the snow deposits.

When using the equipment for weather detection, falling rain, wet hail or snow —
in fact any liquid concentration — will show up. The three stages of a thunderstorm
can be observed. The first appearance of the echoes indicates the beginning. The
echoes grow in size and when the fuzzy edge is replaced by a well-defined edge the
mature stage is reached. At this stage a black hole will be seen when operating on
contour function (see later). The dissipating stage is the process in reverse. The black
hole gets smaller, ultimately disappearing, the cloud echo becoming ill-defined and
weaker.

If a cloud shows up at a very long distance, say a hundred mile range, it indicates
a presence of high liquid concentration — a cloud that must be watched.

Airborne equipment
The airborne equipment consists of the following units:
- (a)   transmitter/receiver
- (b)   an aerial scanning unit
- (c)   an indicator, and
- (d)   a control unit.

Transmitter/receiver
Transmission frequency varies with equipment within the range stated earlier. A
typical ASR, Ekco Type E190 used by commercial airliners operates on a frequency
of 9 375 MHz. This gives a wavelength of 3.2 cm. The pulse length is 2.2 μs and the
PRF is 400. The range covered is 150 nm. The mapping beam is 85° deep and scans a
sector of 90° either side of the aircraft's centre line, ahead of the aircraft. With
some equipment, a scan extending to 120° is available. The beamwidth of the conical
pencil beams (weather beam) depends on the size of the scanner employed. An
18-inch scanner produces a beamwidth of 5° and a 24-inch scanner, 3.5°.

Aerial scanning unit
The scanner unit consists of a paraboloid dish with a centre dipole and the system is gyro stabilised in pitch and roll.

Indicator
A typical indicator is shown in fig. 19.3. Ekco E190 employs a rectangular CRT. Bearings are marked on the face of the CRT with bearing lines at 15° intervals and the range markers are electronically produced. The intervals between range markers vary according to the selected range. On a 150 nm range indicator
> on 20 nm scale, range markers appear at 5 nm intervals
> on 50 nm scale, range markers appear at 10 nm intervals and
> on 150 nm scale, range markers appear at 50 nm intervals.

Similarly on a 120 nm equipment
> on 20 nm scale, range markers appear at 5 nm intervals
> on 60 nm scale, range markers appear at 10 nm intervals and
> on 120 nm scale, range markers appear at 20 nm intervals.

Control unit
The control unit shown in fig. 19.7 is an Ekco E160 control unit. Most makers provide similar facilities.

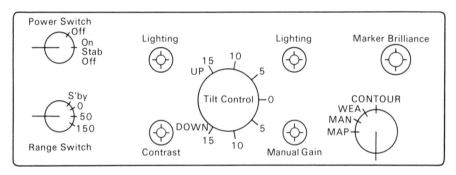

fig. 19.7

Power switch.   A three-position switch, it controls the power supply. In ON position the aerial is automatically stabilised, in STAB OFF position it is locked to the pitch and roll axes of the aircraft.
Time base range switch.   This is a four-position rotary switch; in STANDBY position it maintains the equipment in readiness for instant use. Use this position when ASR is not required during short intervals.
Tilt control.   Permits an aerial tilt from 0° to 15° UP or 15° DOWN. The aerial is normally tilted downward when ground mapping or it is raised up to estimate the heights of cloud base/top.
Function switch
MAP: In this position ground mapping is done by use of the cosecant beam. Manual gain control is used in conjunction with this position. This is because the signal

strength can vary with altitude and type of terrain over which the flight is being made.

MAN: this is the next position after MAP and, again, is used for map painting. But the beam in use is the conical pencil beam and because of the concentration of energy inside a narrow beamwidth, the ranges obtained are greater than when operating on MAP position. And because ground mapping is being done, manual gain control is still operative in this position.

WEA: this is the normal position for observing weather. Manual gain control is inoperative; instead sensitive time control (STC) is brought into operation. It automatically reduces gain at short ranges so that with decreasing ranges the same target continues to produce the same contour separation, or all clouds at short ranges may be compared on equal terms.

CONTOUR: this position is used to examine the cloud structure for severity, and it shows up the turbulent areas on an iso-echo display (see below).

Marker brilliance.   Varies the brightness of the range rings.

Other controls are self-explanatory.

Iso-echo display

Although the operator can see on the screen the complete cloud distribution ahead of him, without sufficient experience he would find it difficult to pick out dangerous clouds from among the less dangerous ones. The iso-echo type of display simplifies this distinction. It is known that strong turbulent clouds produce strong echoes compared with weak, inactive clouds, and this fact is utilised in the production of iso-echo display. All reflections above a pre-determined echo level are cut off from reaching the screen. About the turbulent centre there is usually the remainder of the cloud whose activity is below the pre-determined level. This will be seen on the screen. This signifies that a cloud on the screen with a hole in the centre is dangerous. The hole or the blacked out portion of the cloud is particularly dangerous; the degree of the danger from the remainder of the cloud depends on the steepness of the contour (fig. 19.8).

fig. 19.8

Operation on ground

If the equipment is required to be switched on while on the ground, first check that there are no large hangar or other reflecting objects in the vicinity. The radiation can damage health of persons and the reflections can damage the equipment. And for the same reasons do not select mapping beam on the ground.

Operating on weather
Select maximum range to detect presence of clouds in good time. When the clouds close up to around 50–60 nm, select lower scale and operate on CONTOUR function. Ensure from the beginning that no ground returns are being received – the aerial tilt may be adjusted to exclude them. Any clouds detected at very long ranges are potentially dangerous. Take avoiding action when the range gets below 20 nm. If possible avoid all response areas; if this cannot be done, then at least avoid responses with black holes.

Operating on mapping
Cosecant beam is used for short range mapping. To obtain optimum ranges use pencil beam for reasons given earlier. Give the aerial a large downward tilt initially and then reduce the tilt angle very slowly, keeping a watch on the changing coverage. When no further forward coverage is observed, you have the right tilt for maximum ranges.

Calculating approximate height of the cloud
This is done by tilting the beam upward or downward as necessary until the cloud just disappears from the screen. At this time, the base of the cone is directly on top of the cloud. This gives the angular measure of the cloud height above or below the aircraft's level. We also know the range of the cloud. Thus, we have sufficient information to apply the 1 in 60 rule to calculate the height above/below the aircraft level (fig. 19.9).

fig. 19.9

For example, it is required to estimate the height of the top of an active cloud, 30 nm range.

The first step is to tilt the aerial (fig. 19.9) until the cloud top just disappears. Say, at this time the tilt angle is 3½°. This 3½° defines the centre line of the beam. Therefore, the base of the beam is 1° above the aircraft's horizontal plane. Now the data are put on computer as follows:

$$\text{Angle above a/c} = \frac{\text{Dist. off (Rel. Ht.)} \times 60}{\text{Dist.}}$$

$$1° = \frac{\text{Ht.} \times 60}{30}$$

i.e.
$$\text{Ht.} = \frac{1 \times 30}{60}$$

$$= \text{½ nm or 3 040 feet.}$$

This is the height above the aircraft height. Alternatively, the makers provide pre-computer graphs from which the height is read off against tilt angle.

A rough estimate of the height may be made mentally from the formula: relative height = 100 x range in nm x elevation in degrees. In our illustration it is 100 x 30 x 1 = 3 000 feet.

Height ring

With conical radiation there is an overspill of radiation vertically downwards (fig. 19.9). This is reflected back to the aircraft and the echo appears like a ring. This ring indicates the aircraft's height and therefore it is called the 'height ring'. The presence of the height ring indicates that the equipment is serviceable. Its absence normally means that the receiver requires retuning. It may be possible to retune the receiver in flight — follow the manufacturer's drill and if the height ring is still not visible, the equipment may be considered unserviceable. It should, however, be remembered that there are few reflections when flying over calm water or fine sand particularly when flying above 30 000 feet. Also, as 4.93 nm equals 30 000 feet, if you are flying at that height, the height ring may merge with the 5 nm range marker. To ensure its presence, turn the marker brilliance down. Finally, it is also possible to see a second height ring, at twice the aircraft height. If it is present, it will be faint because it is due to double reflections.

Other uses of ASR

The equipment may be used to ensure a safe terrain clearance over high ground. By tilting the aerial slightly downward, keep a watch as the high ground gets closer. If it does not disappear from the picture at a reasonable range, a climb must be initiated immediately.

If a small feature, e.g. a particular bend in the river or a pier at a seaside town, is recognised, a fix is obtained. If two such fixes are obtained and the heading has not been altered in the meantime, track and ground speed wind velocity may be found, provided the time interval is reasonable, say 20 minutes. If a point is identified but it is not a fix because you are not overflying it, a fix may be plotted by observing two or three relative bearings on the identified point. Finally, you can ascertain your track direction by taking two or three bearings on any single unidentified object. Further, if this track direction is plotted from your last fix to the latest position line, you have a ground speed as well.

(For detailed plotting procedures, consult *Ground Studies For Pilots* volume 2, 'Plotting and Flight Planning'.)

20: Doppler Theory

There are a number of stories about Doppler saying that after he noticed the change in pitch of a passing train's whistle (or was it a sledge or some other vehicle changing its pitch?) he was stimulated by the challenge and produced his theory of frequency shift. Depending on how far the evening has progressed, these stories can make romantic listening. The fact of the matter is, Dr C. J. Doppler was a scientist and a Professor of Experimental Physics in Vienna and he was engaged on a research project to establish the relationship between waveform and motion. His primary interest was to calculate movements of the stars and it was to this end that the theory was immediately put into practice. In 1842 he published his work in a paper titled 'Uber das farbige Licht der Doppelsterne' (no, this is not an exam question) in which he explained the relationship between the frequency of a waveform and the relative motion of an object.

The paper establishes that whenever there is a relative motion between a transmitter and a receiver, a frequency shift occurs. This frequency shift is proportional to the relative movement. It is now variously known as:

Doppler shift, or
Doppler frequency, or
Doppler effect

and is abbreviated 'f_d'. If the distance is closing, the received frequency is greater than the transmitted frequency and it is described as a positive Doppler shift. Similarly, if the objects are moving apart, the received frequency will be smaller and it is a negative Doppler shift.

Why does frequency shift take place?

Consider a radio signal, transmitted from a stationary source at a carrier frequency of f Hz. The receiving object, R will receive f waveforms each second, each say λ metres apart. Further, they are approaching R at the speed of electromagnetic waves, say c metres per second.

Thus, R receives a frequency which is equal to c/λ which in fact is the transmission frequency. Now suppose that the object R is moving towards the transmitter at a speed of V metres/second. Although the waves still travel at the same speed, because of the object's motion towards the source of transmission, each wave will arrive at the receiver at a progressively shorter time interval than its predecessor, the first wave taking the longest time and the last one the shortest time to reach the receiver. This progressive closing up of the waves is sensed by the receiver as a reduction in the wavelength.

Now, the relationship between speed of electromagnetic waves, frequency and wavelength is expressed in the formula $c = f \times \lambda$ (see chapter 1) where c is constant.

Therefore, if λ decreases (as it does when the objects are closing) the value of f must increase to keep the value of c constant. This frequency shift is entirely due to the relative motion between the transmitter and the receiver.

The transmission frequency is c/λ.

The new frequency
$$= \frac{c + V}{\lambda}$$

$$= \frac{c}{\lambda} + \frac{V}{\lambda}$$

$$= f + \frac{V}{\lambda}$$

f being the original transmission frequency, V/λ is the component due to the relative motion between the transmitter and the receiver and is the Doppler shift, which is proportional to the ground speed of R. We express this in the formula

$$f_R = f + \frac{V}{\lambda} \quad \cdots \qquad \cdots \qquad \cdots \qquad (1)$$

where f_R is the received frequency. Note that because

$$\lambda = \frac{c}{f} \quad \text{and} \quad \frac{1}{\lambda} = \frac{f}{c}$$

this formula may be rewritten as

$$f_R = f + \frac{Vf}{c}.$$

Adapting the formula for aircraft operation

Initially, the above formula is modified in two ways.

(a)   In the case of an aircraft, the signals are transmitted from a moving transmitter and are reflected back to a moving receiver. Hence, the relative velocity is two-fold or $2V$ and the formula is modified to read

$$f_R = f + \frac{2V}{\lambda} \quad \cdots \qquad \cdots \qquad \cdots \qquad (2)$$

(b)   The above formula is applicable only when the transmission is directly ahead and the reflection occurs from a reflecting object, also directly ahead. Although such transmission and reception would in theory give a maximum frequency shift, a pilot cannot be persuaded to operate Doppler with a solid reflecting object directly in front of him. Therefore, Doppler equipment must beam its signals towards the earth's surface for reflections. The formula now becomes

$$f_R = f + \frac{2V \cos \theta}{\lambda} \quad \cdots \qquad \cdots \qquad (3)$$

where θ is the angle through which the beam is depressed.

Depression angle

As pointed out above, ideally the signals should be beamed straight ahead for maximum frequency shift. This is, however, impossible. Therefore, the signals must be beamed downward towards the surface at an angle from the horizontal.

The angle of depression may be kept small, for example, to achieve a good measure of the frequency shift. However a signal striking the surface at a shallow angle loses quite a lot of energy by way of scatter *away* from the aircraft (see fig. 20.1).

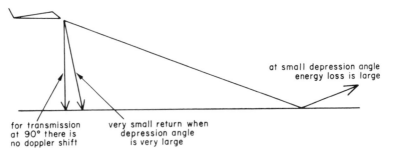

at small depression angle
energy loss is large

for transmission
at 90° there is
no doppler shift

very small return when
depression angle
is very large

fig. 20.1

If the depression angle is made too large on the other hand, strong reflections will be obtained but the value of f_d, that is, $2Vf \cos \theta / c$ becomes too small for accurate measurement. The value of cosine decreases as the angle is increased and if the transmission was vertically downward, the cosine of 90° is 0 and there will be no frequency shift.

Therefore, the depression angle of Doppler equipment is a compromise between strength and frequency shift. Or, it must be an angle which would ideally give the best of both. Most Dopplers operate between a depression angle of 60° and 70°.

Principle of ground speed measurement

Electromagnetic waves are transmitted from an aircraft at a given depression angle either in the form of a series of pulses (pulse radar) or continuous wave (CW radar). On striking the surface these will be reflected. Some of these reflected signals will be received in the aircraft receiver but the frequency of these signals will be different from the original transmission frequency. It will be higher if the signals are reflected from forward of the aircraft, and lower if reflected from the rear of the aircraft. This change in the frequency is due to the Doppler shift and because it occurs due to the relative movement it expresses the aircraft's ground speed. This is continuously indicated on the indicator. The ground speed displayed is 'spot' ground speed, that is, correct only at that instant.

Doppler aerials

Single beam systems.   These represent the earliest thoughts on aerial deployment with Doppler equipment and are no longer in use. A beam is transmitted to the fore of the aircraft to the surface. When the reflected signals are received and f_d is available, the aerial is rotated until the value of f_d is maximum. The angle through which the beam is thus displaced is the measure of drift and the f_d is the direct measure of the aircraft's ground speed.

Twin beam systems.   These may be fixed or rotatable beams.

(a)   Fixed aerials. One beam is directed forward, the other abeam of the aircraft.

The f_d produced by the two beams thus disposed represents the aircraft's speed along its heading and at right angles to it. The two values are compounded to give drift and ground speed.

(b)   Rotating aerials. The two beams at a fixed angular distance are rotated about the fore-and-aft axis of the aircraft until the f_d produced by both the beams is of equal value. Then the bisector of the angle between the two beams is the aircraft's track and the ground speed is calculated from the extension of formula 3

$$f_d = \frac{2Vf}{c} \cos \theta \cos \phi \qquad \ldots \qquad \ldots \qquad (4)$$

where ϕ is half angle between azimuth beams.

Three beam systems.   Where three beams are employed, two beams are directed to right and left forward and the third beam vertically downwards. The system enables the calculation not only of the horizontal velocity components but of the vertical velocity component as well.

Four beam systems

(a)   Fixed aerials. Four beams are transmitted from two transmitters. One transmitter transmits beams 1 and 3 (see fig. 20.2) simultaneously. Beam 1 is

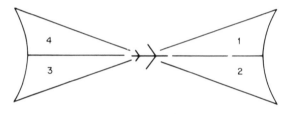

fig. 20.2

directed to forward port and beam 3 to rearward starboard. Half a second later the second transmitter transmits beams 2 and 4 to forward starboard and rearward port. Beams 1 and 3 produce a component of ground speed in direction forward port and beams 2 and 4 in direction forward starboard. Since the angle between the beams is known, drift and ground speed can be computed.

(b)   Rotating aerials. This is perhaps the most popular system. The transmission pattern is similar to the four-beam fixed aerial system. One aerial sends a beam forward and to the right while the other aerial of the pair sends the beam rearward and to the left. A few seconds later the other pair of aerials sends forward left and rearward right. The returning signals from each pair are mixed together to produce a Doppler beat frequency.

When the centre line of the aerial system is along the fore-and-aft axis of the aircraft, and there is no drift, the speed of the aircraft towards both forward reflections is the same. The Doppler frequencies produced by each pair will be identical.

If it has drift, the beat frequency extracted from 1 and 3 aerials and 2 and 4 aerials are explained with reference to figs. 20.3 and 20.4.

In fig. 20.3, the aircraft is experiencing port drift and the aerial is aligned with the fore-and-aft axis of the aircraft. The frequencies received will be something like this:

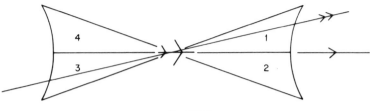

fig. 20.3

From beam 1: it is forward transmission and the return frequency will be higher than the transmission frequency, say +10 kHz. From beam 2, it will still be higher than the transmission frequency, but not as high as the return from no. 1 beam, since the aircraft is drifting away from no. 2 to no. 1 beam. Say, the frequency received is +8 kHz. No. 3 will produce −10 kHz and no. 4 −8 kHz. Beat note from nos 1 and 3 = +10 −(−10) = +20. Beat note from 2 and 4 = +16. This difference between the two is entirely due to the direction of the aircraft aerial and the aircraft's track not being the same. As soon as such a difference arises between the two beat notes, a signal is raised which actuates a motor. The motor turns in the direction of the track, turning the aerials with it and will continue to turn until the difference between the two pairs of aerials is reduced to zero. At this time the aerial is aligned with the aircraft's track (fig. 20.4) and the motor switches off.

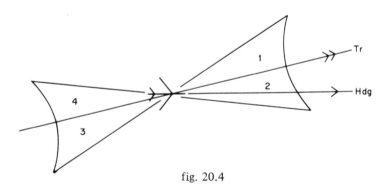

fig. 20.4

The angular move of the aerial from the fore-and-aft axis of the aircraft is the drift which is indicated on a suitable indicator. (It will be noticed in fig. 20.4 that the aerial is aligned with the track and the Doppler spectrum is symmetrical about the track axis.) This is a condition for the ground speed measurement to be correct.

Thus, drift is measured directly and the ground speed is computed from the formula

$$f_d = \frac{4V}{\lambda} \cos \theta \cos \phi \left(\text{or,} \ \frac{4Vf}{c} \cos \theta \cos \phi \right) \qquad \ldots \qquad (5)$$

Notice that in the above formula, $2V$ of formula 4 has increased to $4V$. This is because a four-beam system is being used and the responses from each pair are compared directly and not with the transmitter frequency. Mathematically:

$$\text{front response: } f_{R,F} = f + \frac{2V \cos \theta}{\lambda}$$

$$\text{rear response: } f_{R,R} = f - \frac{2V \cos \theta}{\lambda}$$

$$\text{difference } f_{R,F} - f_{R,R} = \frac{4V \cos \theta}{\lambda}$$

Janus aerials

A name given to the aerials which transmit forward as well as rearward, and comes from the Greek god who could simultaneously look forward and behind. These aerials are used with advantage in various ways.

(a)   Accurate measurement of frequency differences depends largely on the size of such differences. To make them large enough (about 10 kHz), Doppler equipment transmits at a very high frequency. An airborne transmitter working at these high frequencies is unstable and may wander.

With systems which require the reflected energy to be compared with the transmission frequency, the only transmission frequency that is available for the comparison is the frequency actually being transmitted at that instant. If this is not the same as the frequency to which the reflection relates, an error in the beat note will occur.

With the Janus system this coherence is not critical because signals are transmitted simultaneously forward and backward. The signals return to the receiver simultaneously. These two signals contain a component of the transmission frequency f in them and therefore, when mixed, a beat frequency is extracted correctly. With the pulse system the transmission errors may be completely ignored and with CW systems, they can be compensated.

(b)   Pitch errors. In a single-ended system, an error is introduced with the change in pitch angle. For example, when the aerial is pitched up $p°$, the Doppler frequency becomes $\frac{2V \cos(\theta - p)}{\lambda}$, see fig. 20.5. With the Janus system, when the aerial is

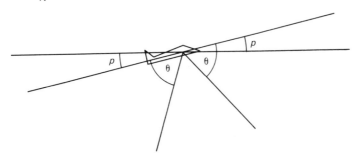

fig. 20.5

pitched up by $p°$, the Doppler frequency from the forward aerial is $\frac{2V \cos(\theta - p)}{\lambda}$ and and the frequency from the backward aerial is $\frac{2V \cos(\theta + p)}{\lambda}$. As these two frequencies are mixed to extract the beat note, pitch errors are reduced but not completely eliminated.

(c)   A Janus aerial, by producing a conical beam pattern ensures an overlap period between two signals by prolonging in time. Thus the equipment will not unlock when flying over uneven territory.

(d)   With this type of beam, when the aircraft rolls, it does so on the edge of the beam and the returned frequencies are not affected.

Doppler spectrum

Although the Doppler equipment transmits signals at a given depression angle, because of the beamwidth, an area of the surface rather than a single point is illuminated. The beamwidth varies between $1°$ to $5°$ depending on the type of the equipment and because of this, the reflected signals are not composed of a single frequency but a spectrum of frequencies. In fig. 20.6, the angle of depression is

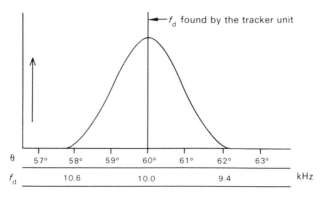

fig. 20.6

assumed to be $60°$ and the beamwidth is $4°$. The polar diagram of the spectrum, that is, the shape of the curve, is determined by the aerial design. In this particular illustration the energy envelope consists of frequencies varying from $\dfrac{2V \cos 62}{\lambda}$ to $\dfrac{2V \cos 58}{\lambda}$. A unit in the receiver called the frequency tracking unit finds the f_d by dividing the energy content envelope in two equal halves.

Doppler problems

1.   If the closing speed of the receiver with a stationary transmitter is 240 metres per second and the transmission wavelength is 5 cm, what is the frequency shift?

$$f_d = \frac{V}{\lambda} = \frac{240 \times 100}{5} = 4\,800 \text{ Hz}$$
$$= 4.8 \text{ kHz}$$

2.   A receiver is moving away from a stationary transmitter at a speed of 360 metres per second. If the transmission frequency is 10 000 MHz, what is the frequency shift? It is first necessary to find the wavelength (in cm) of the transmission frequency.

$$\lambda = \frac{300\,000\,000}{10\,000\,000\,000} \times 100 \text{ cm}$$

$$\lambda = 3 \text{ cm}$$

and
$$f_d = \frac{V}{\lambda} = \frac{360}{3} \times 100 = 12\,000 \text{ Hz}$$
$$= 12 \text{ kHz.}$$

3. A receiver is moving away from a stationary transmitter at a speed of 380 metres/second. If the transmission wavelength is 4.3 cm, what is the Doppler frequency?

$$f_d = \frac{380}{4.3} \times 100 = 8\,837 \text{ Hz}$$
$$= 8.837 \text{ kHz}$$

4. A receiver's motion towards a stationary transmitter is 800 km/h. If the transmission wavelength is 4 cm, what is the frequency shift?

$$800 \text{ km/h} = \frac{800 \times 1\,000}{3\,600} = 222.2 \text{ m/s}$$
$$f_d = \frac{222.2 \times 100}{4} = 5\,555 \text{ Hz}$$
$$= 5.555 \text{ kHz}$$

5. An aircraft transmits on a frequency of 13 500 MHz at an angle of depression of 60°. If its ground speed is 900 km/h, what is the frequency shift?

(a) Wavelength of transmission frequency 13 500 MHz $= \frac{300}{135}$ cm $= 2.22$ cm.

(b) 900 km/h = 250 m/s.

(c) $f_d = \frac{2V \cos \theta}{\lambda} = \frac{2 \times 250 \times 0.5 \times 100}{2.22}$
$$= 11\,261 \text{ Hz}$$
$$= 11.261 \text{ kHz.}$$

6. An aircraft in flight using Doppler equipment observes a frequency shift of 8 kHz. If the transmission frequency is 8 000 MHz and the angle of depression 60°, what is the aircraft's ground speed in knots?
Wavelength of transmission frequency 8 000 MHz = 3.7 cm.

$$f_d = \frac{2V \cos \theta}{\lambda}; \quad \therefore V = \frac{f_d \lambda}{2 \cos \theta}$$
$$= \frac{8\,000 \times 3.7}{2 \times 0.5 \times 100}$$
$$= 296 \text{ m/s}$$
$$= 574.9 \text{ kt}$$

7. An aircraft using a four-beam Janus aerial transmits on a frequency of 8 700 MHz. Its angle of depression is 60° and the half azimuth angle is 30°. If it observes a frequency shift of 10 kHz, what is its ground speed?
Wavelength of transmission frequency 8 700 MHz = 3.45 cm.

$$f_d = \frac{4V \cos \theta \cos \phi}{\lambda}$$

$$\therefore \quad V = \frac{f_d \times \lambda}{4 \times \cos \theta \cos \phi}$$
$$= \frac{10\,000 \times 3.45}{4 \times 0.5 \times 0.866 \times 100}$$
$$= 199.1 \text{ m/s}$$
$$= 716.8 \text{ km/h or } 387.4 \text{ kt.}$$

21: Doppler Equipment

The basic information provided by Doppler equipment is drift and spot ground speed. The basic airborne equipment consists of the following units:
- (a) an aerial system
- (b) a transmitter/receiver unit
- (c) a tracking unit and
- (d) an indicator.

Aerial system
A Janus four-beam aerial system consists of two parallel rectangular slotted waveguides radiating fore and aft to produce the required radiation pattern. The aerial assembly is free to rotate about a vertical axis through a fixed angle, usually between 30° and 40°, depending on the type of equipment. Its movement is controlled by the tracking unit which keeps it aligned with the aircraft's true track. The angular displacement of the aerial from the aircraft's fore-and-aft axis is the drift, and when combined with the heading, the output is in the form of its true track.

Transmitter/receiver
The Doppler transmission takes place on two frequency bands: 8 800 MHz and 13 500 MHz. The use of such high frequencies is necessary for two reasons:

(a)   The transmission beamwidth must be as narrow as possible in order to give a narrow Doppler spectrum. A narrow beam can only be radiated at micro wavelengths.

(b)   The higher the frequency shift arriving at the receiver, the greater the accuracy of the measurements and the result. Higher transmission frequencies produce higher frequency shifts. The use of higher frequencies is, however, accompanied by the inherent disadvantage of being subject to increasing atmospheric attenuation. Therefore, the ultimate operating frequency is decided from the consideration of the power output available and the operational height required.

A typical unit delivers a peak output power of eight kilowatts in a 40 millisecond burst. The pulse recurrence rate is around 25 000 pulses per second.

The receiver, having carried out a search for the returning signals and having accepted them, locks on to them. It delivers the signals to the tracking unit in the form of a Doppler beat frequency spectrum.

Tracking unit
The tracking unit accepts the frequency spectrum from the receiver and finds the mean frequency. It uses this to measure the aircraft's ground speed. It also controls

the rotational movement of the aerial. The operation of the tracking unit is shown in block schematic form in fig. 21.1.

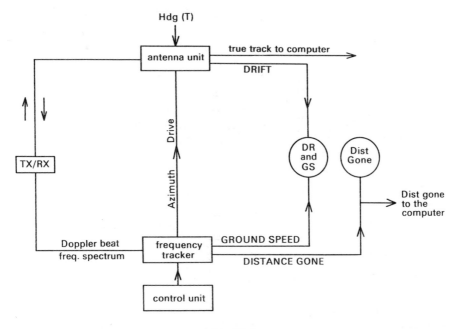

fig. 21.1

Indicators

Drift and ground speed indicators.   These indications may be either by pointer-type indicators or digital displays or a combination of both. Indicators employed by Decca in their Doppler 62 system are shown in fig. 21.2.

With some systems, before the equipment will lock on to the correct values of drift and ground speed the indicator pointers must be set manually, by means of 'inching' switches to the approximate values of expected drift and ground speed. Thereafter, the pointer will pick up the position to indicate correct drift and ground speed automatically, and any changes due to W/V or alteration of headings will be followed.

Distance to go/distance gone indicators.   The facility to obtain alternative presentation is sometimes incorporated in the equipment; otherwise you express your choice when buying the equipment. The counters are initially set to read either 000 or the leg distance. In flight, they are operated by electrical impulses originated in the tracking unit.

The ground speed indicated on the ground speed meter is a spot ground speed and therefore, where a track plot is being maintained, the ground speed should be calculated from the readings taken from the distance gone meter over a period of time.

Memory facility

Most equipment incorporates a memory circuit which takes over when the received signals are weak, that is, below a pre-determined value and the receiver unlocks. In

fig. 21.2 Decca Doppler 62—GS and drift indicator,
'distance to go' meter and control unit

these circumstances, the drift and ground speed pointers remain locked to the last strongly measured signals. When strong signals are received again the pointers are released. If drift and ground speed information is being used to give position indications, the resultant position information is only as accurate as the 'frozen' drift and ground speed shown on the meters. Under these circumstances the position information is only equivalent to the DR plot and when the strong signals return, it must be updated if you have been running it on memory for a long time or substantial changes in the W/V are suspected.

Doppler limitations

As mentioned above, Doppler will unlock when the signals being received are weak. It will also unlock and go to memory mode in the following circumstances.

(a)   When flying over calm sea. Calm sea reflections are not sufficiently scattered to give strong echoes back. It needs at least a 5 kt wind to produce sufficient sea surface irregularities for satisfactory operation.

(b)   Atmospheric conditions. The receiver will unlock if severe thunderstorms are present around the aircraft. The outgoing signals will be reflected by the water drops and admit radio noise whereas the reflected signals will be weakened due to attenuation.

(c)   When flying very low. The Doppler receiver is short-circuited when transmission is taking place. At very low levels, by the time the receiver circuit is in operation again the reflections will have passed the aircraft.

(d)   Limits in pitch and roll. If the limits in pitch and roll as given by the equipment manufacturer are exceeded, Doppler will unlock. Typical limits are $\pm 20^\circ$ in pitch and $\pm 30^\circ$ in roll.

(e)   Height hole effect. For a pulse transmission system, this occurs when the aircraft is at such a height that the time taken for a signal to reach the ground and return is equal to the time interval between pulses, or to a multiple of that time. While a pulse is being transmitted, the receiver is switched off, and the reflections are not received.

This effect is not usually a prolonged one when flying over a landmass because of the surface irregularities. For pulse radar, the effect is avoided by gradually changing its frequency; for CW radar, by further frequency modulating the signal.

Associated equipment

The Doppler's basic information, drift and ground speed, can be used in conjunction with true heading reference from the aircraft's remote indicating compass to provide position information in a variety of ways:

distance flown along track and across track

latitude and longitude

position in terms of a square grid.

With more sophisticated systems, W/V, required track and ground speed, ETA, steering information, etc. may be provided and the Doppler data may be used to run a flight log.

Along/across track.   Fig. 21.3 shows a Marconi indicator with A/A presentation. Track angles and distances may be set up initially. Two green lamps, one on each

fig. 21.3

side of the display unit are used to indicate which stage is active. An amber lamp (marked 10 nm) lights up when the active stage DIST counters read less than 10 nautical miles.

The function switch controls the stage selection and the output from the computer. In position 1, the computer receives Doppler ground speed and track error angle and the computed along and across track distances are indicated on the stage 1 DIST and ACROSS DIST counters respectively.

A block schematic diagram of A/A operation is shown in fig. 21.4.

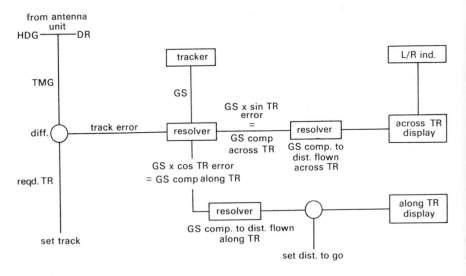

fig. 21.4 A/A resolution

Latitude and longitude

Utilising the ground nautical miles flown and TMG information, the computer solves the following triangle, fig. 21.5, to display latitude and longitude of the aircraft.

fig. 21.5

Errors of Doppler equipment

The accuracy of the basic information is very high: generally, the ground speed accuracy of 0.1% and a drift angle accuracy of 0.15% may be expected. Maximum error (on 95% of occasions) is not likely to exceed 0.5% in ground speed and drift measurement.

Errors in the basic information

(a) *Aerial misalignment.* Any error in the initial alignment of the aerial will give a systematic error in the drift angle measurement. This, in its turn, would give a track angle error. The alignment requirements are such that a 0.1° error is sufficient to affect the equipment's performance.

To study the sense of the error, let us say that there is a misalignment error of 1° to the right, and say that you select a track of 000. Because of the misalignment to the right, the aerial will be resting on heading of 001°. If the track of 000° is maintained, the aerial, which will have moved 1° to its left because that's where the correct track lies, will interpret the rotation as a track error of 1° to the left.

Example: An aircraft is flying from A to B, Tr 090, Dist 100 nm. Track and distance to go counters are set correctly at the start of the flight. If on arrival over B, the distance indication is 0 nm to go, and across track indication is 5 nm to the left, and this discrepancy is due to the aerial misalignment, calculate by how many degrees and in which direction the aerial is misaligned.

The solution is by the 1 : 60 rule.

$$\text{Aerial error} = \frac{60 \times 5}{100} = 3°$$

and since it puts you to the left of the track, the aerial is misaligned to the right.

(b)   *Pitch error.* This error occurs due to the angle which the aerial makes with the flight path in pitch attitude. It is reduced to an acceptable level by the use of the Janus beam. If a still higher accuracy is required, gyro stabilised aerials may be used.

Some inaccuracy will be noticed during a sustained climb or descent due to the difference between the length of the flight path and the corresponding ground distance. The inaccuracy will show up as an error in distance display. Update the indicator after the climb is completed.

(c)   *Sea movement error.* If the reflecting surface itself is in motion, an error will be introduced, since the velocity of a moving current of water becomes the basis of Doppler measurement, and not the stationary bed underneath. You are not likely to be flying over a tidal race for long, and the ocean currents are not fast enough to affect the Doppler. Thus, the error is really effective only when flying along a coastline with a fast tide and for a considerable time. Then the error may show up in ground speed or drift or both, depending on the relative movement of the water and the aircraft.

Other circumstances may be when flying over an open stretch of water for a long time, if there is a surface movement due to wind velocity, the equipment will again give erroneous information. Depending on the wind direction on the surface, both drift and ground speed may be in error. Generally speaking if this information is used to calculate and display as a Doppler position, it will be in error by approximately one-fifth of the surface wind speed and in an upwind direction.

(d)   *Sea bias.* Doppler transmits at a given depression angle, and as the beam strikes the surface, because it has a finite width (usually between 1° and 5°) the reflections come back not singly but from a large number of reflecting points on the surface. The equipment analyses these returns and extracts mean Doppler frequency from this spectrum. This it does by measuring the strength of the various reflections received back, and by dividing the energy envelope of these reflections at its mean position.

Doppler equipment having a beam width of, say, 4° and transmitting at a depression angle of 60°, illuminates the surface from 58° to 62°. Generally, the signals received from the rear edge of the beam (62° in our case) are stronger than the ones reflected from the forward edge of the beam. On the land, this difference is not significant and the equipment finds the Doppler frequency which is appropriate to the depression angle.

Over the sea, however, this bias becomes significant. In producing stronger signals from the rear it distorts the spectrum, and the equipment, in dividing the energy envelope at its mean position slides towards the higher angle of depression (see fig. 21.6). This means that the Doppler frequency produced is too low (cosine of $62°$ is less than cosine of $60°$) and the resulting ground speed consequently too low. This error is called sea bias error.

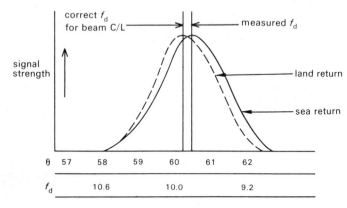

fig. 21.6

To a certain extent this error may be overcome by use of the land/sea switch. When 'sea' position is selected the computer makes a correction for a predetermined error, usually the error found when flying over an average sea. The error can be reduced by using a narrower beam but this is a design problem. It can be done by either increasing the aerial dimensions or decreasing the transmission wavelength.

Errors in associated equipment

(a)   *Heading error.* This error must come first on the list. The heading component is an extremely important part of the Doppler navigation system. It not only transforms the basic information into earth co-ordinates but also has a very major effect on the total system accuracy. Unfortunately, present-day compasses do not match the basic Doppler accuracy.

A magnetic compass itself has its basic errors expressed in terms of deviation. In flight, the detector unit of the compass system is tilted from the true vertical by coriolis effect and gives an error in terms of E–W deviation. Also, as the true heading is required for the Doppler equipment, the correct value of the local magnetic variation must be known.

To reduce the error due to the compass system

(a)   swing the compass very carefully for coefficients A, B and C and reduce the deviations as much as possible.

(b)   carry out a 12-point swing and find the residual deviations.

(c)   compensate for the following on the variation setting corrector of the compass to give true heading: (i) residual deviation as found above (ii) deviations due to coriolis and (iii) variation.

A gyromagnetic compass when well swung is capable of probable errors of $0.5°$ and a maximum of $1°$ on 95% of occasions.

(b) *Latitude error.* The value of 6 080 feet for 1 nm is only the average distance on the earth and the value is only correct near 48° N/S. The Doppler computer is instructed to clock on one nautical mile when 6 080 feet have gone, irrespective of the latitude the aircraft is in. This being a constant calibration value adopted in British Doppler equipment, a small error is bound to occur when the aircraft is not flying around 48° N/S.

(c) *Altitude error.* By definition the length of a nautical mile is the distance subtended at the earth's surface by an angle of 1′ of arc measured at the earth's centre. Since this arc distance opens with height, the distance between any two places at altitude is naturally longer. Actually, above sea level, the length of a nautical mile is $6\,080\,(1 + h/R)$ where h is the height of the aircraft and R the radius of the earth. Thus, the equipment over-reads by a factor $(R + h)/R$. This error is quite significant and amounts to nearly 0.2% at a height of 40 000 feet. Where high accuracy is required, correction tables are available.

Summary of Doppler errors

Factor	Error in the measurement of distance	track
Aerial misalignment	No	Yes
Pitch error	Yes	No
Sea movement	Vector error depending on time over tidal water, direction of tide movement and W/V	
Sea bias	Yes	No
Heading error	No	Yes
Altitude and latitude	Yes (affects lat. and long. information)	No

In the overall performance of the system, heading error outweighs other errors, some of which may be cancelling each other out. Generally, when it finds a wrong track, the indications of across distances could be in greater error than along distances.

To the basic information, the largest source of error is the 'sea bias error'.

Advantages of Doppler
(a) It is an independent aid.
(b) It has no range limitations.
(c) It has worldwide coverage.
(d) It is of high accuracy.
(e) It has area navigation capability.

Updating Doppler
It was mentioned earlier that whenever Doppler unlocks, the equipment goes into memory mode and only provides a DR plot. Occasions when Doppler is likely to unlock were also listed earlier. These errors, together with the system errors and errors in climb/descent accumulate with time. If during the flight a better fix is

available at any time, it is compared with the information being indicated on the Doppler and if there is any discrepancy, the Doppler co-ordinates can be inched up to bring the indication up-to-date. This process of adjusting the co-ordinates to the latest and accurate fix is called 'updating' Doppler.

The fix being used must be of a high accuracy, e.g. a Decca fix or a fix derived from two simultaneous DME ranges. In spite of all these errors of Doppler, when flying at a high level a pinpoint beneath the aircraft is not considered sufficiently accurate for updating Doppler.

22: Loran

Loran, a hyperbolic navigation system, derives its name from 'Long Range Aid to Navigation'. Because of the long ranges obtained, the system is mainly used to cover the vast expanses of the world's oceans.

Hyperbolic systems

A hyperbola is defined as the locus of a point having a fixed difference in range from two other fixed points. What does that mean? Simply this. The system calls for two fixed points — let M and S be such points in fig. 22.1.

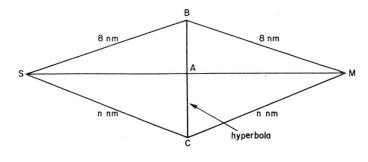

fig. 22.1

Join M — S by a straight line. The straight line thus drawn is called the base line between the two fixed points.

Point A is halfway between M and S and, say, the distances A–M and A–S are 5 nm respectively. The difference between the two ranges = 5 – 5 = 0.

Point B is 8 nm from M. Therefore, it must be 8 nm from S, BAC being the perpendicular bisector of MS. Differential range equal to 8 – 8 or 0.

If point C is 'n' nm from M and S, its differential range is also 0.

Draw up a smooth curve (it will be a straight line in this case) BAC which is a hyperbola. The curve BAC may be extended in both directions and any point on that curve will yield zero differential.

Curve BAC need not be the only hyperbola between M and S. Any number of hyperbolae may be constructed to cover the area. Take point P, a distance of 7 nm from M and 3 nm from S, along the base line (fig. 22.2).

Point Q is 8 nm from M and 4 from S, giving a differential range of 4.

Point P is 7 nm from M and 3 from S, differential range 4.

Point R is 9 nm from M and 5 from S, differential range 4.

Curve QPR is a hyperbola of differential range of 4 nm.

To utilise the system we want equipment in the aircraft which gives us the differential ranges. Loran is one of them. Then, once we know that the differential is 4, for example, we know that we are on curve QPR, a position line. But to plot ourselves on that curve we also need printed hyperbolic charts. Such charts are available for use in conjunction with Loran or any other existing hyperbolic system.

As for the information, it is not necessarily needed in terms of nautical miles as in the above illustrations. It may well be in terms of phases of the signal received in the aerial (Decca) or in the time in microseconds (μs) that the radio wave took to travel to the aircraft (Loran). In either case, the principle still remains the same, that of differential range. For example, if the information is in terms of time, at point R, signal from M will take 55.62 μs (6.18 μs = 1 nm) and the signal from S will take 30.9 μs to arrive at the aircraft. The differential of 24.72 μs will be labelled against the hyperbola QPR instead of 4 nm as in fig. 22.2.

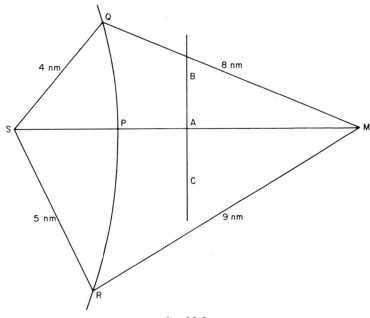

fig. 22.2

Loran

Loran works on the principle of differential range by pulse technique. Two stations called Master (M) and Slave (S) operate as a pair to give a single position line. They are generally placed between 200 and 400 nm apart to give a wide coverage and it is usual to have more than one slave operating in conjunction with a common master to provide 2 or 3 position lines. The operator tunes in the chain and measures off the time difference between two signals on the screen. He then enters the Loran chart with this value and plots a position line. Usually there are two or three chains printed on a Loran chart, each in a different colour so that no confusion arises in selecting the correct hyperbola. Hyperbolae are normally shown at 100 μs interval and it will be necessary to interpolate for values in between them. Up to about 800 nm from the station the hyperbolae are continuous lines; beyond that range they are shown by pecked lines. Pecked lines suggest an extended reception area during night periods.

Transmission sequence

If both the Master and the Slave transmitted synchronously it would be impossible to determine which was which. Therefore, in Loran, the Master transmits first. It transmits a pulse, 50 μs wide (pulse width) in all directions. When this pulse reaches the slave it triggers the slave transmitter. This transmitter, however, does not respond instantly. There is a calibrated delay before the Slave transmission takes place. The transmission again is in the form of pulses radiating in all directions. The Master then transmits again and the sequence repeats. In one second, approximately 25 pulses are transmitted, the transmission PRF. The actual PRF depends on the chain and varies from 25 to 34 as we will see later in the chapter.

Time base

The time base is the time that the 'spot' on the CRT takes to travel from one end of the tube to the other. This movement of the spot appears to the naked eye as a trace and provides a scale for measuring the time difference. Since the measurement is in time, the length of the time base is calculated in microseconds. It is synchronised with the PRF of transmission so that the signals from other chains operating on the same frequency do not remain stationary on a wrong time base. If these signals do break through they will simply sweep across the screen. Assuming a PRF of 25, the transmission takes place every 1/25th of a second. In microseconds this equals

$$\frac{1\,000\,000}{25} = 40\,000\,\mu s$$

Thus, the length of the time base will be 40 000 μs. This length, however, is split up in two traces, as shown in fig. 22.3, each of approximately 20 000 μs.

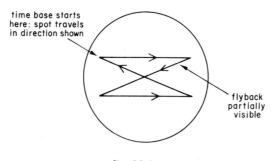

time base starts
here: spot travels
in direction shown

flyback
partially
visible

fig. 22.3

We said 'approximately' because some time is lost in the flyback shown in fig. 22.3. The flyback portion is not used.

The purpose of this split up is mainly to enable the operator to identify the master and the slave signals. It is so arranged, by adjusting the delay at the slave transmitter, that the slave signal always appears more than half the time base away from the master. We will come back to the topic of identification later. Presently, it will be appreciated that the delay required to put two signals on different traces must be at least half of the length of the time base. This is 20 000 μs. In addition to this, there is a further small delay of approximately 1 000 μs called a 'coding' delay, giving a total delay at slave of 21 000 μs. However, when taking the actual reading on the indicator you will not need to deal with such large figures. The time delay of 20 000 μs is automatically subtracted from all indicator readings, making the task easier. Typical readings that will be obtained at various positions are shown in the following calculations, to be studied with reference to fig. 22.4.

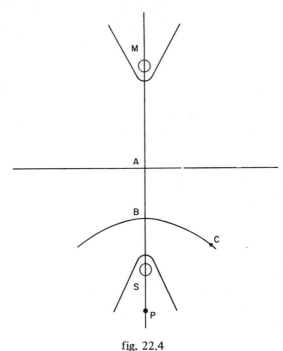

fig. 22.4

Observer at S
1. Time taken for the pulse to travel M − S, distance of, say, 200 nm.
    = 200 × 6.18 = 1 236 μs
        Delay at S = 1 000   (20 000 μs delay is not considered here because it
                                   will not be read)
    Slave transmits at $\overline{2\,236\ \mu s}$
2. At S, therefore S is seen after 2 236 μs
                      M   1 236 μs
        Time difference   1 000 μs Indicated
Observer at P, 50 nm behind S along extended base line M − S
1. M − P   =   250 × 6.18 = 1 545 μs
2. M − S   =   1 236 μs
    Delay   =   1 000 μs
    S − P   =   309 μs
                 $\overline{2\,545\ \mu s}$

3.   Difference 1 and 2 = 1 000 μs, the same value as above example.

Therefore, along the extended base line M − S the differential range obtained is a constant figure and thus, an ambiguous area.

Observer at M

1.   M signal is received instantaneously.
2.   Slave pulse −

M − S	=	1 236 μs
Delay	=	1 000
S − M	=	1 236
		3 472 μs

3.   Difference 1 and 2 = 3 472 μs and the same value will be received anywhere along the extended base line S − M, giving an ambiguous area.

Observer at A, half way between M and S

1.   M − A   =   618 μs
2.   M − S   =   1 236 μs

Delay	=	1 000
S − A	=	618
		2 854 μs

3.   Difference 1 and 2 = 2 236 μs. This is the value of the hyperbola of the perpendicular bisector.

Observer at B, 140 nm from M along the base line

1.   M − B   =   140 x 6.18 = 865 μs
2.   M − S   =   1 236 μs

Delay	=	1 000
S − B	=	371
		2 607 μs

3.   Difference 1 and 2 = 1 742 μs

Observer at C, 160 nm from M, 80 nm from S

1.   M − C   =   160 x 6.18 = 988 μs (approx)
2.   M − S   =   1 236 μs

Delay	=	1 000
S − C	=	494 (approx)
		2 730

3.   Difference 1 and 2 = 1 742 μs, the same value as position B.

Thus, B and C are on the same hyperbola and having located C and a few other points having a similar value, a curve is drawn up joining the points. How did we locate C? It is going back to the basic : differential range. If you notice the ranges of B and C from M and S bear this relationship : MC − SC = MB − SB. Thus, knowing the differential range and one true range, the other one can be calculated.

Frequencies

Loran operates in the upper MF band, and the actual frequencies allocated are four in number, each one being called a 'channel'. These are:

Channel 1 : 1 950 kHz
Channel 2 : 1 850 kHz
Channel 3 : 1 900 kHz
Channel 4 : 1 750 kHz

It will be appreciated that in this state only four Loran chains could operate and if station A was operating with three slaves its neighbouring station B would only have one remaining frequency to operate one single slave. This severe limitation is removed by Loran operating on 16 different PRF in conjunction with each channel, thus extending its scope of operation to 64 simultaneous master-slave pairs. This is considered quite adequate. Two basic PRF are chosen — 25 and $33\frac{1}{3}$, called Low and High respectively, each having a possibility of 8 variations. These variations are called 'rates'. Low PRF of 25 increase by $\frac{1}{16}$ and the high increases by $\frac{1}{9}$. Thus:

Rate No.	Low	High
0	25	$33\frac{1}{3}$
1	$25\frac{1}{16}$	$33\frac{4}{9}$
2	$25\frac{1}{8}$	$33\frac{5}{9}$
3	$25\frac{3}{16}$	$33\frac{2}{3}$
4	$25\frac{1}{4}$	$33\frac{7}{9}$
5	$25\frac{5}{16}$	$33\frac{8}{9}$
6	$25\frac{3}{8}$	34
7	$25\frac{7}{16}$	$34\frac{1}{9}$

There are three controls to select a chain. Say you are selecting a chain which is described as '2L7'. Figure 2 is the channel number suggesting that the frequency in use is 1 850 kHz. Letter L stands for Low and this is set on Low/High control. Figure 7 stands for the rate number, giving the PRF of $25\frac{7}{16}$. This figure is selected on 'Rate Number' control which is marked from 0 to 7. PRF of $25\frac{7}{16}$ gives us the time of the cycle —

$$\frac{1\,000\,000 \times 16}{407}$$

$= 39\,310\ \mu s$ and this figure governs the length of the time base produced.

Operation
Switch on the set and allow it to warm for a period of 4 to 5 minutes. Select the chain number, L or H position on L/H control and the rate number. If you are within the range you should now see two signals on the screen. Other controls are:

L/R Switch	— this positions signals on trace required
Drift Switch	— controls drift of the signals, or stabilises them on the trace.
Rx Gain	— incorporates ON/OFF and gain control
Coarse Delay	— governs coarse movement of the moveable strobe.
Fine Delay	— governs finer adjustment of the moveable strobe.
Amplitude Bal	— gives differential adjustment of signals on positions 2 and 3 of the Function Switch
Function Switch	— this has 5 positions.

Having seen the signals the next step is to identify which is Master and which is Slave. Remembering the fact that the master signal arrives first and the slave arrives at least half the time base distance away, the signals are identified as shown in fig. 22.5.

In fig. 22.5(a), signal A is clearly not the master because signal B is not more than half the time base away. B is the master and it can be seen that A is more than half the time base away, following the time base in the direction of the arrows.

In fig. 22.5(b), A is the master, B being placed more than half the time base in

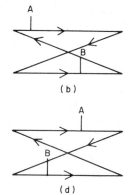

fig. 22.5

the direction of the arrows.

In fig. 22.5(c), B is the master.

In fig. 22.5(d), B is the master.

Having identified the signals the next step is to place both the signals on the bottom trace, slave at the extreme left hand edge. This is done by use of the L/R switch. Fig. 22.6.

fig. 22.6

Starting at position (a) the signals will move as shown until S is at the left hand edge of the lower trace (d). If during this process the signals seem to move, apart from the operation of the left/right switch, this means that the time base is not quite matched to the PRF and the fine tuning is required. This is done by means of the drift control, which is moved in a direction opposite to signal drift until the drift stops. You are on position 1 of the function switch during this operation, and just one more thing remains to be done before moving on to No. 2 position. S, as in fig. 22.6(d), is placed on an invisible strobe. It is necessary to similarly strobe M. This is done by use of the coarse delay control which moves a V shaped visible strobe along the bottom trace. Place the strobe beneath M. Signals on the bottom trace will now appear as shown in fig. 22.7.

fig. 22.7

Position 2.   In this position the space occupied by two strobes is presented in expanded form. Two traces still appear but now the slave is on the top trace, master on the bottom. The time base generated in this position is an exponential time base, fast time being towards the left of the centre. The signals as they appear in this position are as shown in fig. 22.8.

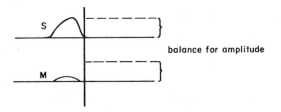

fig. 22.8

First, drift the signals slightly to the left of the centre, i.e. in the fast portion of the time base (this has the effect of opening them up) and then balance them for amplitude so that the two signals look alike or as close as possible.
Position 3.   In this position both signals are superimposed on each other for accurate matching. Match up the leading edges as close as possible — accuracy of time measurement depends on it — by means of fine delay control. (Fig. 22.9.)

fig. 22.9

Note the time and throw the function switch to position 4. This is the time of the position line.
Positions 4 and 5.   Actual count of the time interval is carried out in these two positions, in position 4 the time being read to nearest thousand microsecond, hundreds and tens in position 5.

Later models of Loran eliminate use of positions 4 and 5 by presenting veeder counter reading, counters being placed directly as coarse and fine delay controls are adjusted.

Range
Loran utilises both ground wave and sky waves and the charts are made out with

sky wave corrections printed on the hyperbolae. Normal ranges are given in the table below.

	Ground Wave		Sky wave	
	Land	Sea	Land	Sea
Day	200	850	–	–
Night	very little	500	1 300	1 300

Sky wave utilisation

This navigation aid actually makes use of the sky waves. The first pulse to arrive at the aircraft must be ground wave (if within the range) since it has the shortest distance to travel. Given proper range, the ground signal could be followed by a trail of sky waves at night. Range from the stations is of paramount importance, as is the time of the day. As for the time, from previous studies we are aware that sky waves by day and at twilight are quite unpredictable but at night there is constancy about the height of the E layer and the resulting reflections. In the absence of ground waves, the time difference can be measured between two sky waves, the reading then adjusted to the ground wave measurement on which the charts are based.

The reflections are numerous – one hop E, second hop E, one hop F – and only the first sky wave (one hop E) is used. The others are ignored as they are greatly fallible. The vital problem is to identify the sky waves since on no account must the time difference between one ground wave and one sky wave be taken: measure ground wave with ground wave, sky wave with sky wave. The limit of the sky wave reception is governed by the geometry of the earth's surface together with the height of the E layer. A wave leaving tangential to the surface will produce the maximum range.

Principle of sky wave correction

The difference between the distance that the master sky wave arrives after the master ground wave and the distance that the slave sky wave arrives after the slave ground wave is the error in reading and must be corrected before plotting the position line. The error may be positive or negative, depending on which of the two sky waves is closer to the ground wave. These distances may be estimated from visualising the geometry involved. Follow these principles:

(a)   Aircraft is close to the master and at considerable distance from the slave. As the aircraft gets near to one station, the sky waves will get further behind the ground wave : the solution is triangular – the base of the triangle is the ground wave and the difference between it and the sum of the two other sides (representing the distance of travel of the sky wave) will be greater at short ranges – fig. 22.10.

In fig. 22.10 the difference between ground waves is shown by (x). This is the correct distance which you would have measured had you been measuring two ground waves. The distance between the two sky waves is shown as (y). This is the distance actually measured using sky waves.

d_m is the distance between master ground and sky waves; d_s is the distance between slave ground and sky waves. From fig. 22.10(a) we know that the distance d_m is greater than distance d_s. Therefore, distance (x) must be greater than distance (y); or, the measurement taken on the sky waves must be too small and the correction

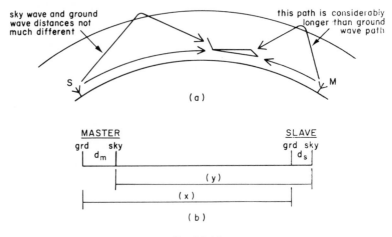

(a)

(b)

fig. 22.10

is positive. $(d_m - d_s)$, the value of the correction, is additive.

(b)   Aircraft close to the slave and considerable distance from the master. Fig. 22.11.

fig. 22.11

Here, the distance required is (x); distance measured using sky waves is (y). d_m is smaller than d_s (being nearer the slave), the correction $(d_m - d_s)$ is negative.

(c)   Aircraft at equal distance from master and slave.
In this case d_m will equal d_s or (x) will equal (y) and therefore no correction will be required.

Accuracy
Accuracy depends on the type of waves being used. With basic accuracy of $\pm 1\ \mu s$, the ground wave accuracy is of the order of $\pm 6\ \mu s$ and the sky wave accuracy of $\pm 16\ \mu s$.

Accuracy also depends on how well the two pulses were matched before taking the count. This matching is necessary because a pulse of $50\ \mu s$ pulse width is being used in Loran. A pulse of this size takes a measurable time in rising and any measurement taken in the meantime will be erroneous. This limitation is overcome by amplitude matching which we discussed earlier in the chapter.

Unserviceability
Should any of the two signals blink or jump along the time base, the chain is unserviceable and must not be used.

Interference
Being an MF aid, Loran is sensitive to weather static.

Problem
1.   The length of the base line M − S is 1 000 μs. An observer A, 250 μs from master along the base line reads a time difference of 2 100 μs. What is the delay at S? (Answer: 600 μs).

23: Decca

Decca is another hyperbolic navigation system, operating on the master–slave basis. It differs from Loran in many ways. First of all, the basic principles employed by the two systems to produce differential ranges are different. Decca measures differential ranges by comparison of phases of the master and slave signals arriving in the aircraft. The presentation of information is different – Decca displays information by means of three decometers, on the dial and pointer system. Decca operates on yet lower frequencies, the LF band in fact, and lastly, Decca is a short range navigation aid.

A standard Decca chain consists of a master transmitter and three slave transmitters, the slaves being known as Red, Green and Purple. The slaves are placed around the master, approximately 120° apart from each other and at a distance of between 70 and 110 nm from the master. One master–slave pair gives one position line, but unlike Loran, information from all three pairs is continuously presented on the decometers and thus, more than one position line may be obtained without having to select another station, as with Loran.

Principle

The principle of Decca is differential range by phase comparison. Let us see first of all, how it is possible to have a knowledge of range simply by measuring the phases of two signals and comparing them. See fig. 23.1.

It is an M–S combination, each transmitting at two cycles per second. At any given instant, the signals relationship is as shown in the figure. Master's signal is shown as wave A, slave's as wave B. Both waves are phased locked, that is, their crests and zero values occur at the same instant.

Let us now consider the phases produced by these two waves at different positions in the area MW. Signal A (master) will produce phases of 045, 090 and 135 respectively at positions a, b and c. At these same positions signal B (slave) will produce phases, 315, 270 and 225. Both signals will produce 0 phases at M and 180 at W.

Now, if we had a meter sensitive to phases, at position M it would read 0 phase from both the signals. Further, if this meter was capable of displaying the result as a difference of the two phases, it would still read 0, as shown by a meter in the figure. If we now move to position a, the phase meter will read a phase of 045 from A signal, 315 from B signal, and the result displayed will be 045 + 360 − 315 = 090.

At b, the phase difference will be 090 + 360 − 270 = 180

At c, the phase difference will be 135 + 360 − 225 = 270

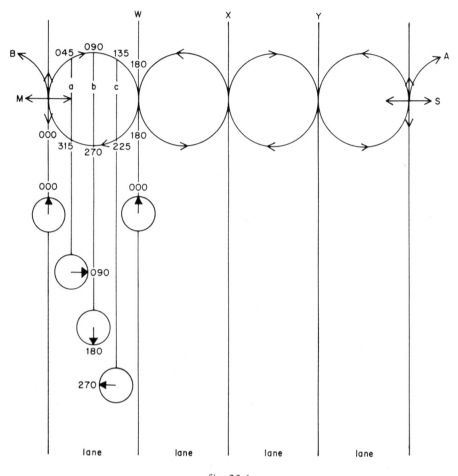

fig. 23.1

Lastly, at W, the phase difference will be 180 − 180 = 0.

Thus, as we moved from M to W, we went through an area of complete 360° phase difference, or the needle in fig. 23.1 completed one full revolution. This is the basis of the principle. We can calculate the distance from M to a point where, for example, a phase difference of 090 or any other given value will occur. We can do this because the distance M−W is the distance of half the wavelength. We know the frequency, therefore, we know the wavelength.

In fig. 23.2 a hyperbolic lattice is drawn up for a two-wave transmission as illustrated in fig. 23.1.

In this figure, master and slave waves are shown every 90°, master's transmission being continuous curves, slave's pecked curves. Hyperbolae are determined as follows:

Starting at M, the phase due to master signal at point a is 90, the slave phase is 270. Difference is 090 + 360 − 270 = 180.

Now we want to find all other points in the vicinity of M which will give the same phase difference, i.e. 180. Take point b. Master's phase here is 180, slave's phase 360, difference 180. Points c, d and e are similarly found. A smooth curve jointing these points gives a hyperbola of 180 phase difference. This means that an aircraft anywhere along that curve will read a phase difference of 180, and a small portion of that hyperbola in the vicinity of the aircraft's position is its position line. (Note: positions a, b and c are not related to a, b and c in fig. 23.1).

By a similar process hyperbolae at any convenient interval may be drawn up between master and slave and then the original wave pattern erased. Note that the perpendicular bisector is a straight line curve. Note also that ambiguity exists behind master and slave.

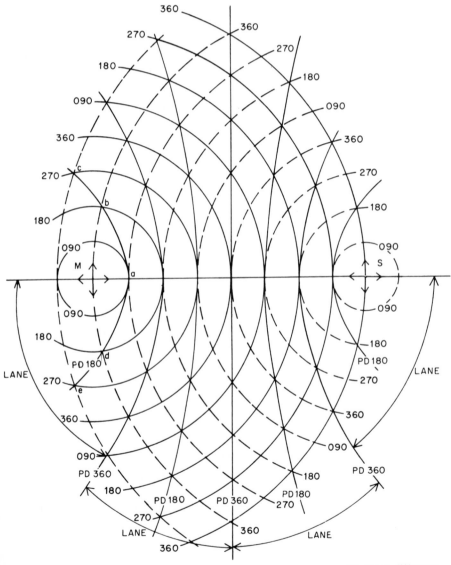

PD phase difference

fig. 23.2

We are now ready to see how this principle is implemented in practice. In our illustration in fig. 23.1, we have both master and slave transmitting on the same frequency. In practice, this is not possible since two signals on the same frequency arriving at the aerial will merge and appear as a single voltage. Unless separate identity is maintained the phase comparison cannot take place. Therefore, a Decca master and the three slaves transmit on different frequencies. Each station (i.e. master and three slaves) has a basic or fundamental frequency called f. The value of f is always in the region of 14 kHz. Master and its slaves then transmit on fixed harmonics of that fundamental frequency. Harmonics are the multiples or divisions of a given frequency and they are easier to produce. These fixed harmonics in respect of the four transmitters are as follows, and they are valid for a Decca chain anywhere in the world.

$$
\begin{array}{lcl}
\text{Master} & - & 6f \\
\text{Red} & - & 8f \\
\text{Green} & - & 9f \\
\text{Purple} & - & 5f
\end{array}
$$

Just to repeat for the sake of emphasis, the multiples remain constant throughout, the value of f varies from chain to chain. A typical chain operating on a basic frequency of 14.2 kHz is shown in fig. 23.3.

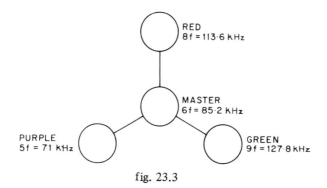

RED
8f = 113·6 kHz

MASTER
6f = 85·2 kHz

PURPLE
5f = 71 kHz

GREEN
9f = 127·8 kHz

fig. 23.3

Comparison frequency

By staggering the four transmission frequencies we solved the problem of keeping the signals separate. But in doing so, we created a new problem. Phase comparison cannot take place between any two signals which are not on the same frequency for the simple reason that they do not bear phase relationship. Now we have two signals in the receiver but not on the same frequency and we cannot compare their phases. So where do we go from here? The obvious solution is to step them up now to a common frequency and then take the phase difference; Decca has done just that. Each master-slave combination is stepped up in the receiver to the value of their LCM and phase comparison is then taken. These stepped up values are called Comparison Frequencies, and they are as follows:

Master and red

M transmits at $6f$
R transmits at $8f$ LCM = $24f$ which is the comparison frequency

Similarly, the comparison frequency for master and green is 18 f and master and purple, 30 f.

Thus, the principle is finally implemented and the result of phase comparison displayed by a pointer on the decometers. The only observation that remains to be made is how the receiver converts the received frequencies into comparison frequencies. This is shown in fig. 23.4 which is self explanatory.

```
Master  6f X 4 = 24f ⎫
RED     8f X 3 = 24f ⎭ compare  — — — — — — — — —

                                         fractional
                                         pointer
Master  6f X 3 = 18f ⎫
GREEN 9f X 2 = 18f   ⎭ compare  — —
                                         lane
                                         pointer

Master  6f X 5 = 30f ⎫
Purple  5f X 6 = 30f ⎭ compare  — — — — — — — —
```

fig. 23.4

Decometers

With the information coming to the Decca receiver in the form of phase differences it is now necessary to create a system of presenting this information in a convenient form so that the operator can rapidly utilise it.

For a start, the very fact that a 360° phase change occurs over a known distance can be adopted to give us a basic unit of measurement. On a decometer (which is a Decca indicator) these 360° phase changes are indicated on the fractional pointer — fig. 23.4. The pointer indicates the position inside any one of the numerous 360° phase change areas that occur between a master and a slave by taking the phase difference between the two signals.

The next step is to be able to locate the exact area we are in. To enable us to do this, these 360° phase change areas, called Decca 'lanes' are numbered, the numbering system being explained below. A lane is defined as an area enclosed by two hyperbolae of 0° phase difference. On a decometer, the lane number is indicated by the lane pointer geared to the fractional pointer.

The physical distance that any one lane would occupy, that is its lane width, depends on the slave's comparison frequency, because it will be remembered that the fractional pointer is placed by the phase difference taking place at this frequency. Along the base line, the lane width is the distance occupied by half the wave at comparison frequency — see fig. 23.1. Taking a typical Decca fundamental frequency, f, of 14.2 kHz, the lane width for the three slaves is calculated as follows.

Red slave: compares at 24f, comparison frequency = 24 x 14.2 = 340.8 kHz.

$$\text{Lane width} = \frac{300\,000}{340.8 \times 2} = 440 \text{ metres}$$

Green slave: compares at 18*f*, comparison frequency = 18 x 14.2 = 255.6 kHz

$$\text{Lane width} = \frac{300\,000}{255.6 \times 2} = 587 \text{ metres}$$

Purple slave: compares at 30*f*, comparison frequency = 30 x 14.2 = 426 kHz

$$\text{Lane width} = \frac{300\,000}{426 \times 2} = 352 \text{ metres.}$$

From the above it will be noticed that the different slaves produce lanes of different lengths, green for example is 587 metres whereas the purple is merely 352 metres. It is further pointed out that no two slave transmitters can be expected to be located at exactly the same distance from the master. In a Decca chain, the green slave may be, for example, 160 km from the master and the red may be 180 km. These variables call for some kind of grouping of the lanes for the sake of standardisation of the calibration of the decometers.

This standardisation is achieved by the establishment of Decca 'zones', so that a zone provides a fixed distance measurement for all three slaves. A zone is defined as an area enclosed by two 0 phase hyperbolae formed by comparison at the basic frequency, *f*. The basic frequency, *f*, being the same for all three slaves in a chain, the zone width for all three slaves will also be the same. Along the base line, the width of a zone is the distance occupied by half the wave at the fundamental frequency, *f*. Zone width for any slave may be calculated as follows:

f = 14.2 kHz

$$\text{zone width} = \frac{300\,000}{14.2 \times 2} \text{ metres}$$
$$= 10\,563 \text{ metres.}$$

Thus, the zone width is independent of the slave colour, but within these zones, the number of lanes enclosed for each different slave will be different, as shown below.

Red: lane width = 440 metres and the number of red lanes in a red zone

$$= \frac{10\,563}{440} = 24$$

Green: lane width = 587 metres and the number of green lanes in a green zone

$$= \frac{10\,563}{587} = 18, \text{ and lastly}$$

Purple: lane width = 352 metres and the number of purple lanes in a purple zone

$$= \frac{10\,563}{352} = 30.$$

Decca equipment employs three decometers, one for each slave and the information provided is in the form of a zone, lane and the fraction of the lane, as below.

Zones. All decometers read up to ten zones. These are lettered from A to J (including I) and the indication is on moving counters. If in a particular chain the master-slave distance exceeds ten zones, the letters then repeat. It will be appreciated that this repetition is not likely to cause an ambiguity because, on average the first ten zones would occupy a distance of around 100 km along the base line (and more elsewhere) before the repetition would occur.

Lanes. As mentioned earlier, the number of lanes in a zone differs according to the slave, and different calibrations for different slaves may be expected. The lane pointer moves round the dial calibrated as follows:

Red decometer — 24 lanes to a zone, numbered 0 to 23 (inc.)

Green decometer — 18 lanes to a zone, numbered 30 to 47 (inc.)

Purple decometer — 30 lanes to a zone, numbered 50 to 79 (inc.).

Fraction of lane.   360° travel of the fraction pointer round the dials is shown in decimals, that is, from 0 to 0.99 rather than as 360 phases. This makes it easier to read and the dial requires fewer calibration marks which enhances the accuracy of the reading.

To recap, when the fractional pointer completes one full revolution, a flight through one lane is complete. The lane pointer which is geared to the fractional pointer will now indicate the next lane. When the lane pointer completes one full revolution, the aircraft will have flown through 24 red lanes or 18 green lanes or 30 purple lanes. The zone indicator which is geared to the lane pointer will now have moved to indicate the next zone. An operator takes the zone reading first, this being the slowest moving counter. The number of the lane is then read, followed by the fraction inside the lane. A typical reading D 41.75 is illustrated in fig. 23.5. D is the zone letter, 41 is the lane number and .75 is the position inside that lane. Or, the aircraft has progressed three-quarters of the way inside lane 41 of zone D.

fig. 23.5

Lane identification

It will be appreciated that the length of a Decca lane is a very small distance indeed. For example, for a purple slave, if the master-slave distance is 100 nm, (and we know that there are 300 lanes in that distance) the length of a lane is a mere 1/3rd of a nm. If you are taking off from an aerodrome and planning to use Decca straight-away, this causes no problem, since you will have set the base co-ordinates in terms of zone and lane (fractional pointer will pick up correct position automatically) before the start. In that case, Decca will continue to indicate the correct reading throughout the flight. The problem arises in cases where temporary failure of the equipment occurs or when entering a Decca chain from outward or when changing over from one chain to another. In these instances accurate information on lane number is required. On Decca, this information is provided on a Lane Identification Meter, a single indicator calibrated in decimals just like the fractional pointers of the three decometers and which caters for all three slaves. The identification meter consists of two pointers, one is wide and is called the Sector Pointer. The other is a six legged one and is called the Vernier Pointer (fig. 23.6).

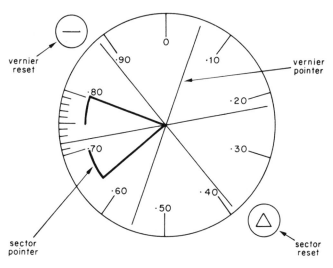

fig. 23.6

In the above illustration the reading is .72. If this was a green reading (that is, a reading taken when green light was on) and we wished to set the lane on the deco-meter in fig. 23.5, we would move the lane pointer to cover .72 on fractional scale. This would put us in lane 43.

As for zone setting, it is wide enough to be ascertained by DR navigation. On later Decca models (Mk. 10) zone identification also takes place automatically.

We shall now look at the theory and see how lane identification is achieved, and particularly, how the lane number ties up with decimals on the fractional scale. Let us forget for a minute the LI meter and concentrate on the decometer in fig. 23.5. As pointed out, the need for LI (lane identification) arises because of the smallness of the lane distances. The obvious answer to this would be to momentarily widen the lanes. In Decca the lanes are widened momentarily for LI purposes by providing suitable ground transmission to phase-compare the signals at $1f$ and $6f$. Fig. 23.7 represents a master and green comparison pattern. 180 lanes are produced which are contained in 10 zones, each zone having 18 lanes in it. This is so during normal transmission. At $1f$, we know from earlier calculations, that there will be 5 waves between master and green (distance 60 nm) or 10 lanes. This $1f$ transmission forming 10 lanes between master and green is also shown in fig. 23.7. Distance X–Y which marks the boundary of D zone (shown exploded for clarity) is now covered by half a wave from master and half from slave. This resembles the wave pattern between M and W in fig. 23.1. Thus, as the aircraft travels from X to Y, 360° phase change will occur and the fractional pointer will complete one revolution.

Under this arrangement the distance X–Y (or original zone D) is a lane, and the fractional pointer at any time indicates position inside this lane in terms of decimals.

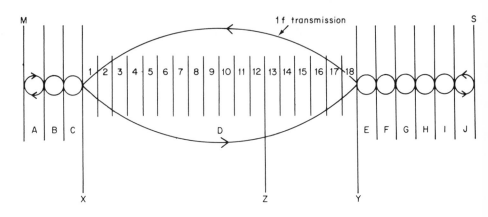

fig. 23.7

For example, when the aircraft is at Z, the fractional pointer of the decometer will have gone round 2/3rds of the dial, say, it indicates .72. Now, if against position .72 on the fractional scale, the decometer was calibrated to give lane numbers under normal comparison frequency, the reading would be 43 (30 + 13) from fig. 23.7. If you examine fig. 23.5, it is calibrated just that way. Fractional value at 1 f indicates lane number at normal comparison frequency. As for the fractional pointer on the decometer, it would be most inconvenient if lane identification readings were fed to it. The needle would jump every minute to indicate a lane. Hence the use of a separate LI meter. The result of 1 f is displayed on the sector pointer.

Comparison for lane identification also takes place at 6 f simultaneously with 1 f. The reason for 6 f comparison is to improve the accuracy of the LI. If you examine the 1 f curve above you will notice that the curve is very gentle and the phases change very slowly. A comparison on its own would only yield an approximate result, and this accounts for the shape of the sector pointer. 6 f will produce six lanes in the original D zone (6 f = 60 lanes in place of original 180. Therefore, the original 3 lanes will equal one new lane or, there will be six lanes in one original zone). So there will be six positions in distance X–Y where the same phase difference will be measured – hence the shape of Vernier Pointer. The leg that falls in the area covered by the sector pointer indicates the lane in decimals.

To enable the receiver to carry out phase comparisons at 1 f and 6 f the transmission pattern has to be modified. The transmission sequence together with frequencies transmitted for LI purposes is as follows, and during this period normal transmission stops.

On the minute: Red Identification
                       M transmits at 6 f and 5 f
                       Red transmits at 8 f and 9 f
                       Purple and Green are switched off

Minute + 15 s	Green Identification
	Master transmits at $6f$ and $5f$
	Green transmits at $8f$ and $9f$
	Red and Purple are switched off
Minute + 30 s	Purple Identification
	Master transmits at $6f$ and $5f$
	Purple transmits at $8f$ and $9f$
	Red and Green are switched off.

Each transmission lasts for approximately ½ second during which time the normal flow of data stops. The identification light is kept glowing for approximately 3 seconds to enable the operator to take the reading. The receiver converts the above transmissions to $1f$ frequency as follows:

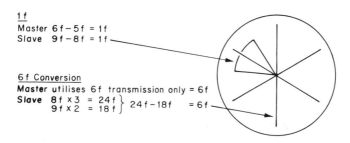

fig. 23.8

Use of Decca

An On/Off switch is provided to switch on the Decca. Amber light on the control unit glows when the set is switched on. Allow ample time for the set to warm up. The set must be 'referenced' when thoroughly warmed up. This is done by throwing the Ref/Op switch on the control unit to Ref position. In this state outside signals are cut off and instead an internally generated 360° phase signal is fed to all three decometers and the LI meter. All three decometer fractional pointers must return to zero phase position (12 o'clock). If they haven't done so, they must be zeroed manually. On the LI meter the sector pointer will be near zero and one of the vernier legs will be at zero. If this is not at zero, it must be zeroed likewise. The purpose of referencing the set is to make allowance for changes in value of electronic components operating in warmed up conditions. Referencing will also be necessary when changing a chain in flight since by selecting a new frequency, new crystals will be brought into operation. Otherwise do not reference the set in flight unless you must, since during the referencing period flow of normal data is stopped and therefore lane identification will be necessary before using the decometers again.

Range

300 nm by day; 200 nm by night.

Accuracy

Accuracy of the equipment is very high indeed. If the phase difference is read to

the accuracy of 6°, the theoretical accuracy for the red slave would be –
Lane width = 240 lanes in 60 nm

$$= \frac{60}{240}$$

$$= \frac{1}{4} \text{ nm}$$

∴ Accuracy $\quad = \frac{6}{360} \times 440 \text{ yds}$

$$= 7\frac{1}{3} \text{ yard}$$

In practice the accuracy is 1 nm on 95% of occasions at maximum range. The degree of accuracy also depends on the area the aircraft is in in relation to the master and slave stations. See fig. 23.9.

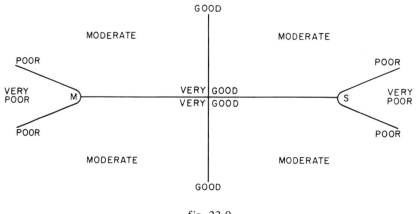

fig. 23.9

Errors
1. *Height Error.*   All Decca charts are made up for ground level propagation. Therefore, a slight error occurs, particularly at very high altitudes. There will be no error, however, when the aircraft is along the perpendicular bisector of the base line, and there will be maximum error when overhead the master or slave station. If high accuracy is required correction charts must be used in conjunction with the readings obtained.
2. *Decometer Lag.*   There is a lag between reception and presentation on the decometer dials. This is greatest when crossing lanes rapidly, along the base line. Purple is the most vulnerable. This error will be rather less than the airman's eye-to-brain agility in reading a decometer, so know about it but don't worry about it.
3. *Night Error.*   Decca assumes that transmissions to the receiver are the shortest distance and the most direct, the ground wave. Being a low frequency aid there will be sky waves present in the aerial at night, when at distant ranges. At night, therefore one must use caution when 200 nm or so from the master. Dusk and dawn are critical periods.
4. *Lane Slip.*   Although Lane Identification signals occupy but half a second, the data flow in the receiver is interrupted for about one second and during this time the decometer concerned will stop. On return of the signal, the decometer starts again quite fast, but if during this time the aircraft has moved through more than ½ lane,

the needle will turn the shortest way to the correct position, and a whole lane could be lost. Lane slip will occur at 240 kt and over but the later marks of Decca take care of this error by automatic Lane Identification. Even Mk VIII has been adapted to include a memory device which takes over at the last rate of decometer movement after the signals are interrupted.

5. *Static.*   Rain static and atmospherics can blot out signals entirely or give incorrect readings through interference.

6. *Interpretation and Interpolation Error.*   Reading the decometers takes a bit of practice : plotting between wide hyperbolae likewise.

Decca chart

The lattice is overprinted in the appropriate colours on a Lambert's chart. The AO, A30 and A50 are the base line extensions of Red, Green and Purple respectively, behind the master. Base line extensions behind the slaves have no zone letters allocated. The area immediately behind the master and slave is ambiguous and must not be used in association with that particular slave. Use of particular Master–Slave combination is shown in fig. 23.10.

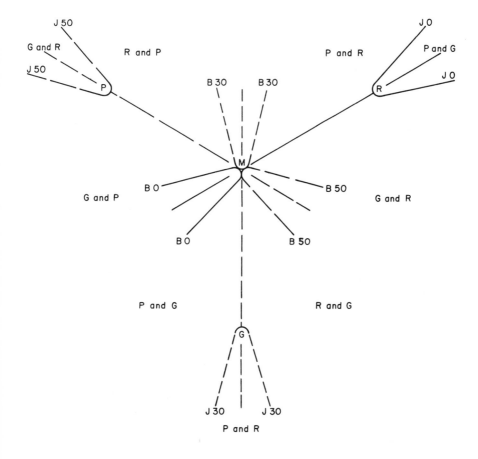

fig. 23.10

Decca problems

1. Given $f = 14.2$, what is the zone width of a purple zone along the base line?

$$\text{Zone width} = \frac{\text{speed of radio wave}}{f} \times \frac{1}{2}$$

$$= \frac{300\,000\,000}{14\,200} \times \frac{1}{2}$$

$$= 10\,560 \text{ metres}$$

2. If $f = 14.26$, what is the width of a purple lane?

$$\text{Purple comparison frequency} = 30f$$

$$= 30 \times 14.26 \text{ kHz}$$

$$= 427.8 \text{ kHz}$$

$$\text{Half wavelength} = \frac{300\,000}{427.8} \times \frac{1}{2}$$

$$= 350.6 \text{ metres}$$

3. Given $f = 14.2$, and there are 14 red zones between the master and the slave. How many kilometres apart are the two stations?

$$\text{Red zone width} = \frac{300\,000}{14.2} \times \frac{1}{2}$$

$$= 10\,560 \text{ metres.}$$

For 14 such zones,

$$\text{Width of 14 red zones} = 10\,560 \times 14$$

$$= 147\,840 \text{ metres or } 147.840 \text{ km.}$$

4. If the width of a Decca lane along the base line is 440 metres, what is the comparison frequency?

Lane width = 440 metres; therefore wavelength = 880 metres and

$$\text{comparison frequency} = \frac{300\,000}{880} \text{ kHz}$$

$$= 340.9 \text{ kHz.}$$

5. A red decometer reading of B 13.6 is obtained when 80 km from the master and 35 km from the slave. If the reading remains at B 13.6 when 110 km from the master, what would be the distance from the slave?

When on hyperbola formed by B 13.6,

$$\text{differential range} = (80 - 35) \text{ km} = 45 \text{ km}$$

When the aircraft is 110 km from the master, it is on the same hyperbola and therefore the differential is the same, that is

$$\text{differential range} = 110 \text{ km} - ? = 45 \text{ km}$$

$$? = 65 \text{ km}$$

The distance from the slave is 65 km.

6. Master and the green slave are 90 nm apart. When 130 nm from the master and 56 nm from the slave, the reading is F 38.3. At what distance from the slave should the green decometer read F 38.3 when on the base line between master and slave? The differential on hyperbola of F 38.3 is $(130 - 56)$ nm = 74 nm. We want to find a point on the base line which divides the base line giving a differential of 74. This is the point through which the hyperbola F 38.3 passes. Let the distance from the master to this hyperbola along the baseline be x nm and the distance from slave to the hyperbola be y nm, the distance we wish to calculate.

Then, $x + y = 90$ (given in the question)

                           $x - y = 74$ (the calculated differential)

                          $2x\quad = 164$

therefore $x = 82$

and $y = 8$

The distance from the slave to the hyperbola is 8 nm.

7.   The distance between master and green slave is 160 km. If the comparison frequency is 256 kHz, give the number of zones (to the nearest whole) that will occur between the master and the green slave.

$$\text{Fundamental frequency } f = \frac{256}{18} \quad \text{(green slave compares at } 18f)$$

$$= 14.22 \text{ kHz}$$

$$\text{Zone width} = \frac{300\,000}{14.22} \times \frac{1}{2}$$

$$= 10\,546.8 \text{ metres}$$

$$\therefore \quad \text{Number of zones between M and G} = \frac{160\,000}{10\,546.8}$$

$$= 15.$$

24: Decca Flight Log

Decca equipment provides zone, lane and fraction of a lane information on 3 decometers. These zones and lanes are geographically fixed areas. This, together with the fact that the decometer information is on a continuous basis makes Decca an ideal system for adaption as a mechanical plotter. That's what a Decca Flight Log is. A moving pen indicates the aircraft's instantaneous position on a chart which also moves, and the pen traces out the aircraft's track made good. The pen and the chart are driven by two Decca slaves, the slaves selected by Decca to give the best result in the area where the flight is taking place.

Charts are specially prepared to meet different flight requirements, e.g. charts for en route navigation, charts for use in congested areas such as Controlled Airspace and approach charts for use in terminal areas. They come in small sections (approximately 2 feet long) and up to 12 charts may be joined up in the right sequence to cover a whole flight. The roll thus made up is loaded on one spool, over the face of the display head and the edge of the start chart fastened down to a spool on the other side.

The chart moves in Y–Y axis, or in a direction up and down this paper. The pen moves in X–X axis, that is, across this paper. Thus, the pen and chart movements are 90° to each other. This causes a problem since the hyperbolic lattice of any two slaves rarely intersect each other at 90° except in the vicinity of the base lines where they do so approximately. Thus, charts for flights near the base line utilise the lattice pattern as naturally produced but elsewhere the lattice has to be straightened out mathematically, and the flight log charts for these areas have an appearance of a square grid. This adjustment is looked after by the flight log computer but the operator has to remember that with this straightening out process, distortion of geographical features is inevitable. On these charts, therefore, estimations of bearings and ranges are not possible. Ranges along a particular track are marked by the Decca company and where applicable, bearings to reporting points around the Track are shown. Only information shown on the chart may be used.

Another factor that one has to take into consideration is the nature of the hyperbolic lattice. Due to their curvature, distances between 360° phase change lines (that is, lanes) are variable distances: shortest distance along the base line, largest distance at the extremity. Thus, 360° phase change fed by a slave to the pen or roller will have different rate of movement on different charts covering different areas. These variables are summarised as follows:
1. Scale of the chart
2. Rate and direction of movement of the chart
3. Rate and direction of movement of the pen.
   These variables for a particular chart are controlled by a Chart Key which is

loaded in a turret switch on the control box. The key code in three letters (e.g. BIP). is printed on the side of the chart together with the number of the Decca chain in use for that chart. The turret switch holds a maximum of 12 such keys to cater for 12 charts and the key in the 12 o'clock position is the one which is operative. When one chart is finished and the other is about to start, the turret switch must be turned until the next key is in the 12 o'clock position.

Operating procedures

     1. Switch on Decca and allow it to warm up.
     2. Switch on the Flight Log (no warming up time required).
     3. Select appropriate turret key.
     4. Adjust the pen and the chart so that the pen indicates the point of start. This may be done from known base co-ordinates or from decometer readings. Simple buttons left/right and up/down permit this setting to be done, with Function switch against correct colour of slave.
     5. Function switch to Standby position for normal operation.

Errors

Normal Decca errors are present plus a small error in flight log due to gear train backlash.

Accuracy

± 1 nm at 120 nm range; ± 2 nm at 200 nm range.

Latest developments

The latest advance in the Flight Log system is the arrival of the Omnitrac computer. It is a lightweight airborne computer and converts the information expressed in hyperbolic co-ordinates into rectilinear co-ordinates. Thus, with the use of this computer the distortions of the flight log charts are avoided. The computer may also be used to establish a direct link between Decca and the automatic pilot and it will correct the aircraft's heading if the Decca receiver detects a deviation from the pre-set track.

Advantages of a flight log

The U.K. Civil Aviation Authority notes the following advantages in having a flight log on board an aircraft (for fuller information see circular 4/1969).
    (a)   Provides a degree of navigational flexibility.
    (b)   The pilot is able to fly by reference to a pictorial display, thereby reducing the workload on the ground radar.
    (c)   The flight log would enable the pilots to commence their descents from the correct geographical position, thus avoiding potential accidents.
    (d)   It reduces the workload on the flight deck. This is particularly so if the system is coupled to the auto-pilot.

25: Secondary Surveillance Radar (SSR)

The variety of aircraft types with wide differences of speed and altitude in a crowded air demands positive identification of each aircraft for adequate safe control by ATC. Primary radar is insufficiently informative, and has the added disadvantages of clutter on the screen and a necessarily high power output for the two-way journey of the wave. Secondary radar, when used in conjunction with the primary radar, does away with these drawbacks, but does demand the co-operation of the aircraft in that the appropriate equipment must be aboard. When such equipment must be carried in designated UK airspace is firmly and legally laid down.

A ground based transmitter/receiver triggers off a reply from an aircraft's receiver/ transmitter when the correct operating procedures are followed: the reply is on a different frequency from the interrogator, this is old stuff to you. The 'interrogator' is the name for the ground equipment, the 'transponder' for that in the aircraft. The aircraft not only identifies itself positively without manoeuvres, but gives its height. On the ground, range and bearing are displayed on the screen, nice and clear, while the aircraft's height is shown either on the screeen or on a veeder counter. With more advanced systems the code is converted to the aircraft's callsign which is displayed on the screen along with the aircraft's blip. All signals are coded; the code of the interrogation signal is called the *Mode*.

Frequency
Ground transmits on 1 030 MHz, receives on 1 090 MHz
Aircraft transmits on 1 090 MHz, receives on 1 030 MHz

Process
The method used is the transmission and reception of pulses, and it is essential to eliminate weak or spurious signals, since the coding system depends on the 'presence' or 'non-presence' of pulses. The interrogator transmits two pulses with a known spacing, and there are four Modes, each mode having a different spacing.

Mode A has pulses (always 0.85 μs wide) 8 μs apart
Mode B 17 μs apart
Mode C 21 μs apart
Mode D 25 μs apart.

Modes A and B are used for identification, Mode C for automatic height information, while Mode D is experimental. The aircraft transponder will reply to an interrogation signal provided the pilot has selected the corresponding Mode. The transponder transmits a code in reply to a correct interrogation (correct in that the aircraft equipment recognises the Mode by the time spacing between each pair of interrogation pulses), a code which is obtained by the inclusion or omission of any of up to 12 pulses. The train of 12 pulses is contained between two framing pulses, 20.3 μs apart, and these are always sent. Between them, the information is sent by transmitting or leaving out any of the 12. The codes available in a twelve-pulse train then are $2^{12} = 4\,096$, and the codes are numbered 0000 to 7777, using all numbers except those containing an 8 or 9. Pulses in the transponder are 0.45 μs wide. A further pulse, the special identification pulse, can be transmitted when the ident button is pressed on the aircraft unit, usually at ATC's request; this pulse is 4.35 μs after the second frame pulse, and will be automatically and continuously transmitted for about 20 seconds after pushing the button.

The Modes and codes are selected by switches on the aircraft control box: a switch for Mode, a window for code, a button for ident, and a switch for automatic height reporting. The Mode and code are pre-allotted before departure usually, or requested by ATC in flight; there are various routine selections such as Mode A, code 76 to be used in the event of radio failure, to quote an example.

Automatic altitude telemetering
On getting Mode C interrogations, the transponder will produce one of 4 096 codes, no matter what code is selected in the window. This code is determined by the output of an altitude digitiser mechanically linked to the altimeter; the sequence of pulses transmitted is thus entirely determined by the aircraft's height. This height is always referenced to 1 013.2 mb, quite independent of altimeter setting; the equipment will provide automatic altitude telemetering up to 128 000 ft, with a change of output every 100 ft. It seems a bit sloppy to be talking about height and altitude when reading a 1 013.2 setting on the altimeter.

Unwanted echoes
The interrogator aerial sends out a wide vertical beam and a narrow one in azimuth: the azimuth beam, though, has side lobes which could produce a transponder response, spreading the echo on the indicator tube and denying the required accuracy of range and bearing. To correct this, an omnidirectional radiation transmission is introduced, whose signal strength is greater than the strongest side lobe but less than the main beam. By fitting a circuit in the transponder for comparing the amplitude of pulses, it can be arranged not to reply to side lobe interrogations; for example, the first pulse of the Mode can be transmitted in the omnidirectional pattern, and the second in the interrogator pattern; the transponder will only reply if the interrogator pulse is equal to, or greater than, the amplitude of the omnidirectional pulse. Or, by a normal transmission of interrogator pulses with an omnidirectional pulse intervening 2 μs after the first: the transponder will not reply if the omnidirectional pulse is greater in amplitude than the interrogator.

General
The aircraft equipment is kept on 'Standby' until required; this keeps the display on the ground clean. The range of SSR is of the order of 200 nm, and the PRF is about 250 per second. Several aircraft in an area with similar flight plans may have been allotted the same code; identification of one would be demanded by ATC, and the resultant echo on the ground display would show as a 'filling-in' of one of the echoes already showing; or ATC might of course order an aircraft to turn to another code.

Advantages

 i.   Longish range.
 ii.   No clutter, no unwanted echoes from cloud, high buildings, high ground, and so on.
 iii. Reply signals give range, bearing and height positively and automatically.
 iv.   No effort required by the pilot — well, very little anyway.
 v.   All other communication channels are left free.
 vi.   Information to ATC is instantaneous and unambiguous.
 vii. No aircraft manoeuvres required.
 viii. Little power needed.

Disadvantage is that the aircraft must carry the necessary equipment.

In U.K. airspace, more stringent regulations for the carriage of SSR transponders are being steadily introduced.

It is now compulsory when flying in the Upper Airspace and whole of the U.K. controlled airspace (notified for rule 21) above FL 100 to carry Mode A 4096 codes and also Mode C. The present requirement when flying in the U.K. controlled airspace notified for rule 21 at and below FL 100 is the carriage of Mode A 4096 codes only.

Gliders, helicopters at and below FL 100 and light aircraft (weighing 2 730 kg or less) below FL 100 flying under special VFR are exempt from the above requirement.

The above requirements for the carriage of SSR equipment will be further amended in the spring of 1980 when the aircraft flying in any controlled airspace where mandatory IFR applies will be required to carry both Mode A and Mode C capability equipment.

Most ICAO States have now published some form of mandatory requirements for carriage of SSR, the details of which are generally available from the State's AIP as well as from the Aerad Supplements.

There is a standard R/T phraseology for SSR, the operative word being 'Squawk'. For example: Squawk Alpha Code 76 means 'Select Mode A Code 76 on your control box, and switch on transponder'. 'Squawk Ident' means 'Stay on present Mode and code, but press the Identification tit'.

26: VLF Navigation Systems

VLF (very low frequency) is the lowest frequency band in the radio spectrum and comprises the frequencies ranging from 3 kHz to 30 kHz. In this band, the signals suffer the least surface attenuation, and travelling between the surface and the ionosphere by the ducting process, they produce very large ranges. Given sufficient transmission power, ranges of the order of 6 to 10 000 nm may be obtained.

Thus, VLF is a very attractive frequency band in which to develop long range navigation systems but it was totally neglected until around the mid-fifties. Interest was aroused following Decca's success. The investigations which followed revealed that such a proposition was feasible and that a global navigation system could be produced in the VLF band. Against the advantages of the ranges, there are two disadvantages inherent in any system working with such a low frequency band: its variable propagation characteristics must be thoroughly understood and such a system calls for colossal ground installations. Two systems emerged, one called 'VLF system' and the other 'Omega'.

VLF system

Instead of transmitting its own signals, this system makes use of the continuous communication signals transmitted by the U.S. Navy, with the Navy's agreement, of course. Its ten transmitters suitably located round the world and transmitting in the frequency range of 15 kHz to 30 kHz provide a world-wide coverage.

The principle of the system is that the signals from different stations arrive at a given position at different times. If the time taken by the signals to travel from the transmission source to a given point can be measured, this time can be converted to the distance from the transmitter and plotted as a circular position line. In favourable circumstances, signals from any two conveniently placed stations would give a navigational fix. In actual practice, because of the high transmission power (from 50 to 1 000 kW) and the use of very low frequencies it is quite common to receive more than two stations anywhere at any given time.

The principle is implemented by use of an accurate on-board atomic time standard which produces a timing pattern identical to the received signals. The necessary navigational data are derived from the comparison of the phase of the incoming signal with the time standard, one station giving one position line.

Several receivers capable of utilising these VLF signals are now on the market: a system known as Ontrac II is briefly discussed here.

Ontrac II.   The airborne equipment consists of a flush-mounted aerial, receiver/computer, an atomic time standard, control head with all its sixteen buttons on the keyboard, a display head and a station indicator.

On switching on the equipment the station indicator lights up to indicate the stations being received. The receiver automatically selects the two best stations for its operation. After around five minutes of warming up time from the initial power supply, the atomic standard will have stabilised and a light signal will indicate that the system is ready to navigate. The computer is initially fed with the accurate start position and a continuous display of the present position is then maintained. Other types of display may be selected: distance to go, distance across, heading to a way point, ground speed, time to a way point and so forth. As the flight progresses the receiver will continue to adjust to the two best signals. Basically a very reliable system, it may lose signals when flying in cloud with high ice crystal content. Then the system will go in the DR mode but it will pick up from where it left off when stronger signals are received again.

Omega system
Ground installations.   The system consists of eight ground transmitting stations, their locations round the world carefully chosen to give a global coverage. The frequencies used are 10.2 kHz, 11.33 kHz and 13.6 kHz. Of these, 10.2 kHz is the navigation frequency and the other two are transmitted to provide lane identification. Of the eight Omega stations, only three stations are on the air at any one time. The transmission is in the form of pulses of 0.9 to 1.2 second duration and there is a silent period of 0.2 second between the end of one set of three transmissions and the beginning of the next one. The whole non-repetitive sequence takes 10 seconds. For interest, the sequence of transmission from the eight stations is shown in the following table.

Station								
Norway	X	Z	Y					
Liberia		X	Z	Y				
Hawaii			X	Z	Y			
N. Dakota				X	Z	Y		
La Reunion					X	Z	Y	
Argentina						X	Z	Y
Australia	Y						X	Z
Japan		Z	Y					X

X: 10.2 kHz   Y: 11.33 kHz   Z: 13.6 kHz

Thus, at the commencement of the sequence, Norway, Australia and Japan transmit together on frequencies, 10.2 kHz, 11.33 kHz and 13.6 kHz respectively. There is a 0.2 second silence and then Norway, Liberia and Japan will transmit, and so on.
Principle of operation.   This is a hyperbolic system and the principle has certain similarities with the Decca system. An Omega receiver, synchronised to 10.2 kHz transmission wavelength measures the phase of the signal being received from the selected station. This information is retained in the memory until the phase of a second signal from a different station is received. The difference between the phases of the two stations gives a hyperbolic position line. With a phase measurement from a third station a three position line fix is plotted as follows:

Phase difference between stations A and B — one position line
Phase difference between stations B and C — second position line, and
Phase difference between stations A and C — third position line.
From the above combinations it will be seen that a fourth station will give a six
position line fix.

Airborne equipment.   The airborne equipment is similar to the VLF system and
consists of a small, flush-mounted aerial, a receiver/computer and a control and
display unit (CDU). At the commencement of the flight, enter the date, time, present
position and the way points in the CDU. The date and time are necessary to make
allowances for the variations in the propagation characteristics and the system will
accept the position accurate to within 36 nm. Subsequently the present position will be
continually indicated as left and right display in latitude and longitude. Depending
on the type of the equipment, other types of display may be selected as follows:

XTK/TKE — Cross track error, track angle error
DIS/ETE — Distance to way point, ETA to way point
W/V
GS/DA — Ground speed and drift
TK/DTK — Track angle for desired track
CH/OFS — Compass heading, magnetic variation.

The system can operate with magnetic, true or grid compass reference, can hold
variation in memory and if less than three stations are being received it would
automatically go in dead reckoning mode. A typical equipment may accept up to
nine way points. The signals may be fed direct to the auto-pilot and the system may
be integrated with Doppler or INS.

Lane identification.   Just as in the Decca, a lane slip may occur if the signals were
temporarily interrupted and a lane ident will be necessary. To enable the lane
identification to be carried out, the receiver is supplied with two identification
signals, 11.33 kHz and 13.6 kHz. By taking a beat frequency of either of these
frequencies with the navigation frequency of 10.2 kHz, the lane may be widened
as follows:

10.2 kHz and 13.6 kHz: beat note = 3.4 kHz and

$$\text{lane width} = \frac{300\,000}{3.4 \times 2} \text{ m} = 44 \text{ km or 24 nm (approx.)}$$

10.2 kHz and 11.33 kHz: beat note = 1.13 kHz and

$$\text{lane width} = \frac{300\,000}{1.13 \times 2} \text{ m} = 133 \text{ km or 72 nm (approx.)}$$

Thus, the system is capable of identifying your lane up to 72 nm and the computer
will take care of it.

Errors of the system.   The errors of the system mainly arise from two sources:
propagation anomaly and ground conductivity. Both these factors affect the
phases of the signals. Propagation anomaly arises from the effect of the sun's
radiation on the ionosphere, which causes the ionosphere level to rise and fall with
time. This up/down movement of the ionosphere level affects the radiation pattern
of the signals contained under the base of the ionosphere and causes variations in
the phase velocity.

Ground conductivity which varies widely over the earth's surface causes varying
attenuation of the signals and changes the speed of the radio waves. This has a similar

effect on the signal phases.

Both these errors have been thoroughly investigated, the variations with time and place are known and are allowed for in the computer. Any resultant inaccuracy of the system arises from incorrect predictions of the behaviour of the signal phases. There is a programme for keeping the propagation characteristics under observation and updating the present information as new data become available.

Apart from the above, there are frequent unpredicted variations in the ionospheric state on account of the sudden flare-up of sun spots, the disturbance reaching us as X radiation. These may simply cause lane slips or at worst, a total disruption of the signals. Even here, however, a limited warning is possible in advance. The warnings of any abnormal conditions are given out in the Notams and in some countries there are regular broadcasts as well. The station status and the warnings of any unpredicted conditions are checked by the crew as a matter of pre-flight briefing. The overall accuracy of the system is given as 1 nm during the day, 2 nm at night.

Glossary of Abbreviations

A/A	along/across Track distances
a.c.	alternating current
a/c	aircraft
ACC	Area Control Centre
ADF	automatic direction finding equipment
AF	audio frequency
AIP	Aeronautical Information Publication
AM	amplitude modulation
amsl	above mean sea level
ASR	approach search radar
ATC	Air Traffic Control
ATCC	Air Traffic Control Centre
BFO	beat frequency oscillator
Brg	bearing
CAA	Civil Aviation Authority
CAVOK	weather fine and clear
CDU	control and display unit
C/L	centre line
cm	centimetre/s
CRT	cathode ray tube
CW	carrier wave/continuous wave
dB	decibels
DDM	difference in depth of modulation
Dev	deviation
DF	direction finding
diff	difference/differential
Dir	direction
Dist	distance
DME	distance measuring equipment
DOC	designated operational coverage
DR	dead reckoning
°E	degrees east
EHF	extremely high frequency

f_d	Doppler shift
FM	frequency modulation
ft	feet
GHz	gigahertz
GNM	ground nautical miles
GP	glide path
GS	ground speed
Hdg	heading
HF	high frequency
Hdg(M)	heading magnetic
Hz	hertz
ICAO	International Civil Aviation Organisation
IFR	instrument flight rules
ILS	instrument landing system
INS	inertial navigation system
kHz	kilohertz
km	kilometre/s
LF	low frequency
LOC	localiser
LMM	locator middle marker
LOM	locator outer marker
LUHF	lowest usable high frequency
m	metre/s
MF	medium frequency
MHz	megahertz
min	minute/s
MKR	marker
MM	middle marker
MN	magnetic north
MUF	maximum usable frequency
NDB	non-directional radio beacon
nm	nautical mile/s
OBS	omni-bearing selector
OCL	obstacle clearance limit
OM	outer marker
°P	degrees port
PAR	precision approach radar
PPI	plan position indicator
PPS	pulses per second
PRF	pulse recurrence frequency
PRP	pulse repetition period

QDL	series of bearings
QDM	aircraft's magnetic heading to steer in zero wind to reach the station
QDR	magnetic bearing from the station
QE	quadrantal error
QGH	landing procedure clearance
QTE	true bearing from the station
QUJ	aircraft's true track to the station
°R	degrees relative
RAD	approach surveillance radar
RBI	relative bearing indicator
RC	radio compass
Rel Brg	relative bearing
RF	radio frequency
RMI	radio magnetic indicator
ROD	rate of descent
RT	radiotelephony
RVR	runway visual range
°S	degrees starboard
SHF	super high frequency
Sig	signal
SSR	secondary surveillance radar
Stbd	starboard
T, (T)	true
TAP	terminal approach procedures
TAS	true airspeed
TR	track
TVOR	terminal VOR
TX	transmitter
μs	microsecond/s
UHF	ultra high frequency
U.K.	the United Kingdom
UKAP	the United Kingdom air pilot
VDF	VHF direction finding
VFR	visual flight rules
VHF	very high frequency
VLF	very low frequency
VOR	VHF omni-directional radio range
VOT	a test VOR
°W	degrees west
W/T	wireless telegraphy
W/V	wind velocity

Index